BRIGHTER
CLIMATE
FUTURES

BRIGHTER CLIMATE FUTURES

A Global Energy, Climate & Ecosystem Transformation

by

Dr. Hari Lamba

REGENT PRESS
Berkeley, California
2020

Paperback
ISBN 13: 978-1-58790-528-5
ISBN 10: 1-58790-528-0

E-book
ISBN 13: 978-1-58790-529-2
ISBN 10: 1-58790-529-9

Library of Congress Cataloging-in-Publication Data

Names: Lamba, Hari, 1948- author.
Title: Brighter climate futures : a global energy, climate & ecosystem
    action plan / by Dr. Hari Lamba.
Description: Berkeley, California : Regent Press, 2020. | Includes
    bibliographical references and index. | Summary:
Identifiers: LCCN 2020027831 (print) | LCCN 2020027832 (ebook) | ISBN
    9781587905285 (trade paperback) | ISBN 9781587905292 (ebook)
Subjects: LCSH: Climatic changes--International cooperation. |
    Environmental policy--International cooperation. | Energy
    policy--International cooperation.
Classification: LCC QC903 .L35 2020 (print) | LCC QC903 (ebook) | DDC
    363.738/46--dc23
LC record available at https://lccn.loc.gov/2020027831
LC ebook record available at https://lccn.loc.gov/2020027832

Printed in the U.S.A.
REGENT PRESS
Berkeley, California
www.regentpress.net

**Besides this book, details of the transformation plan
can also be found at the following website**

www.brighterclimatefutures.com

In addition to providing descriptions, information and guidance to activate you and help you do more for solutions to Climate Change, the website will also be used in a manner so as to define other solutions to Climate Change in a constructive manner, and to highlight successes and failures to date. The main aim is to have the world agree to a sufficient plan and implement it!

Note: For readers that are not familiar with many of the terms that are used, it is advised that they visit the Glossary of Terms FIRST at the end of the book before reading the book. Here are some of the most commonly used ones.

Greenhouse Gases: Gases that trap the heat resulting from sunlight in the atmosphere, like the glass of a greenhouse traps heat. When sunlight falls on the earth's surface it is re-emitted mainly as heat radiation (infra-red light), which normally would escape back into space. But greenhouse gases are types of gases that trap this heat, and as the amount has been increasing, they have been heating the atmosphere more than normal.

Solar PV: Solar Photo-Voltaic just means solar panels that are made in such a way that they are able to turn the sunlight (Photo) falling on them directly into electricity (Voltaic).

Carbon Dioxide: Is the main greenhouse gas that is a chemical molecule that consists of one atom of carbon and two atoms of oxygen (CO_2) joined together. All of us breathe out carbon dioxide, and plants and trees mainly absorb carbon dioxide, and breathe out oxygen.

Contents

Introduction – Upping the Ambition 1

1. The Status of Climate Change and Setting the Goals 11

2. The Global Energy and Climate Plan 29

3. Massive Carbon Sinks – Forests and Coastal Ecosystems .. 100

4. Advanced Disaster Management for Climate Change 119

5. Adapting to the Consequences of Climate Change
   and A Regenerative Agriculture 133

6. National Energy, Climate and Ecosystem Plans for the
   US and California, Including the Green New Deal 152

7. National Energy, Climate and Ecosystem Plans for other
   Major Emitter Nations – China, India and the
   European Union 205

8. Organizing Globally – An Implementation Plan That
   Will Be Adequate, Timely and Effective 234

9. Investments We Need and Ways of Financing Them 239

10. Overcoming the Obstacles – Climate Deniers and
    Fossil Fuel Financial and Political Interests 261

11. Global Plan for Reducing Other Greenhouse
    Gas Emissions 284

12. Jobs and Economy Aspects of the Plan – Including
    Just Transition and Energy Democracy 293

13. What the Transformed World Will Look Like
    After the Plan 305

Conclusion – Making it Happen 310

Glossary of Terms 312

Abbreviations and Units 315

Notes / References 319

What You Can Do 324

Index 331

About the Author 336

Introduction

Upping The Ambition

Climate Change represents the biggest long term threat to our world and possibly, even our civilization. But instead of books that convey a picture of gloom and doom, this book provides a total practical and time bound plan of a type that will help us achieve the needed solutions in a timely manner. In the succeeding chapters, all of the needed ingredients are brought together in terms of global energy growth and transitions strategies, carbon emissions reductions, massive electrification, enhanced energy efficiency, methods for global organization and cooperation, economic and environmental justice, and the massive restoration of forests and coastal ecosystems to absorb carbon. The book aligns its aims with the goal of keeping the global average temperature rise below 1.5 degrees Celsius (or 2.7 degrees Fahrenheit), avoiding the worst consequences of Climate Change, dealing effectively with remaining problems through adaptation and advanced disaster management, and coming out of all this much better than we ever thought we would. The time for hand wringing is over. What we need is totally adequate planning and effective global implementation.

Climate Change is both a threat and a challenge. The threat is destruction of the life support systems of Planet Earth, on which we all depend, and the challenge is to do this in a relatively short time – in the coming decades. Globally, nationally and individually, what is needed is to limit the worst consequences of global warming and eventually reduce them. The build-up in the atmosphere of gases emitted by human activity, that trap more and more heat, is having severe consequences which are growing worse. Besides temperature rise, there are sea level rise, increasing ferocity of storms and hurricanes, catastrophic rains, melting of glaciers and polar ice, wildfires of increasing severity, drought (with deadly heat waves), water shortages, and coastal storms and flooding (the increased evaporation from higher temperatures). The understanding is growing that the solutions are all doable and could be a combination of renewable energy, energy efficiency improvements, and the expansion of carbon sink ecosystems. We need to move rapidly to save and then rejuvenate the carbon sinks (vastly improve their health and vitality so they can absorb more carbon), namely the global forests, land vegetation ecosystems, coral reefs, iced masses, and land, freshwater and coastal ecosystems.

There have been many climate movements that have occurred and the worldwide climate rallies organized throughout the world that have applied pressure on governments to proceed with actions on Climate Change. The United Nations leadership and organizations have tried to motivate the nations of the world to up their ambitions.

This book outlines a Global Climate Action Plan that is doable. Because of the influence of its leadership or absence thereof, a more detailed plan is presented for the US. To be effective, it is necessary to present plans for some of the other major emitter nations, such as China, India and the European Union (EU28 – or union of 28 nations). Because of the massive reversal of strategy in the US, and yellow vest riots in France, it has become clear that the solutions and plans presented must be politically doable, not only to the rich and the powerful, who are going to fight it tooth and nail anyway and who have benefited immensely till now, but also the vast masses of the middle and lower middle classes and the poor. Otherwise, the political backlashes will derail what may be thought of as even the best of strategies. Opposition to fair Climate Change solutions will show up as extreme politics of the right and the left, but more probably as fascist type dictatorships, which unfortunately will delay actions unless resolved. Some of the main opposition to solutions to Climate Change are described as well as how these will need to be overcome.

The most crucial part of the plan is the energy transition, as the world must have enough energy in a manner that helps us achieve the carbon reductions, and which, together with energy efficiency still enable us to have the chance of a decent global existence for all of the people of the world. If the world proceeds on the path we are today then not much will be achieved and solutions will be outside our grasp. Even other plans that have been proposed only partially get us to where we need to be, and some plans are good at descriptions and evaluations of possible solutions, but do not give us all the parts of the Global Plan that we need.

At the same time, it has become clear that the activities represented by the giant global economic system have to go through some fundamental and far reaching transformations in all aspects – the way the cities (and their buildings, houses, developments and areas) are designed, the way people and goods move (transportation), the way energy is produced, how agriculture is conducted, the way forestry is practiced or enhanced, how global fishing operates, how much meat we eat, how much paper we use and recycle, and all other human activities. Together these represent the transformation to a clean energy zero carbon economy and the rejuvenation of carbon sink ecosystems so they can absorb more carbon.

As the terrible symptoms that have already shown up from the natural disasters of Climate Change start to take a toll, there will be several things that will happen: (1) The so-called rich "Developed" nations will see themselves being devastated to the point of rapidly becoming undeveloped with large scale suffering of their populations and unsustainable financial losses, (2) The poorer nations will suffer such devastation that they will be unable to feed their populations, and large scale famines, and migrations will exceed their capacity to cope, (3) Living conditions will become intolerable as heat waves, storms, flooding, pollution, sea level rise, freshwater availability, ocean degradation, and wildfires devastate much of the world and make it very difficult to grow any food or even live, and (4) These devastations will lead to such upheavals, conflicts and wars, that the world will suffer the twin problems of total environmental and economic devastation on one hand and the expanding conflicts and war (even with weapons of mass destruction) as the rich struggle to survive and suppress the rest. **This is the devastation that awaits us if we do little or nothing.**

The nations of the world have been increasing fossil fuel use for a long time, and have continued to do so even since 1992, when the first global warming treaty was signed that was officially known as the United Nations Framework Convention on Climate Change (UNFCCC). Some parts of the world have stepped up to their responsibilities, but the powerful global, political, financial and military interests have stonewalled significant efforts to proceed towards solutions, even though the United Nations and its affiliated organizations have urged action for some time now (at least 30 years). **The aim of this proposed Plan is to make sure the people and concerned organizations of the world *understand* that there is a Plan that is Technically Feasible (that it CAN be done), that it is financially viable (within the financial grasp of global society to do), that will be much more beneficial for all humans and life, and that it will make our planet Earth much more beautiful. The challenge is to convince enough of the nations of the world so that it becomes politically feasible. The accompanying challenge is to fashion the details of implementation is such a way that the vast majority of the people of the world benefit from the process, and not just the rich and powerful.**

That's why the three components of the Plan are Energy, Climate and Ecosystems. *Implementing the Plan will avoid devastation and instead restore and rejuvenate our planet Earth.* It will provide enough clean energy and a good life for all, a TOTAL solution of the Climate Change problem, and make the Earth much more beautiful than even today with a restoration of all forms of life and biodiversity, while making all natural systems healthier and more productive for all humanity.

The Wider Environmental or Ecological Crisis involves not just Climate Change, which is the biggest crisis, but also the following: (1) Ozone layer destruction, (2) Poisoning of the air, water and soil with toxic and hazardous chemicals from industry and agriculture, (3) The vastly increasing amounts of solid waste from mining, agriculture, industry, construction, sewage treatment and municipal waste, (4) The increasing amounts of high level radioactive waste from nuclear reactors (from 41,000 metric tons in 1985 to an estimated 450,000 tons by 2050, even if no new reactors are built) and from the nuclear weapon activities of nations, (5) Environmental and industrial accidents that occur on a daily basis, (6) The sixth massive extinction of species in the planet's 4.6 billion year history (this time all caused by human activity and now Climate Change), (7) Destruction of forest (deforestation), water (wetlands), soil (fertility), coastal (shrimp farms), ocean (coral reefs) and desert (desertification) ecosystems, and (8) The massive air and water (including ocean) pollution. The overall environmental crisis problems and solutions, which are not covered in this book, are described in the author's earlier book, *Rethinking Progress*. However, solving the climate crisis as per the Plan laid out in this book, will begin to solve many of the problems of the environmental crisis listed above, which ultimately will require its own attention.

From the way solutions to Climate Change are often presented, it is claimed that it will lead to a total reversal of all progress and large-scale privation that we have to cut back. However, as this book aims to show, the opposite is true. People will need to change what they do and how they live and move, but the net result will be much better. The world will become much greener and more beautiful, and the productive capacity of nature (soils, crops, forests, fisheries, and agriculture) will be so much better as planet Earth will have been truly rejuvenated. We will have our major ecosystems not only restored but also thriving – our coral reefs, our forests, our mountains, our glaciers, our lakes and rivers, our coastal ecosystems, and even our deserts and drylands. Although solving the wider ecological crisis is not the central aim of this book, some of the massive species extinction, where every few hours species become extinct, will have been reversed and some biodiversity and species that are being hurt by Climate Change will begin to thrive, so that we begin to benefit again from the restoration of the health, beauty and productivity of live nature.

Living conditions will be much better as there will be less air and water pollution, less noise, more wholesome, healthy and cleaner food, safer and cleaner transportation (the high level of deaths and injuries on global highways and roads will have been partly reversed), and healthier and happier living communities where people can live, eat, move, work and thrive in cities, towns and habitats that are so much more desirable to live in. The creativity and productivity of common people and their businesses will have exploded as they implement, operate and innovate new ways of doing things. Cities will have been transformed so that they are truly eco-cities that are beautiful places to live and work and play! Cities will have been redesigned or reorganized or transformed so that travel distances are reduced, and the new transportation system is cleaner, safer, quieter, and healthier, with all types of transportation integrated and linked.

Energy production will be totally with renewables like solar, wind, hydro (with environmental adjustments) and geothermal, not only to produce electricity, but also ways will have been found to run all transportation from renewable energy by different energy storage methods. All of fossil fueled electricity production will have been transformed to a combination of renewable energy (often mainly solar PV or photo voltaic – using the solar panels most people are familiar with) and battery systems, with innovative means found to supply energy at other times, that are outlined in this book. This will address coal-fired power plants, followed by oil-based power plants, and then natural gas based power plants. Next all of the fossil fuel based activities in industry, buildings, transportation and agriculture, will have been electrified and the added electrical energy supplied all by renewables. The remaining energy needs can be met with energy dense, storable and transportable non-carbon fuels such as hydrogen and ammonia that store renewable energy. This where global society needs efforts at research and development.

Agriculture, forestry and fisheries will be totally transformed, and thrive even more because the health and productivity of our natural systems will have been rejuvenated. Agriculture will have been totally transformed as the productive capacity and fertility and carbon absorptive capacity of soils will have been rejuvenated and agriculture will rely on cleaner methods that require less water, fertilizer and chemicals, and are totally based on crop biodiversity (many different types of the same crop originating from traditional varieties) as opposed to crop mono-cultures. Forestry will have been transformed so that major areas of the world will have been reforested, and while a lot of this will be left alone to grow as natural and ecosystems forests where wildfires are easy to control, they will be significant areas that will enable forest products to be used on an extractive basis as planting and harvesting go on together under the democratic control and husbandry of local people (sustainable forestry principles). As coastal ecosystems will have been restored and rejuvenated, the habitats for sea species will be so much better that if fish catches are regulated, the productive capacity of fisheries will have been restored and never allowed to deteriorate (sustainable fisheries principles), and ocean wildlife will thrive again. **That will recreate for us a clean, biodiverse, productive and beautiful Earth.**

In the US, there has been talk of a Green New Deal that is a combination of solutions to Climate Change and economic and social justice, i.e. solving the climate crisis is such a way that it improves the lives of the many. **First, it is described how the Plan proposed herein will help implement the mobilization goals of the Green New Deal, and turn it into a practical reality.** Next, California has led the charge in the US in renewable energy, electric cars and even hydrogen fuel cell vehicles – so there is much that the world can learn from California (and from the efforts of the European Union). So, California's successes are described as also the remaining challenges, after which a Plan is described for California. Then, even though China, India and the European Union (of 27 nations) have begun significant moves towards renewable energy, they are still too dependent on coal and other fossil fuels. So, detailed plans are described for these nations, as their transformations will not only make things better for them, but also help solve Climate Change which is hurting them.

Following that, a strategy is described that may be called a **Global Green New Deal.** What is presented is a transformed global economy where many new businesses and jobs will have been created that will lead to new and different ways of doing things, with economic power much more decentralized, and common folks all over enabled to live clean wholesome lives that rather than maximizing blind consumption, maximize the value that everyone gets from things produced and consumed. For this to be an orderly transformation, businesses, companies and workers will need the assistance, guidance and investment to transform their lives and skills, and will need to be provided the resources to help them transform to the new post-Climate Change world. This book presents a Plan and framework that is intended to help the world do exactly that.

With this Plan, the aim is to do the following:

1. **GET THE PLAN ACCEPTED AND SOMETHING LIKE THE PLAN IMPLEMENTED**
2. Convince the nations of the world that the Plan is technically feasible and economically viable, and something like it is needed.
3. Provide an incentive to major emitter nations to up their am-

bitions and then lead the world in implementing such a Plan.

4. Show that we can have plenty of clean renewable energy for all our needs, use energy wisely and efficiently, and get rid of polluting fossil fuels that are causing Climate Change.

5. Invest in the R&D (Research and Development) and infrastructure development that will enable large amounts of solar and other renewable energy to be stored in batteries and in non-carbon storage fuels like hydrogen, for use at other times when the sun is not shining.

6. Show that we can expand our carbon absorbing ecosystems. Expand and rejuvenate our forest, coastal and agricultural ecosystems, so that they not only act as much bigger carbon sinks but also restore much of the Earth's beauty, the natural health and productivity of its ecosystems and the diversity of life.

7. Show how we can practically implement the US Green New Deal, and provide a practical way of implementing a Global Green New Deal.

8. Show how we can take care of the consequences even if we achieve an average global temperature rise of no more than 1.5 degrees Celsius – through adaptation and advanced disaster management.

9. Get all greenhouse gas emissions, carbon dioxide (down to zero), methane and nitrogen oxide down enough so as to not allow the global average temperature rise to be more than 1.5 degrees Celsius or 2.7 degrees Fahrenheit, by 2050.

10. Convince the nations of the world that we need a greatly strengthened and empowered version of the UN organization (United Nations Framework Convention on Climate Change, UNFCCC, based in Bonn, Germany) that can plan, organize, coordinate, fund and implement the transformation in an effective and timely manner by 2050.

Globally, the world will need to come together in a way that it has never done so before and the energy transformation that we are about to embark upon is unlike anything humanity has ever done. The Plan proposed herein will make it happen if the political, financial and technical resources are brought to bear on the issue with a sense of urgency and a "can do" attitude. This book outlines a Plan of a type that has a high probability of success, but will need to be modified as we go along – it provides a good starting point. The future after the transition will be much better than where we are now, and infinitely better than where we are headed. We now proceed to describe the transformation Plan in the rest of this book.

Chapter 1

The Status of Climate Change and Setting the Goals

Human Caused Global Warming Damage
Is Already Here and Will Get Worse

The devastation of Climate Change has already arrived. Coral reefs are where the life on our planet Earth first exploded in the sea, when there was no life on land. Coral reefs when fully alive are the one of the most beautiful places on Earth and where there is enormous diversity of life, like in our rain forests. In 1997-98 was the previous global bleaching event when many of the coral reefs bleached (died) because of high ocean temperatures. Some of those have come back a little, especially in non-polluted areas. In 2016, because of El Niño and hotter sea temperatures, another major global bleaching event happened, mainly in the Pacific and Indian Oceans.

Some of the other events and symptoms are that because of the El Niño climate phenomenon, average surface temperatures over sea and land were the hottest during the 2011-2015 years – surface temperature rise reached about 1.0 degree Centigrade by 2018. Hurricanes and cyclones are getting more and more devastating in all parts of the world, because of the increase in temperatures and hence thermal energy in atmosphere. Many parts of the world have experienced yearly increases in temperatures. The summer temperatures in the middle east and in India get hotter every year – leading to increasing deaths caused by heat waves. Major floods and occasionally landslides have occurred over the past decade in Honduras.

It is projected that by the year 2100 the following events will become more likely. There will be higher maximum and minimum temperatures – more hotter days and fewer colder days, leading to the Increased frequency, duration and intensity of heat waves. These are already getting worse every year in most parts of the world. Then there will be further increases in precipitation – meaning much heavier rains, more and more extreme flooding. Recently the large Indian city of Chennai (Madras) had suffered a massive rain and flooding unlike ever seen before. Most of the city became like islands. Then in 2019 this large city ran out of water! There will be increasing intensity duration and frequency of cyclones or hurricanes. Many regions around the world now know and are preparing for hurricanes and cyclones that they expect will get worse over time. Along with this there will be increases in extreme sea events leading to coastal storms of increasing intensity. Most low lying regions like Bangladesh and Florida will be subjected to these large storm surges, before they eventually get submerged after a few decades. Many low lying islands like the Maldives in the Indian Ocean will disappear.

To summarize, there is very little uncertainty that human caused Climate Change has started to cause great damage and is only getting worse. Natural disasters like hurricanes, cyclones, typhoons, coastal storms, extremely heavy rains, floods, heat waves, and wildfires are getting much worse due to Climate Change. Longer term effects like droughts and sea level rise continue to worsen.

There is scientific consensus that the heating of Earth's atmosphere is being caused by increasing emissions of Greenhouse gases, mainly by the burning of fossil fuels. These gases trap the heat resulting from sunlight, and as the gases in the atmosphere are increasing, they are trapping more and more heat. The concentration of carbon dioxide (CO_2) in the atmosphere in 2018 had increased to about 410 ppm, up from about 280 ppm (parts per million) at the pre-industrial level. The UN based Intergovernmental Panel on Climate Change (IPCC) is the most credible global organization that has published many Assessment Reports since 1990. Only climate deniers and their financial and political supporters continue to deny the above.

SUMMARY HISTORY OF GLOBAL ACTIONS

- ❏ In 1992, at Rio de Janeiro, Brazil, most of the nations of the world signed the Global Warming Treaty that was officially called the United Nations Framework Convention on Climate Change (UNFCCC), which was only a statement of principles.
- ❏ In 1997, at Kyoto, Japan, most of the nations of the world

signed the Kyoto Protocol, which was an agreement to actually do something. The richer industrialized or Annex I nations had to reduce their greenhouse gas emissions to the 1990 levels by about the years 2008-2012, and the others were not required to do so.

❏ By about 2000-2005, it had become clear that most Annex I nations were not meeting their commitments. Canada withdrew from the Kyoto Protocol in 2011 and the US never ratified it because the Republican party controlled both Congress and Senate.

❏ Rather than a mandatory approach, a voluntary approach was begun. This resulted in the Paris Agreement of December 2015, that was signed by most of the nations of the world. Each nation who signed submitted an Intended Nationally Determined Commitment (INDC) of what they could do voluntarily. All commitments made at Paris would still lead to a rise of the global average temperature rise to 3.5 degrees Celsius.

SETTING THE GOALS

❏ In October of 2018, the IPCC (United Nation's Intergovernmental Panel on Climate Change) submitted a report titled, *Global Warming of 1.5 Degrees Celsius*, which stated that if the worst consequences of Climate Change were to be avoided, the global average temperature rise should be no more than 1.5 degrees Celsius.

❏ In order to achieve this, they calculated that carbon dioxide emissions needed to be reduced 45% from 2010 levels by 2030, reaching net zero by 2050. This has been adopted as the goal for the Plan in this book.

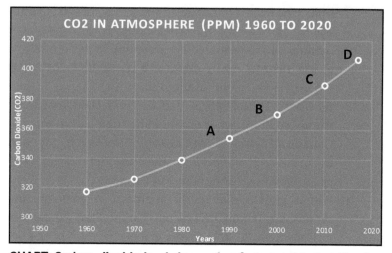

CHART: Carbon dioxide in air increasing faster and faster. Need to get it down to about 350 ppm (parts per million).

We show here how the concentration of carbon dioxide in the atmosphere (or the air we breathe) has been increasing at an ever increasing rate.

Increasing Amounts of Carbon Dioxide in the Air

Increasing concentration of carbon dioxide (CO_2 – in chemistry language, a molecule with one atom of carbon and two atoms of oxygen). The four labels of A, B, C and D correspond to the dates when the world could have decided to do something. Parts per million (ppm) of say 400 means that if you could count a million molecules, 400 of them will be carbon dioxide. **If the world had started at point A (1990), it could have leveled off at a significant level of carbon dioxide emissions from fossil fuels and could have continued to have a significant level of fossil fuel use. However, by delaying to point D (where we are today), the carbon dioxide emissions need to decrease to zero – the same as what IPCC is saying.**

Next, we show how the concentration of the main greenhouse gases need to decrease if we are to keep the temperature rise below 1.5 degrees Celsius (or 2.7 degrees Fahrenheit).

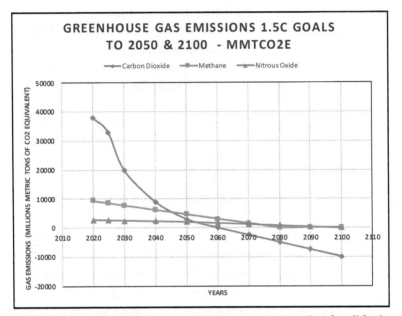

CHART: Goals we need to meet. We have to stop burning fossil fuels and dumping in the air.

Simply Put – The Goals for Greenhouse Gas Reductions

Simply put, the goals the Plan aims at achieving reductions by 2050. Beyond, we have to continue to do better. Methane (CH4) and Nitrous Oxide (N2O) are reduced by a given percentage each. The vertical axis is MMTCO2e or millions of metric tons of CO2 (carbon dioxide) equivalent. That means that the emissions of all gases other than CO2 were converted into how much these gases would trap heat compared with CO2 (this is based on Global Warming Potential or GWP of each gas – explained later and in detail in Chapter 11).

Methane (CH4): Consists of one atom of carbon and four atoms of hydrogen. This is emitted by agricultural activities, waste facilities, energy use (leakage at oil and gas facilities), and burning of biomass.

Nitrous Oxide (N2O): Consists of two atoms of nitrogen and one atom of oxygen (although there are other nitrogen oxides), and is primarily emitted by fertilizer use, and the combustion of fossil fuels.

The reductions in the emissions of these gases are covered later in Chapter 11. Most of the rest of this book looks at how to eliminate carbon dioxide emissions that result mainly from the burning of fossil fuels.

We now present the science of Climate Change and the status in more detail.

The Science and Status of Climate Change

The fields of atmospheric chemistry and physics, which are the main scientific fields that affect Climate Change, are established scientific fields, where research is done and peer reviewed scientific papers are published (peer reviewed means that people who are experts in the field review the work and vote on whether or not it should be published). Many scientists have made similar scientific measurements with scientific instruments and come to similar conclusions. As early as 1896, the scientist Arrhenius predicted on the principles of atmospheric chemistry and physics that carbon dioxide and water vapor trap solar heat. As sunlight falls on the earth's surface, it is re-emitted as infra-red light (the heat part of the spectrum of light), which is trapped by these gases. The amount of heat a particular gas traps is based on its molecular structure. It is now known scientifically what the Global Warming Potential (GWP – extent to which a gas traps solar heat) of these different gases are, and all of them are compared with carbon dioxide, which has a lower GWP than methane gas, but as much more carbon dioxide is emitted, it makes a much larger contribution to global warming.

For example, methane (Chemical Formula CH4 – which consists of one atom of carbon and four atoms of hydrogen), has lifetime of 12.4 years, and its GWP over a 20 year period is 86. Hence, during the 20 years, it absorbs or traps 86 times more heat than carbon dioxide (chemical formula CO2 – one atom of carbon and two atoms of oxygen). Carbon dioxide and methane can be naturally occurring or emitted by human activities. However, the other green-house gases, hydrofluorocarbon, chlorofluorocarbon (both refrigerants), nitrous oxide, carbon tetrafluoride, and perfluorotributylamine (PFTBA – used by the electrical industry since the mid 20th century for electronic testing and as a heat transfer agent), **do not occur naturally in nature and are ALL MAN MADE! Except for nitrous oxide, the GWP of most of these other chemicals are in the thousands. The effects of these chemicals on their heat trapping effects in the atmosphere are well defined scientifically!**

The next scientific field is that of the study of the weather systems of planet Earth, which spins around its axis once every 24 hours, and the Earth currently rotates around the sun about 365.24 days every year. Then, the Earth currently has a 23.5 degree angle relative to its plane of orbit around the sun, which according to scientific weather dynamics of our atmosphere, gives us our seasons. Over geological time, the earth's axis tilts between 21.4 and 24.4 degrees, a cycle that lasts 41,000 years, and which has been scientifically predicted to cause the ice ages. Anyway, the angular spin of the earth and the seasons lead to changes in the aerodynamics (science of the motion of air) of the atmosphere and of the currents in the oceans. The evaporation, and precipitation as rain or snow of water, and the weather patterns are now predicted by global circulation models (GCMs) on computers that can analyze temperature patterns and predict future heating and cooling patterns – these GCMs are getting better and better.

The study of the Earth's climate system has also become a very developed science, with studies of the atmosphere (the air and the wind patterns), the hydrosphere (interactions with water – oceans, and water ecosystems), the biosphere (the interactions with all forms of life), and the geosphere (the interaction with geology or the earth's crust). To this one can add the "energy sphere" or the manner in which energy from the sun actually has powered almost all forms of direct and indirect energy for plants, fossil fuels, and the resultant heating and cooling of air and water.

All of these "spheres" are studied and are known scientifically to be interacting with each other – the life forms produce all of the oxygen we breathe, the water and rain patterns give us our freshwater or flooding, the fossil fuels were buried in the Earth's crust when carbon dioxide was removed from the atmosphere and buried geologically as decomposed forms of life that had grown thanks to solar energy – specifically as fossil oil and fossil coal (geosphere), the oceans and land together affect all forms of life, and the atmosphere and hydrosphere interact to give us our climate and weather patterns, our storms, our hurricanes, our floods and our droughts.

The scientific basis of Climate Change or global warming is very well understood, and the scientists who are rigorous practitioners of the related fields, whose articles and papers are subjected to peer review before publication, have a high level of agreement on what is happening, and who and what is causing it. This is the same level of rigor that is practiced in ALL other fields of science that the whole scientific and technical worlds rely on **and on which ALL engineering and technology is based.** ALL of such scientists have come to the firm conclusion globally that emissions of greenhouse gases by human activity is causing Climate Change and global warming and that it is having predictable and severe consequences for not only humans but all life on the planet.

Someone who really understood all this and was an expert in atmospheric physics, was James Hansen. He had a great interest in all aspects of atmospheric physics and chemistry and in global circulation models (GCMs) that could model the effects of greenhouse gases and predict what would happen considering the Earth's atmosphere and the rotation of the planet about its axis. In 1981, at the US Goddard Institute of Space Studies, Hansen had already been measuring and studying surface temperatures and comparing those with past Earth surface temperatures. In a testimony to the US Senate in June 23, 1988, Hansen had reported that there was a 99% certainty that the surface temperatures (1981-1987) were warmer than in previous recorded history, that for this there was a clear cause and effect relationship with warming caused by greenhouse gases, and there was a high probability of the occurrence of worsening extreme and freak weather.

He was very critical of climate denier groups such as the Competitive Enterprise Institute that attempted to mislead the public and of politicians that accepted fossil fuel money and then described global warming as a "great hoax". Hansen has been a climate activist, especially after retiring and in 2009 published a book, *Storms of My Grandchildren – The Truth About Coming Climate Catastrophe and Our Last Chance to Save Humanity*, in which he warned that

the massive species extinction already occurring was being worsened by global warming and that it might lead to an extinction of the
human species. As the title of his book suggests, catastrophic and
stormy weather will get more severe if fossil fuel use continued. Others before had warned about global warming, but at least as early as
1988, Hansen had warned us about global warming and the need for
effective solutions that would improve things in a big way, but were
being delayed by climate deniers and their political allies. [1]*

**Global warming is not some distant future problem. It has al-
ready begun to devastate the US and the world.** To understand that,
one needs to understand that one of the key things that happens is
that when air temperature rises, there is greater evaporation from
the sea, and the air has more energy. This leads to two effects: it
increases the energy and hence the wind velocity of weather related
phenomena like hurricanes, tornados and coastal storms, while increasing the amount of rain most of the time. We have seen both.
The hurricanes are getting stronger and more devastating. Katrina
($120 billion losses), Superstorm Sandy ($75 billion losses), etc., the
list continues to grow. Each time the devastation is greater and the
hurricane leaves more damage and grief. Caused by a coastal storm,
the catastrophic floods in South Carolina (October 2015) are now
known to have given one of the highest levels of rainfall in US history, giving 15-19 inches of rain in a 24 hour period ("One in a 1,000
year storm"). Out of 59 sites recording rainfall, six sites set all-time
records (NOAA data – U.S. National Oceanic and Atmospheric Administration). In recent years, many rainfall events in the Chicago
area have led to very high levels of rainfall – some to flash flooding.
More and deadlier tornadoes, and severe rainfall events are likely to
damage the region. Global warming is not some future problem – its
devastation has arrived!

When I started talking publicly about Climate Change or Global
Warming in 1991 in Chicago, I was in a minority. In 1992, The United
Nations (UN), with the leadership of the Canadian Maurice Strong,
played a key role in getting the nations of the world together at the
Earth Summit, or the UN Conference on Environment & Development (UNCED) at Rio de Janeiro, Brazil. At that time I had organized
an informal group in Chicago, called the Earth Summit Network, that
consisted of about a dozen organizations and about a dozen other
people, coordinated by Tom Spaulding of the YMCA (Young Men's

Notes/References are found beginning page 319.

Christian Association) and myself. We organized a number of tele-conferences and public events to educate the Chicago and the Il-linois public about the global issues being discussed at the Earth Summit, especially Climate Change and Biodiversity. At the first teleconference that we organized at DePaul University north of Chi-cago in 1991, Senator Al Gore spoke to us about the importance of agreeing to and signing the first Global Warming Treaty. Our "Net-work" attempted to apply pressure on the then Senior Bush US Ad-ministration to be more flexible at the Global Warming talks at Rio. Anyway, we do not know if it was because of our pressure or not, the US did sign the United Nations Framework Convention on Climate Change (UNFCC – or Global Warming Treaty), the Biodiversity treaty, and Agenda 21 (or the global agenda for the 21st Century).

The United Nations Framework Convention on Climate Change (UNFCCC) was signed by many nations including the US at the Earth Summit at Rio de Janeiro, Brazil in 1992. All nations who signed and then ratified the treaty got their legislatures and leaders to agree of-ficially, then joined a "Conference of Parties (COP)" that became the governing body for the monitoring, implementation, and furthering of its aims. The treaty came into force on March 31, 1994 when the required minimum of 50 nations came back and ratified the treaty (got it approved by their home governments). As of December 2015, the treaty had 197 nations (parties) belonging to the convention. The United Nations Secretariat that supports the Convention is located in Bonn, Germany. Since 1994, the Conference of Parties has met mostly annually with each meeting being designated by a sequential number. For example, the Paris Agreement was signed at COP21 or the twenty-first meeting of the Conference of Parties.

A convention or a treaty by itself is non-binding, and it is only when a Protocol is agreed to that the latter contains action plans and possible targets and timetables. So, during the COP3 meeting, the nations that were parties to the treaty met in Kyoto, Japan, to adopt a Protocol to the treaty (the Kyoto Protocol) which required industrialized countries to reduce greenhouse gas emissions to 1990 levels by about the year 2010. However, very few nations met these commitments and by 2012 it was clear that no progress had been made in reducing emissions of greenhouse gases.

The Paris Agreement

Both, the treaty and the mandatory approach of the Kyoto Protocol were not successful in reducing greenhouse gas emissions in any significant way (more on this below). So, the parties to the treaty decided to try a voluntary approach that included everyone. For this, the Conference of Parties met at COP 21 during November 30 to December 11, 2015 in Paris, France, in which 192 nations participated – about 150 presidents and prime ministers were there at the opening. After the poor results from UNFCCC and Kyoto, something different was needed. Both in terms of reducing their own emissions, and in helping the poorer nations with financing and technology, the developed industrialized nations had fallen far short of their commitments. But this had been a mandatory approach, in which the Annex I industrialized nations had to make commitments and meet them.

The agreement in Paris provided some basis for hope. The main items agreed to were that the nations would aim for the goal of keeping global temperature rise below 2 degrees Celsius, while trying to keep it below 1.5 degrees Celsius. However, it was estimated that the voluntary commitments made at the time of the Paris Agreement were only enough to limit temperature rise to below 3.5 degrees Celsius. The aim was to for the developed nation's emissions to peak soon, with those of developing nations to peak later. The approach was more bottom-up than one mandated from above. Each nation proposed what it would do, and it became what they committed to and how they would do it.

Although the goal was $100 billion per year contributed by the developed nations to assist developing nations, the year this was to be achieved was extended from 2020 to 2025. Although no liability obligations were agreed to by the richer developed nations, there was agreement that some form of help would be given, especially to low lying island nations for loss and damage caused by global warming. Besides the nations, there were many non-state actors that participated that launched their own initiatives – these included governors, mayors, CEOs and philanthropic billionaires. This was historic agreement that was encouraged by and resulted from the pressure that has built up because of global actions of various people and organizations, by people's climate marches and by people's movements agitating for change.

The highlights and outcomes were:

1. Each of the nations committed to Nationally Determined Contributions (NDCs) based on what they had proposed themselves – which they committed to implementing domestically. Each nation would continue to report regularly on the progress they were making in achieving their NDCs, and be globally reviewed. These nations cover more than 90% of global emissions, which makes the commitments meaningful. These were called Intended Nationally Determined Contributions (INDCs).

2. All nations committed to submitting new NDCs every five years, with the hope that they would try to build on the initial NDCs and do better.

3. The richer or developed nations reaffirmed their original treaty commitments to help the developing nations, many of whom gave commitments for the first time.

4. From a market viewpoint, although the market based approaches like carbon trading did not get direct reference, a new trading mechanism is to be set up to replace Kyoto Protocol's Clean Development Mechanism.

5. The initial taking of stock, or how the nations are progressing, took place in 2018, with nations encouraged to start doing better, as presented in new NDCs. A full stock-taking is scheduled for 2023.

6. Agreed to in Paris is a new approach to transparency in which all nations will be required to submit their emissions inventories, and other information so that their progress can be tracked as per their NDCs.

7. It was also agreed that there would be a new mechanism to facilitate and help compliance – as aided by a committee of experts who would facilitate nations, and it would not be adversarial or punitive.

8. In regard to financially helping the poorer developing nations, there was a renewal of commitment by developed nations, and an added commitment by richer developing nations to provide a combination of public and private finance totaling about $100 billion a year as a goal up to 2025, and extend it beyond that as a $100b minimum.

9. Then since the bad effects of global warming are already

under way, and expected to get worse, special attention was paid to adaptation – so that developing nations hardest hit would be assisted in their adaptation efforts.

10. Also, for loss and damage that might occur due to extreme weather events and slowly developing events like sea rise, developing nations, especially island states, would be helped with early warning systems and risk insurance. However, losses and damages incurred would not be used as a basis for liability or compensation.

11. Lastly, the nations would be going back to their home bases and getting domestic approvals, and when approved, would come back for ratification. After at least 55 nations accounting for more than 55% of emissions have signed, then the agreement would go into force, and regular meetings could be held. In the meantime, an ad hoc working group would be formed to take the process forward.

12. On the sidelines, nations offered additional financial pledges of $19b. In addition, India and France led 120 nations in forming a Solar Alliance aimed at helping solar energy development in developing nations. About 20 developed and developing nations launched a Mission Innovation initiative for governments to invest in research and development of clean energy. Bill Gates and 27 other major investors, worldwide, launched Breakthrough Energy Coalition for private capital investment in clean energy. The Compact of Mayors delivered commitments of over 360 cities to deliver over half of the urban emissions reductions by 2020.

13. France encouraged all of the non-governmental actors to enter their pledges into the NAZCA Portal set up under the Lima-Paris Action agenda (Non-state Actor Zone for Climate Action). By the time of the Paris meeting, there had been nearly 11,000 commitments entered by non-state actors. As of early 2020 there are 25,961 commitments made by companies, cities, investors, regions and organizations, of the 191 nations participating.

14. Article 15 of the Paris Agreement provides the mechanism (means) by establishing an expert committee to facilitate implementation and promote compliance.

About 194 UNFCCC member nations signed the Paris Agreement, and 172 of which ratified it (which means they went back to their home governments and got the necessary approval from an official governing authority).

However, the science of Climate Change and actions, described in a summary fashion above, continue to be challenged and attacked. It is important to document here what is credible.

The Intergovernmental Panel on Climate Change (IPCC)

Why it is the Most Credible Source Globally

As early as 1988, feeling the need for evaluation and guidance from experts on the worsening problem of Climate Change, the United Nations formed the Intergovernmental Panel on Climate Change (IPCC) in order to provide it with an objective and scientific understanding, that would inform better political and economic decision making. Formed in 1988 by the World Meteorological Organization (WMO) and the United Nations Environment Program (UNEP – currently known as UN Environment), IPCC was later endorsed by the UN General Assembly, that consists of all nations. Much of what follows comes from the IPCC website.

The IPCC, which currently has 195 member nations, with the Secretariat in Geneva, Switzerland, was established to provide the United Nations and the world with scientific assessments of Climate Change, what was involved and the risks, as well as provide guidance on solutions for mitigation (reducing emissions) and adaptation (adapting to Climate Change). The IPCC does not do research itself, or monitor the phenomena itself, but it assesses research reports. **Thousands of scientists from all over the world contribute to assessing, writing and reviewing reports, which are based on assessments of mostly peer reviewed research papers, but even non peer-reviewed papers. The reports of the IPCC, besides being subjected to its own internal reviews, are reviewed typically by over 120 countries. The IPCC consists of scientific experts from all over the world, and drafts of its reports are reviewed at several stages, thus enhancing transparency and objectivity. It is an internationally accepted authority on Climate Change, as accepted by leading climate**

scientists globally, as well as by governments.

Reports of the IPCC are based on literature from mainly peer-reviewed scientific and technical journals, but also reports from government institutions, industry and research institutions, international and other organizations and conference proceedings. **Many thousands of sources were cited in the Fifth Assessment Report, which shows the wide nature of research literature it draws upon to reach its conclusions. IPCC Reports aim at the highest standards of scientific excellence, balance and clarity, and after multiple stages of reviews, the reports are submitted to expert reviewers and governments to review further.** The First Order Draft of every report is prepared based on peer-reviewed scientific journals and similar publications, and after reviews is revised to prepare a Second Order Draft. After further simultaneous reviews by experts and governments, the authors prepare the final report. Endorsements of reports and especially the Summaries for Policy Makers (SPMs) go through three stages: approval, adoption and acceptance. Assessment and Special Reports are approved and accepted by the responsible Working Group, with the government representatives to the panel coming together in a Plenary Session of the Working Group. It is necessary for the Panel to review a report at a session and formally accept it.

IPCC Assessment Reports – Climate Change, the Past, the Present and the Future

For over 30 years, the IPCC has been providing the reports that have guided global strategy on Climate Change. Formed in 1988, the IPCC came up with its first Assessment Report in 1990, which informed the Earth Summit in Rio de Janeiro, Brazil in 1992, where the first global warming treaty (UNFCCC – United Nations Framework Convention on Climate Change) was signed. The second Report of 1995 informed the people and governments that agreed to the Kyoto Protocol of 1997. The third Assessment Report (2001) looked at the impacts of global warming and the need for adaptation. The fourth Assessment Report (2007) tried to guide whatever agreement would follow after the Kyoto Protocol period (2008-2012). The Fifth Assessment Report (2013-2014) provided the information for the Paris Agreement (December 2015). Much of what follows comes from Wikipedia descriptions of the IPCC and from its own reports.

The Assessment Reports are the best source for understanding how the problem of Climate Change has evolved and what solutions have been proposed since 1992. **The Third Assessment Report published in 2001 had predicted** that global greenhouse gas emissions would rise by 9-12 billion metric tons of carbon equivalent by 2020, and to 11-23 billion tons by 2050 (to calculate carbon dioxide equivalent, these numbers need to be multiplied by 3.67). The average temperature was projected to rise by between 1.4-5.8 degrees Celsius (2.5 – 10.5 degrees Fahrenheit) by 2100, and the average sea level projected to rise by 9-88 centimeters (3.5-34.5 inches) by 2100. The actual numbers are all coming in between the minimum and the maximum.

Next, we come to the Fourth Assessment Report (AR4), published in 2007, which took 6 years to produce and which involved 130 countries, 2,500 scientific expert reviewers, 800 contributing authors and more than 400 lead authors. *Next came the IPCC Fifth Assessment Report (AR5) which was published during 2013 and 2014. It stated in even more forceful terms that global warming was indeed occurring and that the changes were of a type and magnitude not known before in the preceding decades before the 1950s and the preceding millennia (thousands of years). The greenhouse gases had increased to levels not known at least in the last 800,000 years. The probability that it was human activity that was causing the warming was increased to the 95-100% level – almost stating that it was certain that human activity was causing it. The impacts from increasing global warming were stated as going to be severe, widespread and irreversible.* The report feels that the overall risks could be reduced if the rate of change in climate could be reduced.

After the Paris Agreement, the UNFCCC requested a special report on how the total temperature rise above pre-industrial levels could be kept below 1.5 degrees Celsius. This was the stated goal of the Paris Agreement. Considering that by 2015 the global temperature rise already recorded (very high confidence) was about 0.87 degrees Celsius. The global average temperature rise in the Arctic was recorded as being about 2-3 times higher. The IPCC completed and furnished the report in October 2018. The report stated that doing this was possible providing the world made rapid, aggressive and extensive steps towards transitioning energy, land, urban, infrastructure and industrial systems. **In order to achieve this, the carbon dioxide emissions needed to be reduced by 45% from 2010 levels by 2030,**

and down to net zero by about 2050, with other green-house gas emissions reduced on a similar timetable. However, even a warming of 1.5 degrees Celsius was stated as leading to large scale drought, famine, heat stress, species extinctions, loss of entire ecosystems, and adding about 100 million people to those in poverty. **This report is called the IPCC 1.5 C report.** [2]

Setting The Goals

Based on the above IPCC 1.5 C Report, for the Global Climate Action Plan outlined in this book, the carbon dioxide (CO_2) emissions are targeted to be reduced by 50% from 2021 to 2030, and then down to zero by 2050.

So for meeting the goals of global average temperature rise no more than 1.5 Degrees Celsius (2.7 degrees Fahrenheit), or for short "1.5C Goals", the Plan adopts the following goals:

❏ The Climate Plan meets the greenhouse gas (GHG) emissions to avoid the worst consequences of Climate Change.

❏   Three Main Greenhouse Gases (gases that trap heat by the greenhouse effect) are:

    ❏ CARBON DIOXIDE (CO_2)

       ❏ Emissions from fossil fuels down by 50% by 2030 and 95% by 2050

       ❏ (Plan counts only 5% absorption by forests, coastal eco-systems, etc.)

    ❏ METHANE (CH_4) – 50% reductions in emissions by 2050

    ❏ NITROUS OXIDE (N_2O) – 25% reductions in emissions by 2050

*As per IPCC (United Nations, Intergovernmental Panel on Climate Change) 1.5 C Report.

Achieving this goal means that the global average temperature rise will be no more than 1.5 degrees Celsius. To draw on a corona-virus (COVD-19) analogy, we will have peaked. We will have gone from increasing carbon dioxide (CO_2) concentrations to peaking in the year 2050 (or a zero increase in concentration in parts per million of CO_2). Till then we have to rely on fossil fuel emissions reductions to get us there. Thereafter, till 2100, in order to cool things back and get the carbon dioxide concentration to near 350 ppm (parts per million), we will have to rely on carbon sinks on land (forests, grasslands, etc.) and sea (ocean ecosystems), which hopefully will have matured by then. Possibly, other measures to directly remove carbon dioxide from the atmosphere will have been demonstrated and proven.

The reductions in the emissions of other greenhouse gases are covered later in Chapter 11. Most of the rest of this book looks at how to reduce carbon dioxide emissions that result mainly from the burning of fossil fuels.

Chapter 2

The Global Energy and Climate Plan

F or the world, we first take a look at current energy use and that projected for the coming years by the International Energy Agency (IEA) in its World Energy Outlook 2018 Report (Hereafter referred to as WEO2018). [3]

Pie charts: In the following pages, we will present pie charts that show quantitatively in percentages the amount of each energy source used. The title at the top shows the total energy used (equal to 100%).

CURRENT ENERGY USE (AS OF 2017)

So where is the world as of 2017? The latest data available from the International Energy Agency (IEA) from its World Energy Outlook 2018 report (WEO2018) shows a very high reliance on fossil fuels that has been growing recently. In 2017, the world supplied 13,972 Mtoe (million tons of oil equivalent – that means all energy sources converted the same heat energy as metric ton of oil or petroleum) or 162 PWH (petawatt hours, in electrical energy units – One PWH is 1,000,000,000 MWH – megawatt hours). The actual energy consumed is less than this, as some part of this was expended in getting the energy to the end user. Anyway, the following pie chart shows where we were in 2017, causing global carbon dioxide emissions of 32.6 giga tons (or 32.6 billion metric tons, where one metric ton is 1,000 kilograms or 2,200 pounds).

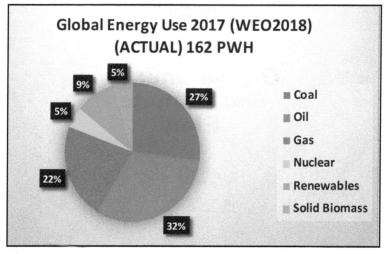

Energy Actually Consumed by World in 2017

Pie chart showing the Energy (including electricity) that the whole world used in 2017. Renewables include hydro, bioenergy, solar and wind. Fossil fuels are clearly still dominating, supplying about 81% of the world's energy. Coal use is still high. The total is 162 PWH (peta watt hours). To calculate energy value for any energy source, simply multiply total with the percentage (For example, coal use is 162 x 0.27 = 43.74 PWH).

ENERGY USE PROJECTED TO 2030 and 2050
IF CURRENT POLICIES CONTINUE

The World Energy Outlook 2018 Report from the international Energy Agency (IEA) projects the energy use by the world in 2025 and 2040. From this, the energy use for the years 2030 and 2050 are calculated by linearly interpolating and extrapolating (drawing a straight line on graph and picking points for these years) for these years from the 2025 and 2040 year data. This gives us what the "Projected" energy use will be for these years, which is the best information that we have from an international organization that specializes in this activity. But these projections are estimates by them assuming that the current policies by all the nations will continue. So here are what we can expect if nothing changes and we continue doing what we are doing now for 2030 and 2050.

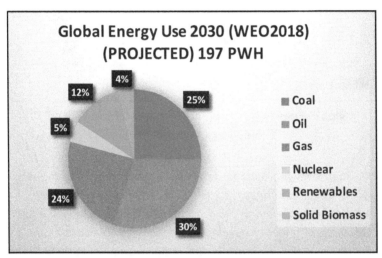

**Global Energy Use Projected for 2030
from WEO2018 Projection**

Pie chart showing the Energy (including electricity) that the whole world is projected to use in 2030 if we continue current policies. Energy use is projected to grow from 162 PWH to 197 PWH, and renewable energies that include hydro, bioenergy, solar and wind, increase a little, but fossil fuels still dominate at 79%.

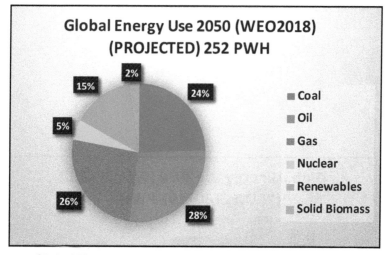

**Global Energy Use Projected for 2050 from WEO2018
Projection – Current Policies**

Pie chart showing the Energy (including electricity) that the whole world is projected to use in 2050 if we continue current policies. Energy use is projected to grow from 162 PWH to 252 PWH, about a 55% growth (most in developing economies), but fossil fuels still dominate at 78%. Meanwhile, the carbon dioxide emissions continue to grow from 32.6 giga tons (giga is 1,000 million) in 2017 to projected (extrapolated) emissions 47 Gt by 2050.

The International Energy Agency looks at another case which it calls the Sustainable Development Goals (SDG) case which goes to the maximum it considers practical in terms of reducing fossil fuel use and increasing production of energy by renewables (including hydro, wind, solar and bio energy), but not including biomass.

The best case projected by the WEO2018 Report of the IEA still shows fossil fuels contributing 47% of the total, and carbon dioxide emissions less than 17 Gt (giga tons) of carbon dioxide. Note that the energy use projected here (158 PWH) is less than that in 2017 (162 PWH) – so total energy use is down.

Before the Plan is presented, it is fair to describe the other scenarios and "plans" that have been put forward or proposed by others.

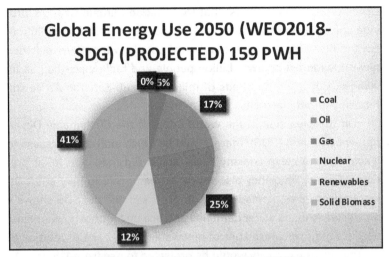

Global Energy Use 2050 (WEO2018-SDG) (PROJECTED) 159 PWH

- Coal
- Oil
- Gas
- Nuclear
- Renewables
- Solid Biomass

0% 5% 17% 41% 25% 12%

Global Energy Use Projected for 2050 from WEO2018 projection – SDG Case

Pie chart showing the SDS energy scenario that is described by WEO 2018, while halving the role for coal, still continues to show a great reliance on all the fossil fuels (coal, oil and natural gas), and with a doubling of the role of renewable energy from the current policies level of 37 PWH (petawatt hours or billion MWH) to 65 PWH by 2050 (extrapolated). However, it still shows that fossil fuels would provide 60% of the total energy and the carbon dioxide emissions would still be at a level of 17.6 giga tons in 2040 – an unacceptable level, that will not meet the goals of keeping the global average temperature increase below 1.5 degrees Celsius (2.7 degrees Fahrenheit), compared to the pre-industrial level.

Other Global Plans and Comparisons

World Energy Outlook 2018 – International Energy Agency (IEA)

The quantitative energy information shown above is taken from the World Energy Outlook 2018 (WEO2018) Report provided by the International Energy Agency (IEA). [2] The WEO2018 report also highlights what it calls a Sustainable Development Scenario (SDS) that is based on trying to meet the requirements of the UN Sustainable

Development Goals (SDGs) that try to tackle Climate Change, provide universal energy access and reduce the effects of air pollution. For the first time ever, the number of people without any electricity worldwide fell below 1 billion people and India electrified all its villages. But many hundreds of millions in sub-Saharan Africa still remain without electricity.

On the plus side, if the world adopted the Sustainable Development Scenario (SDS), there would be much increase in access to electricity and clean cooking fuels, and a big reduction in air pollution. Energy efficiency also much a greater role to play and SDS emphasizes investments in it. Another plus is that the SDS shows a big decrease in the water demands and use by thermal power plants because of the increased use of renewable energy. The proportion of energy use as electricity would be projected to rise from 19% in 2017 to about 28% in 2040. But the energy related carbon dioxide (CO_2) emissions would only fall to net zero by 2070.

International Renewable Energy Agency – IRENA – Road Map to 2050

The International Renewable Energy Agency is an intergovernmental agency that exists to promote and assist nations in their transition to renewable energy of all kinds. According to them, renewable energy as a part of Total Final Energy Consumption, according to their ReMap plan is projected to grow from about 15% in 2015 to about 65% of the total by 2050, and is estimated to create about 11 million additional jobs. The carbon dioxide emissions reductions would be achieved 41% by renewable energy, 11% by switching to electrification and about 40% by enhanced energy efficiency. In their ReMap case, there is significant emphasis on bioenergy, especially for use in the aviation and shipping areas. Because of energy efficiency, the Total Primary Energy Supply (TPES) is projected to stay at the 2015 level of 500 EJ/year (500 Exa Joules are equal to 11,942 Mtoe, million tons of oil equivalent or 138.9 PWH – Peta Watt Hours, Exa = 10E18). But the ReMap plan still projects carbon dioxide emissions of about 9.7 Giga Tons by 2050 and aims for a 2 degree Celsius temperature rise. [4]

The WWS Plan Proposed by the Solutions Project
Led by Mark Jacobson

The Wind, Water and Solar (WWS) plan proposed by the Solutions Project is the most comprehensive plan that is out there to date. Although other renewable technologies are considered, most of the expansion proposed is in wind, hydro and solar PV power. The project has proposed plans for 139 countries, that calls for electrification of all energy sectors (transportation, heating/cooling, industry, agriculture/forestry/fishing) with technologies that are already available, and providing this power and energy with the three WWS energies. The plan claims to meet the carbon emissions reductions to keep the global average temperature rise below 1.5 degrees Celsius, avoid millions of deaths due to air pollution, create about 24 million net new jobs (added jobs created minus those lost in fossil fuel activities), reduce power requirements by about 40% due to higher efficiency (less energy lost in extracting, processing, storage, transporting, etc. of fossil fuels, and less heat energy lost in electricity production), and meet the world power and energy requirements by 2050.

As stated, for energy production and use, the three main technologies that are relied on are wind, hydro and solar, and it is shown that the land areas needed for these are only about 1.5 million square kilometers, out of a total land area of about 120 million square kilometers of the 139 nations. It presents the numbers mainly in terms of the power or Watts (MW or TW) needed rather than in energy or watt hours (kilo, mega or tera, KWH, MWH, or TWH). The total new WWS power added as per the plan is estimated to be 50 terawatts (or TW – 50 million megawatts or MW). The plan estimates that the total power demand of about 12 TW in 2012, which would be totally replaced by 12 TW of WWS energies by 2050, and about 8 TW would be saved as compared to Business as Usual (BAU) scenario through avoidance of energy losses in combustion (of fossil fuels), improvements in end user efficiency, and avoidance of energy lost in fossil fuel extraction, processing and distribution. [5]

The total power to be added of about 50 terawatts (or TW – 50 million megawatts or MW) would need a total investment of about $125 trillion (about $2.5 million/MW), compared with a Business as Usual (mainly fossil fuel investment) needed of about $2.7 million per MW, or about $3.5 trillion investment per year. This is of the order of magnitude of other plans discussed above. Plus, the WWS renewable energy based plan has zero fuel costs (the fuel is free), as compared with a significant fuel cost for fossil fuels (in the Business as Usual Scenario.

The Drawdown Plan

The book *Drawdown* presents a most detailed descriptions of most of the solution areas to Climate Change, and for each area, for the quantitative level proposed, the reductions in carbon dioxide emissions, the net cost and the net savings of each of those. For each of the major categories of energy, food, women and girls, buildings and cities, and materials, it presents excellent descriptions of all the categories and their sections. It also provides a ranking of all the different activities, so as to provide some idea as to the relative importance to be given to each area. At the end of the book the eighty areas are ranked, and top fifteen are highlighted. In its Optimum Scenario it emphasizes 100% renewable energy by 2050, and emphasizes that this is without biomass, landfill methane, nuclear and waste-to-energy. All of the above is very commendable and the book is a great resource. [6]

However, it ignores the big elephant in the room – fossil fuels. It does not even look at the prospect of eliminating or even reducing the use of coal, oil and natural gas. It does not even mention the need to *replace* fossil fuels with renewable energy – although the assumption may be that these are to be replaced by alternatives. **Also, the book does not present a plan on what is to be done when, by who and by which means, how the transition will be financed, what is to be done for fossil fuels and the nations that produce them, what is to be done for the mobile fuels and mobile needs (which need transportable fuel with zero carbon emissions), how the world will cooperate, and how the poorer nations will be able to afford or be helped to do what they need to do without blowing the global carbon budget.** Nonetheless, the book is a very good reference book if one wants to look at what a particular activity is about, and if it is done, what the carbon dioxide emissions reductions are, and what the costs and savings would be.

Getting to Carbon Neutral for California

The US state of California has set itself the goal of being carbon neutral by 2045 – meaning that after it achieves a reduction of 60% in fossil fuel emissions earlier, it is willing to look at options to offset its remaining carbon emissions with any means that absorb carbon. From the 2020 goal of 431 MtCO2e (million metric tons of carbon dioxide), which it has already met and meets the Kyoto target of reducing its emissions to 1990 levels, the emissions goal for 2030 is 260 MtCO2, and that for 2050 is 86 MtCO2 (80% reduction). So, a number of people at the Lawrence Livermore National Laboratory (LLNL) in the San Francisco area, have put forward a study titled, *Getting to Neutral – Options for Negative Carbon Emissions in California*, January 2020. In order for California to reach its goal of being carbon neutral by 2045, the study is proposing three options that it says can achieve 125 MtCO2 of negative emissions (or net carbon dioxide absorption). [7]

The three options are carbon absorption by natural and working lands (25 MtCO2 absorption), convert waste biomass to fuel and store the CO2 (84 MtCO2 absorption), and direct CO2 air capture and storage (16 MtCO2 absorption). While the natural and working lands option (forests, wetlands and agriculture) is guaranteed to work but quantitative absorptions are uncertain, it is not recommending a large amount of reforestation or afforestation. The waste biomass option mean collecting all or most of California's waste biomass and combusting it to generate energy and then absorbing the carbon dioxide. The major proposal (that both the second and third options need) is to collect and pipe large amounts of carbon dioxide gas to underground storage sites and store it there permanently, with each year adding to the total. This proposal is similar to what has been proposed in Europe as BECCS (Bio Energy Carbon Capture and Storage), which is described in a later chapter on the European Union. The important point here to make is that aside from small projects, there has been no large scale demonstration that Carbon Capture and Storage works, what it costs and the consumption needed to do it, and whether long term storage of carbon dioxide gas underground will work. Will the gas stay there, or will it leak?

Substantial Suggestions by Climate Reality
– Al Gore

Both as US senator and as Vice-President, and later as private citizen, Al Gore highlighted the problem of Climate Change, and went around the world, providing information and promoting action. His leadership contributed significantly to the definition and the agreement that led to the Kyoto Protocol in 1997 at Kyoto, Japan. It was a disappointment to him that the two nations that did not ratify the Kyoto Protocol were the US and Australia. For his efforts, he received the Nobel Peace Prize is 2007, along with the IPCC (Intergovernmental Panel on Climate Change). His most well-known 2006 book *An Inconvenient Truth* highlighted the problem of Climate Change and indicated significant solutions. In the latter part of his book he defined solutions in terms of renewable energy (biomass, wind, solar, hydro and geothermal), electric and fuel cell vehicles, increased end use energy efficiency, and personal actions to conserve. Since then, he founded the Climate Reality Project, the aim of which was to provide information and promote action on Climate Change. The Climate Reality Project has been very good for mobilization, training and leadership development, and has been responsible for developing many people who have taken up local leadership in many areas. (https://www.climaterealityproject.org).[8]

Substantial Suggestions by 350.org
– Bill McKibben

Bill McKibben is a well-known author who has written extensively on Climate Change. His books, articles and speeches on nature and Climate Change have been very influential in inspiring a whole range of people globally. The organization, 350.org was formed by a number of university students in the US in 2007, with the leadership of Bill McKibben. From 2008 to 2010, 350.org organized worldwide demonstrations in over 180 nations, linked organizations globally, provided information, and applied pressure worldwide. The organization states that we need to reduce the concentration of carbon dioxide (CO_2) in the atmosphere from the current level of over 400 ppm (parts per million) to below 350 ppm, which many scientists say is needed to escape the worst consequences of Climate Change – hence the name 350.org. They helped organize the People's Climate March on September 21, 2014, which occurred at 2,000 places around the world. Inspired by Greta Thunberg, 350.org was one of the leading organizations that organized the Global Climate Strike on September 20-27, 2019, that was the largest climate related mobilization, in which about 7.6 million people participated in about 185 nations. They have organized thousands of volunteers in over 188 nations, and have formed alliances with over 300 organizations globally. They strongly advocate the replacement of fossil fuels with renewable energy and are very active globally. (https://350.org).[9]

We now present the Plan described in this book.

THE PROPOSED GLOBAL ENERGY
AND EMISSIONS PLAN

This chapter lays out a time bound plan for the world to achieve the energy transition and the carbon emissions reductions in the time frame set forth in goals in Chapter 1. The principle areas for which the plan will be proposed are: electricity production, energy production, energy efficiency, transportation, buildings/homes, industry, agriculture, forestry, fisheries, tourism, shipping and aviation. Rather than electricity production being just enough to substitute for fossil fuels, the renewable energy sector plan will be shown to grow to meet increased electricity demands of a growing economy, after accounting for significant energy efficiency improvements. More detailed proposed plans for the larger carbon emitting economies, the USA, Europe, China, and India and others will be described in a following chapter. Also in following chapters we describe the ecosystem aspects of the Plan – forests, coastal ecosystems and agriculture – the carbon sinks that are treated as a bonus and act as an insurance, and so that the life supporting systems of the planet are enhanced. These account for only 3-5% of energy use, and only about 5% of carbon dioxide emissions.

As shown below, while we are not proposing that all of the world's energy be produced by solar energy, there is little doubt that ALL of the world's energy CAN be produced by solar energy, and the main issue that would remain is what to do when the sun is not shining. While the plan shows how other renewable energy sources, like wind energy, can also grow significantly, the main plan calls for a multi-dimensional energy strategy that relies heavily on solar PV (photo-voltaic) to generate electricity. There is little doubt that solar, wind, geothermal and hydro (mainly – supplemented by some nuclear in the short term), can produce all of the electricity we now consume, as well as the increase in electric energy demand till 2050, with some increase in energy efficiency that leads to a slight reduction in demand and also reduced GHG (greenhouse gas) emissions.

What the current Plan calls for is a massive increase in electrification of most other currently non-electric energy uses, some reliance on battery storage, but a big increase in electricity production, mainly with solar, to generate storage fuels like hydrogen, ammonia, methyl cyclohexane, and aluminum. The big electrification and generation of storage fuels can be done by about a three-fold increase in electricity production, mainly from solar, and the storage fuels can be transported by pipelines, tankers, trains or trucks to wherever needed. Every large solar electricity plant would generate an excess of a *storage fuel* as well as charge a battery storage system – one that would provide level or increased electric output by either batteries or storage fuel powered generators, whenever there is cloud cover or when the sun goes down, or the wind is not blowing. So let's begin with a quantitative reality check for solar energy.

The proposed plan is shown in the pie charts below for the years 2030 and 2050. Essentially, by 2030 fossil fuels begin significant reductions but still stay at about 53% of the total energy use (down from the current 79% as of the 2017 data), but solar PV and efficiency start kicking in significantly. However, by 2050, coal is gone and a small remaining use of oil and natural gas remain, so that fossil fuels are only 3% of the total energy use, and solar PV and efficiency energy use reductions have grown in a big way. In both cases, if energy efficiency can be counted as a quantitative benefit (which it is), then the total energy use as per the Plan proposed in this book is the same as that projected by the International Energy Agency (IEA) for energy use growth based on current policies (252 PWH).

First let us put things in perspective in regard to solar energy and world's energy consumption.

SOLAR ENERGY FACT CHECK

World Total Energy Consumption in 2017 (WEO 2018 Report – IEA)
- ❑ 13,972 Mtoe (Millions of Metric Tons of Oil Equivalent).
- ❑ 162,494 TWH (Terrawatt Hours, 1 TWH = 1,000,000 MWH) = 162.5 PWH (Petawatt Hours).
- ❑ **All fossil fuels only use an average of about 40% of their share (efficiency). The rest is wasted (coal: 35%, oil: 38%, and natural gas: 45%).**

Area Needed to Make This Energy with solar PV (Photo-Voltaic)
- ❑ MW – Megawatts, MWH –megawatt hours (or 1,000 KWH or kilowatt hours – shows up on your electric bill).
- ❑ 1 MW of POWER produced for 1 hour gives 1 MWH of energy
- ❑ 1MW solar panels typically generate 2,000 MWH of energy in a whole year.
- ❑ So 162,494 TWH/2,000 – Needs 81.25 TW, or 81,250,000 MW capacity size.
- ❑ So, 81,250,000 MW worth of solar PV panels could generate ALL of the world's energy for the year 2017.
- ❑ Typical utility scale solar PV system, 1 MW needs 0.0154 square kilometers area.
- ❑ So solar panels of 81,250,000 MW size need **1.25 million square kilometers.**
- ❑ At 40% efficiency, 162.5 PWH of fossil fuel energy only generates 0.40 x 162.5 PWH worth of electric energy (65 PWH), which only needs 32,500,000 MW.
- ❑ Which in turn only needs **0.5 million square kilometers.**
- ❑ Even if the numbers are off a little bit, that's about what we need
- ❑ The total land area of the world is **148.9 million square kilometers (58 million square miles).**

SUMMARY
- ❑ **WE ONLY NEED 0.3% TO 0.8% LAND AREA TO MAKE *ALL* OF THE WORLD'S ENERGY WITH SOLAR ENERGY. Even if solar panels only generate half the energy, the point is that the land area needed is very small.**

With this as background, the following Plan is proposed for the world.

THE PROPOSED GLOBAL PLAN

As shown below, while we are not proposing that all of the world's energy be produced by solar energy, there is little doubt that ALL of the world's energy CAN be produced by solar energy, and the main issue that would remain is what to do when the sun is not shining. While the plan shows how other renewable energy sources, like wind energy, can also grow significantly, the main plan calls for a multi-dimensional energy strategy that relies heavily on solar PV (photo-voltaic) to generate electricity. There is little doubt that solar, wind, geothermal and hydro (mainly – supplemented by some nuclear in the short term), can produce all of the electricity we now consume, as well as the increase in electric energy demand till 2050, with some increase in energy efficiency that leads to a slight reduction in demand and also very little GHG emissions.

What the Plan calls for is a massive increase in electrification of most other currently non-electric energy uses, some reliance on battery storage, but a big increase in electricity production, mainly with solar, to generate non-carbon storage fuels like hydrogen, ammonia, and others to be produced, which when burnt do not lead to the release of carbon dioxide, and which are described later in this chapter. The big electrification and generation of storage fuels can be done by about a three-fold increase in electricity production, mainly from Solar, and the storage fuels can be transported by pipelines, tankers, trains or trucks to wherever needed. Every large solar electricity plant would generate an excess of a storage fuel as well as charge a battery storage system – one that would provide level or increased electric output by either batteries or storage fuel powered generators, whenever there is cloud cover or when the sun goes down, or the wind is not blowing.

The proposed plan is shown in the pie charts below for the years 2030 and 2050. Essentially, fossil fuels begin significant reductions by still stay at about 53% of the total energy use (down from the current 79% as of the 2017 data), but solar PV and efficiency start kick in significantly by 2030. However, by 2050, coal is totally gone and a small remaining use of oil and natural gas remain, so that fossil fuels are only 5% of the total energy use, and 5% or less of greenhouse gas emissions, and solar PV and energy efficiency energy use reductions have grown in a big way. In both cases, if energy efficiency can be counted as a quantitative benefit (which it is), then the total energy use as per the Plan proposed in this book is the same as that projected by the International Energy Agency (IEA) for energy use growth based on current policies. For the Plan between 2030 and 2050, it is proposed that there is a big increase in the "green" production and use of non-carbon storage fuels. The Plan only allows 5% carbon dioxide emissions from fossil fuels, and relies on carbon sink ecosystems to absorb only this amount of emissions, and if they absorb more, that will be considered a bonus.

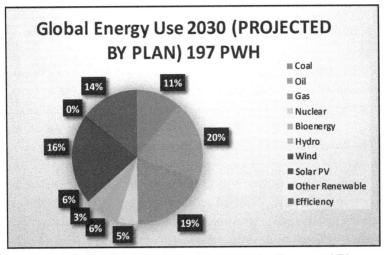

Global Energy Use Projected for 2050 by Proposed Plan

Pie chart showing the new Energy Plan proposed in this book (including electricity) for the year 2030 that the whole world will use if it adopts this plan. Fossil fuels are down to 53% of the total use compared to the 79% of total projected above by WEO2018 if we continue current policies.

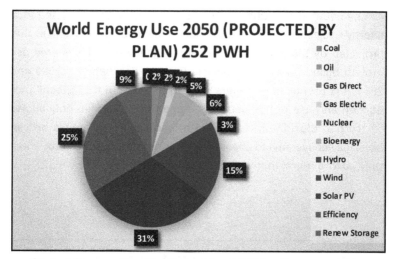

Global Energy Use Projected for 2050 by Proposed Plan

Pie chart showing the new energy plan proposed in this book (including electricity) for the year 2050 that the whole world will use if it adopts this plan. Fossil fuels are down to 5% of the total use (essentially gone) compared to the other projected use of 78% of total if we continue current policies, as projected above (WEO2018) – with fossil fuel based greenhouse gas emissions correspondingly down. There is a massive expansion of renewable energy (mainly wind, but solar in a big way). This plan relies quite a bit on energy efficiency efforts that use less energy to accomplish the same use. Also shown is Renew Storage, or the production of storage fuels (Fuels like hydrogen and ammonia produced with renewable energy) as 9% of the total. If energy efficiency targets are not met then they can be met through expansion of solar PV and storage fuels.

The above Plan energy projections were calculated in the following way:

1. Fossil fuels were totally replaced by other energy sources – mainly wind and solar as per below.
2. Nuclear energy growth was assumed to be about the same as projected by WEO2018 (International Energy Agency).
3. Hydro-electric energy was assumed to be about the same as projected by WEO2018.
4. Bioenergy was assumed to about the same as projected by WEO2018.

5. Wind Energy Projection was much higher that WEO2018, and about equal to that projected by the Jacobsen plan.

6. A number of others have suggested that a 25% goal for global energy efficiency is realistic, considering how the European Union and California have been doing.

7. Then, based on the fact check for solar energy, the rest is all solar PV energy, although other solar technologies like Concentrated Solar Power (CSP) can certainly substitute for it. Solar PV energy is about twice that proposed by the Jacobsen plan for the combined utility scale and roof top solar. This includes direct solar charging of vehicles. Renew Storage at 9% for 2050 is considered a realistic goal if the world steps up to the Research and Development tasks needed for producing storage fuels using solar PV and other renewable energies, and their end user technologies. The energy dense and mobile non-carbon fuels replace gasoline (petrol) and diesel.

We now look in greater detail at all the different parts of the Plan.

SOLAR PV POWER PLANTS ALREADY IN OPERATION WORLDWIDE

❑ For comparison, most nuclear reactors are of 200 MW size (usually in sets of 5).

❑ As of Jan 2020, there were about 62 solar PV Power Plants larger than 200 MW – Wikipedia.

❑ About 27 of these were already operational in the US – the largest number in any nation.

❑ Besides having the largest plant (2,050 MW at Pavagada), India already had 7 power plants larger than 500 MW – total 9 larger than 200 MW.

❑ China had 6 power plants larger than 500 MW, and total 10 larger than 200 MW.

❑ The main issue with solar PV is that it only produces power when the sun is shining.

❑ We look at how we overcome this below.

Image Credit: LA Times

Example of the largest solar PV power plant as of January 2020.

   As of early 2020, the largest solar PV power plant was the 2,050 MW (megawatt) power plant in the state of Karnataka in India. This is the Pavagada Solar Park that is located in the middle of the peninsular area of India in a dry region. Completed at the end of 2019, this project cost $2.1 billion to build, which amounts to a system cost of about $1.02 per watt, one of the lowest costs in the world, at a location that has a very high solar insolation (high average hours of sunlight per day). Shown here is a photo of this power plant.

Courtesy MCE

An example of a smaller scale Utility type solar PV plant in the city of Richmond, California is shown here.

This is their Solar one project consisting of 10.5 MW (megawatt) solar PV panels. MCE (Marin Clean Energy) is California's first Community Choice Aggregation (CCA) not-for-profit organization operating in the San Francisco, California area that supplies renewable energy. More on CCAs later in the book.

TRANSITIONING OUT OF FOSSIL FUELS

NOTE: For each million BTU (British Thermal Units) of heat energy, fossil fuels emit the following amounts of carbon dioxide (CO_2) on the average (US Energy Information Administration):

Coal (Average of Different Types):
210 Pounds, Lb. (or 95 Kilograms, Kg)

Oil (Gasoline or Diesel):
160 Pounds, Lb. (or 73 Kilograms, Kg)

Natural Gas:
117 Pounds, Lb. (or 53 Kilograms, Kg)

The biggest problem with coal power plants is with their massive carbon emissions. Airborne toxins and pollutants releases include mercury, lead, sulfur dioxide, nitrogen oxides, particulates (smoke), and heavy metals. These cause health problems like breathing problems, brain damage, heart problems, cancer, neurological disorders and premature death. In the US, coal use leads to 100 million tons of ash waste every year that pollutes all the waterways.

Plan for Transitioning Out of Coal

1. All existing coal fired power plants globally be REPLACED by Utility Scale solar PV plus battery systems. In the short term, for evening and nights, electricity can come from other locations (nuclear, hydro or natural gas power plants), or small natural gas power plants that turn on only at night.
2. Construction of all new coal power plants be halted, and those planned, be canceled.
3. All planned coal investments be diverted into solar PV + battery power plants,
4. The solar PV stations produce an excess of storage fuels during the day, which are then used to generate the electricity at night.
5. Coal uses in industry be electrified or fueled by storage fuels, all made with renewable energy

Plan for Transitioning Out of Oil

1. Where oil is used for energy or heat, the same strategy will be used as for coal above.

2. However, since oil or petroleum is the main fuel for transportation, the Plan proposes solar-electric highways and roads, and railways (see following pages)

3. Shipping will need to switch totally to storage fuels and have total plug in capability in ports – so their engines shut off.

4. Aviation needs a separate strategy – as there is little attention being paid to it

Plan for Transitioning Out of Natural Gas

1. For electric power production, natural gas use should expand slowly till about 2035, in order to support the solar PV plus battery power plants proposed above.

2. After 2035, storage fuels (like hydrogen and ammonia) that are produced at solar PV power plants (or other renewable sources) will completely replace natural gas for peak electric power production.

3. All other uses for natural gas – homes, buildings, industry, and transportation to be replaced by electric uses, or by use of "storage fuels," all with high energy efficiency.

For reference, it is useful to describe how a coal fired plant operates that generates electricity. The illustration below helps understand this. Basically, coal is mined far away in a coal mine that is either underground or is a strip mine that uses large drag shovels to

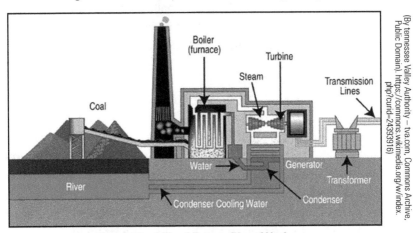

How A Coal Fired Power Plant Works

dig up hill or mountain sides. It is then shipped by rail (by very heavy and large trains in open hopper cars) or to a sea port and then by ship to the power plant. Although there is some dust control on the way, there is often a significant amount of coal dust that blows away from rail cars and finds its way into the air of communities that live along the rail lines. The coal is then stored in open piles at the plant site, often for many weeks, before it is loaded into the plant. All of this causes bad health effects on the communities and people that live along the way.

There is usually a river or a large lake near the plant from which water is taken, and the coal enters a furnace where the coal is burned together with incoming air, and the water is boiled and converted into superheated steam. The steam then enters the steam turbine, which is then powered by the steam to rotate at a fairly high speed, which then rotates a large electric power generator that converts the mechanical energy of rotation into electrical energy using the electrical wires and magnets inside it (designed to output an electric current). The electrical current is then fed to a large transformer that converts it into high voltage electrical energy that is then fed into the transmission line. After powering the steam turbine, the steam condenses back into water which is usually at a higher temperature than the intake water, which is then fed back into the lake or river (this is called thermal pollution). Besides the air pollutants that are emitted by the furnace into the air going up the smoke stack, there is a solid ash that remains. So-called clean coal power plants scrub the exhaust air so as to try and reduce the air pollution and the ash has to be disposed properly otherwise it pollutes the surrounding water and soil. The air exhaust consists of high levels of carbon dioxide, nitrous oxide, smoke particles and toxic pollutants.

GLOBAL COAL USE

World coal production grew from 3,255 million tons of coal equivalent (Mtce) in the year 2000, to about 5,360 Mtce by 2017 (WEO 2018 Report). From the years 2000 to 2017, China increased its production and consumption of coal from 955 Mtce to 2,753 Mtce, a really huge increase. So, in spite of the bad effects of the burning of coal on climate, there seems to have been no let-up in the growth

of coal use. As shown in the pie charts above, coal use was about 27% of total world energy use in 2017, and if current policies of governments continue, even by 2030 and 2050, the coal use will still be 25% of a larger number. Coal used for electric power generation is at 40% of world electric energy production. Even with a "Sustainable Development Scenario" or SDS, the WEO 2018 report projects that the world's coal consumption will still be about 2,282 Mtce (million tons of coal equivalent), which is still too high. Although it is normally used for base load type operation, so that the power plant is run at a high and constant level, more recent coal plants can be run more flexibly where power output can be varied as needed by the load, or demand by consumers.

Coal use is continuing to grow globally. The four biggest exporters are Australia, Indonesia, Russia and the US (which, in 2018, produced about 686 million metric tons and exported about 102 million metric tons). Coal use is causing massive air pollution in China and India, with some residents describing this as "gas chambers". China based its entire expansion and progress from 2000 to 2020 on coal. India plans to do the same by using its domestic reserves. **Clearly, the biggest challenge globally is to head off the increased use of coal, and convince all of the nations of the world to transition out of coal to renewable energy.**

PROPOSED PLAN FOR COAL

REPLACE ALL COAL USES BY RENEWABLE ENERGY AND REDUCE COAL USE TO ZERO BY 2050

SOLAR PV POWER PLANTS – THE TOTAL ENERGY SOLUTION

Solar PV Combined + Battery System + Storage Fuels

Small, medium and large utility scale solar PV plants will be established throughout the world (except of course in nations such as Iceland that already have met all of their needs with other renewable energy). When the sun is shining there will be three loads that would be supplied: (1) Direct supply for electricity for immediate use through transmission lines; (2) The charging of a local battery system that would provide short term smoothing and backup; and (3) the production of a storage fuels such as hydrogen or ammonia (fuels that can store renewable energy), for reuse at the plant and for excess production and supply to the rest of the economy. When clouds come over, the battery system would kick in immediately to make sure the supply is smooth. If the sun stops shining for a longer period of time, in the early stages of the plan, a generator such as one based on natural gas would start up and kick in to provide electricity during that time and at night. At the later stage of the plan, when the storage fuel technology is well developed and storage fuel is being produced and stored during the day, the storage fuel generator would provide electricity when the sun is not shining or at night. When this happens, the natural gas generator would be retired and be no longer needed.

The accompanying block diagram shows how such a concept would work.

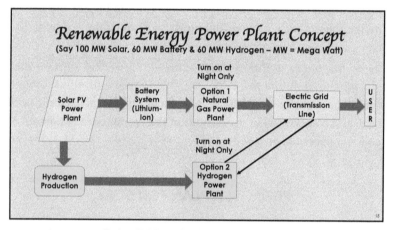

Solar PV Plus Battery Power Plant

A US National Renewable Energy Laboratory (NREL) report shows that solar PV plus battery power plant systems at the same location have become practical and cost effective.[10]

SUMMARY

The new solar PV plants, from smaller community ones to larger state and regional utility scale plants would supply currently needed electricity, and the added electricity for battery charging and the production of storage fuels. The total electric capacity of all the new renewable energy power plants (in terms of power and energy) will be anywhere from two to five times the current electrical capacity, in order to meet the needs of the total electrification of the whole global economy.

LOCATIONS

To minimize the size and expense of the transmission grid (covered in following pages), it is best that the solar PV power plants be located near the end users and end user communities. In this way, the transmission line lengths will be much shorter. All solar-electric charging stations for vehicles will have the solar and battery systems located as close to the station as possible. Similarly, the solar PV based storage fuel production stations will be as close to the end user locations as possible. Solar PV plus battery power plants that REPLACE coal fired power plants will be located very near the original plant so as to use the same transmission lines.

CAISO, the California Independent System Operator of the state of California, USA, coined the term "DUCK CURVE" to point out the problem created for non-renewable power sources when solar PV was added at mid-day in a big way.

The customer demand over a 24 hour period is shown schematically below. (This is not actual data, but the shapes of the curves represent what happens). Then, mid-day as solar energy kicks in, the other energy sources (currently non-renewable energy sources – mainly natural gas power plants in California), have to ramp down very fast. Then, towards evening as the sun sets, these same sources have to ramp up fast. This is all in addition to what happens early morning and late at night as energy demand from customers fall.

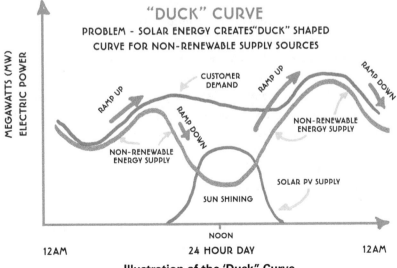

Illustration of the 'Duck" Curve

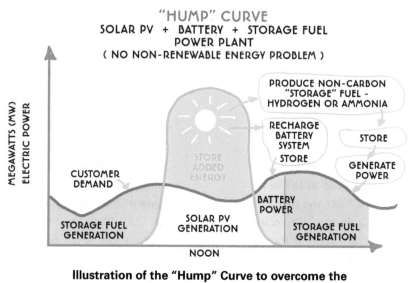

Illustration of the "Hump" Curve to overcome the variability of solar energy,

The "HUMP CURVE" proposed by the Plan completely overcomes the problem if solar PV is the only source of electric energy. The solar PV plus battery plus "storage fuel" power plant is sized such that when solar PV power is being generated, it is enough to not only meet the mid-day demand, but it fully charges the on-site battery system, and produces adequate quantities of a non-carbon storage fuel, which is stored for evening and night use. Then, as solar PV power and energy are going down as the sun is setting, the battery system cuts in and meets the late afternoon increased power demand. Then, after the battery system has discharged to a defined level that is good for battery level, the storage fuel electric power generator (gas turbine or fuel cell) kicks in and produces power and energy for the rest of the evening, night and early morning, till the sun rises again.

Other major storage sources can also play a role here in providing the power – compressed air, water pumped storage, molten salts at CSP (Concentrated Solar Power that use heat to generate power, but can also melt the salt) or other storage methods. For storage fuels, the maximum amount that might need to be produced in advance and stored would be, say 6-7 days' worth, in case there were a number of overcast or days with less sunshine. Also, before storage fuel green production and use is fully developed, natural gas power plants can be used from evening to early morning, or electricity can be imported by the grid from elsewhere (hydro, geothermal or wind).

The issues with high levels of solar energy that occur in the US in states such as California, do not occur in the middle of the United States which are more dependent on wind energy. Wind energy tends to be steadier and can blow at all times, so that it creates more of a flat curve during the day. Some have called it the "ALLIGATOR" curve that actually is closer to consumer demand most of the day, and only causes a small hump during the day when nearby solar PV power kicks in (utility scale or roof top solar). **So, it is important to encourage wind and geothermal energy that can provide power when the sun is not shining, and energy from hydro-electric power plants can also add to this.** There are other good ways of managing the issues and that is by demand side management, or reducing the demand on the user side by various means.

Other Strategies on the Demand Side

Energy Efficiency has been covered elsewhere in this book. Besides a customer buying and retrofitting the most efficient appliances and cooking units in the house or commercial building, the government organization that controls the utility companies must REQUIRE the company to be continuously reducing demand, so that (as often happens in the US), utilities offer rebates to customers when they install high efficiency furnaces and air conditioners that exceed a certain level of efficiency. The author got such rebates when he lived in the Chicago area when he replaced his old 90% efficiency natural gas furnace and electrically powered 12 SEER air conditioner with a 97% efficiency furnace and a 16 SEER (Seasonal Energy Efficiency Ratio) air conditioner. In this way, he went from being an energy inefficient customer to being a very energy efficient customer and both his electric and natural gas bills went down significantly. There are many other ways in which users can reduce their energy use by getting audits conducted by a professional energy auditor.

Demand Side Management is a "Smart Grid" Approach that is another way that can reduce the demand and hence overcome some of the disadvantages of the "DUCK" curve. Utilities, in order to ensure that they do not run out of power when demand is high (like on a very hot day when everyone turns on their air-conditioners), usually have been using "peaker plants", or generators that just turn on only for the few hours that power demand is high. These tend to be very expensive and also tend to be more polluting. One simple example of demand side management is if the utility installs a remotely operated receiver controller on the air conditioning units and then cycles the power between customers (turning off each customer's air conditioner for, say, no longer than an hour), **so that all the air-conditioners in an area are not operating at the same time.** Another way is for the utility to subsidize a battery system for the customer (say a hotel or large store), so that when demand is high, the battery system provides the added power, and the utility does not need to charge extra for higher than normal demand (in the US they call this a "demand charge"). With these strategies the need for a "peaker plant" is eliminated.

Consider the following advantages of solar energy over coal

1. No energy needed in mining – no pollution and destruction at mining sites.
2. No energy needed for transportation – no pollution transporting the fuel.
3. No water pollution at the power plant – no heat emitted to air and water.
4. No fuel cost at the power plant –THE FUEL IS FREE!
5. No toxic and other air pollution at plant site – no toxic ash to dispose off.
6. No actions needed at any site – once solar panels and power plant is installed, it produces electric power when the sun is shining – automatically!
7. The main disadvantage is that it stops producing when the sun goes down – but as shown above, solar energy can be stored in batteries or other mediums and used later for a properly sized solar system.
8. The cost of solar has been going down steadily and in most nations the installation and operating cost of a solar PV power plant is lower than a coal-fired power plant (more on that later).

Minimizing the Environmental Impacts of
Solar PV Power Plants

It is totally true that once solar PV power stations are installed, there are no added carbon dioxide or other greenhouse gas emissions. However, there is strong need that every effort be made to minimize the impact on the global environment. Most solar panels use the metal silicon and trace amounts of other metals, but the production involves toxic and poisonous chemicals which must be handled properly and disposed of in a safe manner. Then, there needs to be a strong emphasis on recycling the materials if solar panels get damaged or at the end of their life – hopefully into the next generation of higher efficiency solar panels. Thin film solar sheets though involve a number of other chemicals like gallium arsenide, copper-indium-gallium-diselenide and cadmium telluride. These also need to be handled and disposed of properly, and being scarce metals, recycled. Next, it is important that the life cycle emissions of the silicon solar panels be minimized through the use of renewable energy in all stages of their manufacture, transport, installation and final recycling. Current estimates of the life cycle emissions of solar panels are 0.017-0.18 pounds of carbon dioxide equivalent per kilo-watt hour (KWH) – compared with 1.4–3.6 lbs of CO2e/KWH for coal.[11] It takes no more than 2–4 years of solar energy production to fully recover the energy consumed in their production.

Then for solar PV plants there are issues of land use, land costs, water use, and the environmental impact on local species of plants and animals. Water use is very little, but may be significant in dusty areas which require that the solar panels be washed frequently. Land use and land costs are important, and should fully take care of and respect local community rights. Further, adjustments need to be made in the design of these projects so that the need of local animal species be taken care of – possibly with gaps in the solar arrays having wetlands or grass areas. As the small to large solar PV projects are implemented, the need to do these in environmentally friendly ways is very important.

EXAMPLES OF RENEWABLE ENERGY
REPLACING FOSSIL FUEL POWER PLANTS

Replacing Coal Power Plant in
Utah with Natural Gas and Then Hydrogen by 2045

The Los Angeles municipal utility (LADWP – Los Angeles Department of Water and Power) plans to replace a large 1,800 MW
(megawatt) Utah coal fired power plant (see accompanying photo
Intermountain Power Project), from which it imports electricity, to a
natural gas power plant by 2025, and then replace that with a totally
green hydrogen power plant by 2045. The hydrogen will be produced
using renewable energy available in the region (solar, wind, and geothermal). The power plant is interconnected on the grid to 370 MW
(megawatt) wind, with added power to be available from wind, solar
PV and geothermal. The power plant is going to be the first power
plant that uses renewable energy to produce hydrogen (green hydrogen) through electrolysis, by which water (chemically H_2O) is
split up into hydrogen (H_2) and oxygen (O_2) using electricity. [12]

The plant will produce hydrogen and then store the gas in underground caverns that are available, in a quantity adequate enough
for a year's generation of electricity. The three technologies needed
for the 840 MW (megawatt) project are making hydrogen from renewable energy using electrolysis (in adequate quantities and at an
acceptable cost), storing the hydrogen, and then using the hydrogen
to produce electricity. Initially, when the 840 MW natural gas plant
is established in 2025 (when the coal plant ceases operation), hydrogen will be capable of making 30% of the electricity when mixed
with natural gas. Both electrolysis to produce hydrogen from renewable energy (production of the storage fuel) and modifying the Gas
Turbine to burn on 100% hydrogen (End-user technology) are technologies that need RDD&D (Research, Development, Demonstration
and Deployment), an issue that will be taken up in regard to storage
fuels in pages that follow.

Existing 1,800 Megawatt Coal Power Plant in Utah.

Replacing Fossil Fuel Power Plants With
Solar PV Plus Battery Power Plants

Possible Natural Gas Power Plant In S. California to be
Replaced with Battery System — Study Indicated it Can Be
Replaced With A Solar PV Plus Battery System

Southern California Edison (the local Gas and Electric Utility Company) had proposed a 262 MW (megawatt) Natural Gas Peaker Plant at Puente for the area around the coastal city of Oxnard, California. Earlier, a battery system when proposed had been estimated to cost three times as much, but it turned out that these estimates were outdated. Instead, it is being substituted by a large battery system (although a solar plus battery power plant that will meet the same electricity needs as the natural gas power plant). Targeted for completion by December 2020, a company called Strata Solar will build and own a 100 MW (megawatt) lithium-ion battery system with a four hour energy capacity (hence 400 MWh – megawatt hour, or 100 MW for four hours) at Oxnard, California. **Since the year 2000, whenever California needed additional electrical energy or wanted to enhance grid reliability, it simply installed new natural gas power plants. This was going to happen again in 2013, and state energy regulators were ready to approve a 262 MW natural gas power plant at Puente, California.**

An independent study conducted by the Clean Coalition showed that a combination of solar PV and battery energy storage system would meet the same needs as the Puente power plant, and be more cost effective. The study demonstrated that a power plant consisting of 120 MW solar PV and a 75 MW battery storage system (of about 225 MWH energy capacity) would meet the whole requirement. If the solar PV power plant was ground mounted, the total cost would be $267 million (as of 2017), and if mounted overhead on poles (built environment) would cost $370 million. This was compared with a Puente gas power plant cost of $299 million, with an added cost of $16 million for natural gas infrastructure. A slightly larger system would also meet the needs posed by another nearby Peaker Plant at Ellwood, California. [13]

Other Major Renewable Energies

While solar PV has the distinct advantage that it is available everywhere and can be located near the ultimate user (hence minimizing transmission costs), there are other major renewable energies.

Wind Energy

Large onshore horizontal axis wind turbines (or wind mills that look like propellers) have increased many fold in recent years. In many places around the world, these can be seen as propellers on top of tall towers or varying height. In the US, there are many wind "farms" in the Midwest of the country and in Texas. IRENA in their GET 2018 Report (International Renewable Energy Agency) reported that worldwide in 2017 there was 167 GW (gigawatts) of renewable power added in 2017, of which 94 GW was solar PV and 47 GW was wind energy. In 2018 they reported that there was 109 GW of solar PV added and 51 GW of wind power added (more than the electric power addition from non-renewables). From 2017 to 2018 the cost of electrical energy from wind and solar had gone down from 6 and 10 US cents per KWH (kilowatt hour) to about 2-3 US cents per KWH. IRENA is projecting big increases in wind energy electric power generation capacity, so that it is projected by them to grow from about 411 GW (gigawatts) to 5,445 GW by the year 2050.[14]

In the Global Plan that is shown for 2050 in the pie chart before in this chapter, the world would about 38,000 TWH (terawatt hours) of wind energy (or about 38,000,000 gigawatt hours). Because this number is based on a replacement for fossil fuels (that are only about 40% efficient or about 60% energy is wasted), the world would only need 15,200 TWH of energy to replace the 38,000 TWH of fossil fuels, unless the world uses the difference to produce non-carbon storage fuels. So for the wind power needed to generate 15,200 TWH of energy, would be about 7,000 GW – about 30% higher than projected by IRENA above. However, if more wind energy is added to produce storage fuels like hydrogen and ammonia (which then have their efficiency losses as well), then the world may need even more wind energy. As for all renewable energies, wind mills need to be designed so that birds can see them and are not killed by flying into them. One way is for the speeds of these large blades to be reduced – for some designs the full capacity speed is 17 RPM (17 revolutions per minute – which means each blade rotates 17 times in each minute), which is a slow enough speed for birds to see them.

The other option for wind energy is to site the wind mills in the sea (**offshore**). This is projected to be about 10% of all wind energy but is a higher cost. Another option for smaller scale generation is to have **vertical axis wind turbines**, which look like the rotating vents on top of buildings. Some of these are like Darius Rotors. These wind generators are much smaller (usually less than 100 kilowatts), and can be located in urban areas, ground mounted on poles or mounted on the roofs of buildings. Coastal areas, where the wind blows often at the ground level are also well suited for these small vertical axis wind turbines, which can be a good supplement to small solar PV electric units on homes or buildings.

Plan for Wind Energy: Besides maxing out for wind (the maximum in terms of worldwide wind potential) in terms of quantity, since wind energy is generated most of the 24 hour period although at varying speeds, it is recommended that it be used in combination with solar PV. In this case, wind will provide a base load (or a nearly constant amount of electricity as is provided today by nuclear, coal and natural gas power plants), and the solar PV power plant still designed to provide the "Hump" energy for battery and producing storage fuels.

Geothermal Energy

Our Planet Earth was a molten ball when it formed about 4.6 billion years ago as a part of the formation of our solar system. Since then, as the surface of the planet cooled, it formed the crust on which we live, the atmosphere we breathe, and the oceans that give us water.

Geothermal energy is that which taps into the subsurface heat in the Earth's interior. To tap geothermal energy one need only go up to small depths where hot rocks are available, and sometimes near the surface as evidenced by surface hot water geysers as can be seen at the Yellowstone National Park in the US.

Geothermal based electric power generation may be simply tapping into a reservoir of subsurface hot water or steam that is ported to the surface to run a turbine and generate electricity, or it may involve injecting water which then gets heated and is ported to the surface. Even if not enough to generate electricity, the hot water may be used to heat buildings or for other uses. Near the surface, the constant temperature of the ground from 3 to 50 meters (10 to 160 feet), can be used by **geothermal ground source heat pumps**, in which an environmentally friendly liquid like polypropylene glycol flows through pipes buried horizontally or vertically to about 50 meter (165 feet) depths. The geothermal ground source heat pump works a little like a refrigerator in exchanging heat energy. When it is winter, it extracts heat from the ground and blows it into the house, and when it is a hot summer it dumps heat down there and cools the house. Heating and cooling costs can be reduced by as much as 75% with the use of this in homes or buildings. However, both geothermal for power generation and for ground source heat pumps have higher up-front costs, but the long term savings are definitely there. Another issue is that if rock cracking techniques are used, this can lead to mild earthquakes.

In 2013 about 11,700 MW (megawatts) of utility scale geothermal power plants were in operation worldwide, and there were plans to double this capacity. These produced about 68 billion KWH (kilowatt hours) of electricity, and produced about 25% of the electricity generated in Iceland and El Salvador. With about 3,300 MW capacity, the US leads the world with the state of California having 80% of this, so that geothermal produced about 7% of the state's electric energy. The US also has thousands of homes and buildings that use geothermal ground source heat pumps. [15]

Plan for Geothermal: For power generation, wherever ground resources are available, Plan calls for the use of geothermal to provide a base-load as the power is available 24 hours of the day. It is recommended that this be used in combination with solar PV, where the "Hump" generation by solar power be used to charge batteries and produce storage fuels, although geothermal can be used for the latter too.

Concentrated Solar Power

Concentrated Solar Power (CSP) is basically some type of reflecting mirrors concentrating the heat segment of solar light to either a trough (horizontal) or a tower (vertical), by moving with the sun during the day, in order to heat a medium that then is used to create steam, which runs a steam turbine, that is tied to a generator that produces electricity. Sunlight consists of a full spectrum of light, from ultra-violet to visible (which splits up into a rainbow, which we see) to infra-red. Concentrated solar power uses the Direct Normal Irradiation (DNI) that is found in tropical or desert regions, and solar PV uses Global Horizontal Irradiation (GHI), which is found everywhere. CSP also has an option whereby it can melt a salt or a synthetic oil during the day, which can be insulated and be available for heat or generating electricity when the sun goes down. Like geothermal, CSP can then be a "dispatchable" form of energy as it can also help overcome the disadvantage of a "DUCK" curve in late afternoon or evening when demand peaks.

As of 2018, the world had 5,400 MW (megawatts) of power being generated from CSP, with Spain leading with 2,300 MW, the US next with about 1,700 MW, and South Africa, Morocco, China and India each having a power of more than 200 MW. [Wikipedia]

Plan for Concentrated Solar Power (CSP): Plan proposes a greater use of CSP when used with its option for producing a molten salt or a synthetic oil even while it is generating electricity during the day for the customer. The molten salt or oil can then be used after the sun goes down in order to produce electricity from the evening through the night. In this way, the CSP station can complement a nearby solar PV plus battery station and performs the same function as geothermal and storage fuels can locally. For desert or similar regions it has the advantage over geothermal that it can be located anywhere where sunlight is available.

Solar Thermal for Other Uses

Solar hot water and space heating: Heating hot water by using the sun has been done for ages. If one just places a black water tank in the sun, the water in it will heat up, just as your skin heats up in the sun. Solar hot water heating in its simplest form can simply be a number of copper tubes attached to copper sheets (as copper conducts heat better than most other metals), painting them black and placing them in a box with a glass case. If the water in it is connected to a hot water tank, that also has water in it, as the water in the glass case (let us call it solar hot water panel) gets heated, it rises and the cooler water in the pipes flows to enter the glass case. The heated water in the pipes heats the water in the water tank, which can then be used. This is simple convective flow – hot water rises as it becomes lighter, and cold water falls. Simple hot water heating panels can be made very easily with a few tools and hardware. In this way, the heat component of solar energy can be used to preheat the water in a tank.

However, on a commercial scale, when one hires a contractor to install a system, the options available are many, as there can be a system with an electric pump to circulate the heated water, the liquid in the panel can be another environmentally friendly liquid that heats the hot water tank, and the tubes can be evacuated tubes (just like a thermos bottle), that reduces heat loss in a cold climate. As with all renewable energy hardware, all commercially sold hit water panels are tested for heat efficiency and other requirements. The biggest fact about solar hot water heating panels is that they usually cost less than solar PV electric panels, and with the amount of energy they provide, one gets one's money back sooner in energy cost savings.

On a wider level, concentrated solar power has been covered above, but solar thermal systems can be used for water heating, space heating (ventilation systems), as part of furnaces for heating homes and buildings, for solar cooking and even for cooling. The reason this is covered here is because these methods can be employed by individuals on a wide scale. Solar hot water heating systems for homes and buildings have been increasing throughout the world and the Plan calls for their widespread adaptation, as they can save on electrical and other energy used for the same purpose.

Rooftop or On-site solar PV

Lamba System: The author has used rooftop solar PV to generate some of his own electricity, wherever he has lived over the last 35 years. His previous house in the Chicago area had installed a 1kW (kilowatt) pole mounted grid tied solar system in 2003 that was fixed at an angle of about 40 degrees to the horizontal and facing south, that produced a significant amount of electrical energy over more than a decade. This kind of system uses a grid tied inverter that converts the DC volts (direct current that only varies with the solar electricity generated) electrical energy from the solar PV panels to 120 Volt AC (alternating current that changes in a waveform that varies at

60 Hertz or cycles per second – which is used by all households and buildings in North America). After moving to California, the author has gotten a larger 3.5 kilowatt (KW) solar PV system directly on his south facing angular asphalt shingle roof that generates more than his annual electricity than he consumes – because as per this book, he plans to electrify all the natural gas units in his house and buy a battery electric car, which will need to be charged. In the winter, the sun trajectory in the sky is low so the electricity production per month is less at a low of about 250 KWH (kilowatt hour or electricity units), and a high of about 600 KWH (kilowatt hour) in summer, when the sun is high and there are more hours that the sun shines on the panel. For a year (May 2019 – April 2020), his home solar PV panel system produced 5.25 MWH (megawatt hours of energy) – each kilowatt produced 1,500 KWH (or 1.5 MWH) of energy for the year. The author paid about $8,500 for the system, for which in the US there was a 30% federal tax credit for solar PV, so the system cost him about $5,000 – this unit cost was $2.4 per watt or a $1.4 per watt after the tax credit, and his electric bill has gone to zero, except for a transmission charge, so he does not have to be concerned with any future electricity cost increases.

Worldwide the total growth of solar PV power grew from 178 GW (gigawatts) in 2014 to 512 GW in 2018 (with about 180 GW of that being large or utility scale systems described elsewhere) with projected growth to about 770 GW in 2020. This growth has been exponential, meaning that the growth of added electrical capacity has been faster and faster each year. The six leading nations in 2018 with solar PV were China (175 GW), European Union (115 GW), USA (62 GW), Japan (55 GW), Germany (46 GW), India (27 GW), and Italy (20 GW). Rooftop solar has grown fast also, but faster in commercial and municipal sectors than in the residential sector. Still, even by 2024 IEA projects that there will be an added 100 million homes that will have solar PV installed. [2]

Plan for Rooftop and Distributed Solar

Plan calls for the requirement that all commercial and industrial buildings be net zero electricity buildings in that they produce as much electrical energy through solar PV as they consume annually, and that all new residential buildings (apartments or homes) also be net zero in electrical terms. All communities should plan to generate as much of their electricity through solar PV as they can locally, near their communities, by small scale solar PV plus battery plants, so that transmission costs are decreased, especially as they electrify. All of these should be tied to the electric grid so that they feed back excess energy and draw energy when producing less. The Plan for solar PV that is presented earlier in the pie chart for the world includes Utility Scale Systems, Concentrated Solar Power and rooftop/distributed solar.

We now turn to the proposed Plan for storage fuels.

NON-CARBON FUELS NEEDED
THAT ARE PRODUCED BY RENEWABLE ENERGY

The world needs a way of storing renewable energy in portable, storable, energy dense fuels that are zero carbon and whose burning or use do not cause carbon emissions. This is essential to decarbonizing ALL sectors of the economy. As the next section shows, it will not be possible to electrify everything – so for all of those uses we will need fuels in which we can STORE renewable energy. This Plan refers to these fuels as *storage fuels.* The two fuels that are very good candidates are hydrogen (H_2) and ammonia (NH_3), both of which are currently used commercially in relatively large quantities but are both made using fossil fuels and hence involving large greenhouse gas (mainly carbon dioxide) emissions.

Hydrogen is one of the lightest gases available, and it is actually everywhere as it is part of the water molecule (H_2O – as two atoms of hydrogen and one atom of oxygen). Hydrogen gas (which consists of two atoms of hydrogen) is mostly made by the steam methane reforming of natural gas (which contains methane) at a high temperature, with the byproduct unfortunately containing carbon dioxide. However, to make commercial hydrogen the world actually uses natural gas, oil, coal and electrolysis in the proportion of 48%, 30%, 14% and 4% respectively. As of 2017, the world hydrogen market was about $115 billion, and in early 2019, the world was using 70 million tons of hydrogen annually for industrial processes (such as oil refining), the production of ammonia (to be discussed next), and methanol (a lower cousin of traditional alcohol or ethanol). So, the world knows how to handle and use hydrogen.

For information, it should be noted that hydrogen can be used in its gaseous form or at a very low temperature can be liquefied and stored in special insulated containers. As a gas, hydrogen has a high energy density by weight (about three times the energy content than gasoline of the same weight), but its energy density by volume is only quarter that of gasoline – so a much greater volume (or size of cylinder) is required for the same energy. However, hydrogen, when used to fuel an Otto-cycle internal combustion engine has a maximum efficiency of about 38%, about 8% higher than for gasoline in the internal combustion engine used in cars. A fuel cell and electric motor combination is 2 to 3 times more efficient than an internal combustion engine, that wastes most of the energy as heat in the exhaust.

As of 2015, it is known that by current electrolysis processes (in an electric cell that splits water, or hydrogen oxide, into hydrogen and oxygen), it takes about 50 KWH of electrical energy to produce 1 kilogram (Kg, or 2.2 pounds) of hydrogen gas. If the price of electricity is $0.06 per KWH, the price of hydrogen would be $3/Kg. This is about double the current price of $1.20-$1.50 per Kg for hydrogen. If the cost of electricity from solar or wind Energy could be less than about $0.03/KWH, it would be economical to produce this by electrolysis. If one considers the cost of carbon dioxide emissions by current production process, it will tilt it in favor of producing "Green" hydrogen using electrolysis that is powered by solar or wind energy. Pure hydrogen is currently used to provide the fuel for fuel cell cars, and for some other vehicles in small quantities today. Hydrogen is much safer than gasoline or natural gas as it is much lighter than air and shoots up when released and is gone. Gasoline vapor and natural gas are about the same weight as air so hang around and can cause explosions. Hydrogen in enclosed spaces can lead to an explosion if there is a spark. However, the world has learned how to use hydrogen safely, and it now has begun to be used in fuel-cell cars.

Plan for hydrogen
❏ Most hydrogen (H2) gas is produced today by Steam Methane Reforming that usually uses natural gas, but produces a lot of greenhouse gases too.
❏ Today, hydrogen is mainly used in refining petroleum, treating metals, producing fertilizer (via ammonia) and processing foods.

❑ As of 2017, about 70 million metric tons of hydrogen was used globally, and because its production used fossil fuels, it resulted in carbon dioxide emissions of about 830 million metric tons (more than the total emissions of Germany).

❑ Electrolysis is a method by which an electric current is used to split water (H2O) into hydrogen (H2) gas and oxygen (O2) gas. Currently, hydrogen produced by this method is more expensive, but research is under way to reduce the expense. The main challenge is electrodes that last.

❑ Hydrogen is produced, stored and used today in large quantities – the world knows how to safely handle and use it today.

❑ A photograph that follows shows one the first Stations in California that supplies Green Hydrogen.

❑ The Plan is calling for RDD&D (Research Development, Demonstration and Deployment) for producing Green Hydrogen, or hydrogen made with solar PV electricity or other renewable energy – see schematic that follows

❑ There are some significant demonstration projects under way to use electrolyzers of a few megawatts to produce significant quantities of hydrogen. If these projects are successful, they can be scaled up commercially.

❑ The use of hydrogen in cars and buses has already begun, and along with electric vehicles needs to be expanded to jointly cover all vehicles. The combination of solar powered electric charging stations and hydrogen refueling stations will need to replace most of the gas stations of today. Hydrogen will also power other forms of transportation like ships.

❑ In electric generation, hydrogen will be produced with solar PV energy during the day and, together with larger battery systems, produce electricity from evening to early morning, so the full cycle is all renewable energy – although energy during those times when the sun is not shining can also be provided by other renewable energies like wind, geothermal and hydro.

Ammonia (NH3, which has one atom of nitrogen and three atoms of hydrogen) has also been described in the Global Plan in Chapter 2. It is produced currently first by producing hydrogen using Steam Methane Reforming (SMR) which emits carbon dioxide, and then combining the hydrogen with nitrogen from the air (which is about 78% of the air we breathe), using the Haber-Bosch process. In 2016, the world produced and handled about 175 million tons of ammonia, most of which was used as fertilizer for agriculture. Ammonia has the advantages over hydrogen in that it is easier to handle because it doesn't require high pressure (which saves money). It has twice the amount of energy per unit of volume than hydrogen, it can be stored more easily in a smaller volume, it has a distinctive smell making it easier to detect (hydrogen is odorless), and it doesn't embrittle steels like hydrogen thus making the job of designing storage tanks easier. The main safety aspect that needs special handling is the toxicity of ammonia to human respiration. Plus ammonia is already handled, stored, transported and used in large quantities – about 175 million tons worldwide in 2015. In 2012, the US produced about 8.73 million tons of ammonia and imported some for its own use.

Plan for Ammonia

- ❏ Ammonia (NH_3) gas is an alternative to hydrogen and a close relative of it.
- ❏ As of 2016, the world used 175 Million Metric tons of it, mostly as fertilizer for agriculture.
- ❏ Ammonia is made by taking nitrogen from the air and combining it with hydrogen using the Haber-Bosch process to produce anhydrous (dry) ammonia
- ❏ The infrastructure (storage, pipelines, and transport, etc.) already exist in a big way for it.
- ❏ Ammonia has its own distinctive properties – it is easier to store and transport than hydrogen.
- ❏ Again, the Plan is calling for RDD&D at both ends – that of making ammonia by Green methods, using Renewable Energy and for end-user technologies by which ammonia can be used as a fuel in fuel cells, internal combustion engines and gas turbines.
- ❏ Because of its toxicity to humans for respiratory purposes, ammonia needs special attention in regard to its safety, so that humans are not significantly exposed to it. Strict safety procedures are to be enforced wherever it is used, especially when humans and animals are in close proximity to where it is stored and used.

Ammonia has a very distinctive pungent smell that is easy to recognize. Its advantages are that it can be liquefied easily (much easier than for hydrogen). Because of its physical properties it can stored in an inexpensive pressure vessel. Then, since ammonia has a large percent of hydrogen (17.65%), its density per unit of volume in the liquid form is about 45% higher than hydrogen, so more of it can be stored in a given volume. Lastly, it can be decomposed over a catalyst to produce hydrogen and nitrogen (that is not a greenhouse gas).

Other advantages of ammonia are that it is an excellent storage fuel (for storing renewable energy). It can power an internal combustion engine (like gasoline for cars), although this technology is still under development. It can power an alkaline fuel cell, or be cracked to provide hydrogen that can power a non-alkaline fuel cell. Ammonia's storage, transportation and distribution are much cheaper than hydrogen, and its use in an engine or fuel cell would not produce carbon dioxide. Also, since it carries more hydrogen per volume, it is better in terms of on-board storage in cars, is easier to crack than other hydrocarbon fuels, and no greenhouse gases are emitted.

The special character of ammonia does require attention for on-board storage in vehicles. It expands with rise in temperature, has a high tendency to react with water, reacts with some container materials and has a high toxicity of the vapor when released to air. Proton exchange membrane (PEM) fuel cells used for hydrogen cannot tolerate ammonia, so it needs to be effectively filtered if it is cracked to hydrogen. Storage tanks need attention to these aspects of ammonia. Ammonia is currently transported by pipelines, sea tankers, railcars and trucks. The US currently has about 5,000 Km (kilometers) or about 3,000 miles of pipeline for it. For large scale storage for the energy purpose of this Plan, ammonia has the lowest cost and space needed for long term storage times (100 – 10,000 hours).

One promising technology is the Proton Exchange Membrane (PEM) technology that converts water to hydrogen at one electrode and then takes hydrogen and combines it with nitrogen at another electrode to produce ammonia. Although Japan and Australia are very active, there are significant activities in Europe and in the US for producing ammonia by Green methods (using only renewable electric power and no fossil fuels and no carbon emissions).

The Flow Chart above shows how hydrogen and ammonia can be produced anywhere where there is solar energy. The Plan calls for

PRODUCING GREEN HYDROGEN & AMMONIA
From Solar Energy

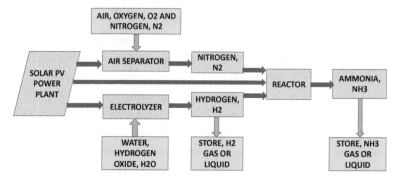

RDD&D (Research, Development, Demonstration and Deployment) for all aspects of the above.

The US state of California has developed about 40 retail hydrogen refueling stations, and one is located near Honolulu, Hawaii. These have been opened by a company to serve Toyota Mirai car drivers who lease their fuel cell vehicle cars through Toyota. Most of these refueling stations are located near the Los Angeles area, but others are spread throughout the state. As of the time of the writing of this book (early 2020), there are about another 24 hydrogen stations that are at various stages of permit, planning, construction and commissioning. Other car manufacturers that have developed fuel cell vehicles are Honda (2018 Clarity Fuel Cell) and Hyundai (2019 Nexo) – the latter offers 5 passenger seating and a 380 mile (612 kilometer) range. Hyundai says that it plans to build 500,000 fuel cell vehicles powered by hydrogen by 2030. The former Governor of California, Jerry Brown, had signed executive orders that that set targets of 200 hydrogen refueling stations by 2025 and 5 million zero emission (electric or fuel cell) vehicles by 2030.

The main challenge of hydrogen fuel is that they need to ALL be green, or use renewable energy sources to produce the fuel. The photo to the right shows a 100% green or renewable hydrogen station installed in 2019 in the city of San Francisco, that was developed by Shell and funded by the California Energy Commission (CEC). This is open 24 hours a day, has a capacity of 513 kilograms (about 1,130 pounds), has two refueling nozzles that supply hydrogen gas under pressure, to fill the vehicle tanks. The government of California

A 100% green hydrogen refueling station in San Francisco, California.

requires that at least 33% of the hydrogen fuel supplied at each station comes from green sources, and that a station that supplies at least 40 % green hydrogen qualifies for its Low Carbon Fuel Standard ZEV (Zero Emission Vehicle) Infrastructure credit. **[California Fuel Cell Partnership – Cafcp.org]**

Electrification of The Whole Global Economy

SOLAR-ELECTRIC HIGHWAYS – EXAMPLE OF THE USA

VARIATIONS OF THIS TO BE APPLIED GLOBALLY

❏ The Entire US Highway Transportation system can be electrified by solar PV powered electric charging stations throughout its entire highway and road network.

❏ Indirect electrification will be by fuels that are produced by solar energy, and then stored for later use – we call these storage fuels – more on these in next few pages.

❏ These vehicles will use either fuel cells (like the hydrogen fueled vehicles of today), or have internal combustion engines (like those used in vehicles today).

❏ Calculation for the US based on its energy use on roads and highways in 2017 **(US Energy Information Agency).**

❏ The US used 27 Quads (quadrillion BTUs) or 7,930 billion KWH of energy.

❏ Information from the US Energy Information Agency Report.

❏ On the average, vehicles consume this energy with only 40% efficiency.

❏ About 60% is wasted and leaves out of the muffler.

❏ So, for Electric Energy, we only need 3,172 billion KWH (40% of 7,930).

❏ For most latitudes of the US, this energy needs 2,115,000 MW (megawatt) of power. Each MW of *power* annually assumed to give 1,500 MWH (megawatt hours) of *energy*.

❏ **If Charging Stations are 10 MW is size we need 211,500 of these.**

❏ **At 0.015 square kilometers per MW, this needs 0.15 sq. Km. or 38 acres area.**

❑ Each Solar-Electric charging station can also store and sell storage fuels, produced on-site or transported from some other location.

❑ Each Station can also have an on-site unit that produces one or more storage fuels using solar PV energy using the same solar panels.

❑ These storage fuels can either be hydrogen or ammonia.

❑ Since the US has 47,000 miles of Interstate Highways, one station each 20 miles means 2,350 of these stations on the Highways alone.

❑ The photo on the next page shows a Solar Powered Electric Charging Station.

❑ Or the solar panels could be elevated construction along the center strip of the highway.

❑ See the page after next for a Concept of such a Solar-Electric Charging, including "storage fuel" on-site production as an option.

❑ Over a period of 30 years (2021-2050), these Solar-Electric Charging Stations can replace the 111,000 "Gas" Stations currently in the US (for gasoline and diesel).

SOLAR-ELECTRIC ELECTRIC VEHICLE CHARGING STATION

In April 2019, Marin Clean Energy (MCE), a local non-profit organization in California, that was established for Community Choice Aggregation (CCA* – see next page) completed a solar PV Powered Electric Charging Station in cooperation with a company called American Solar Corporation, that is of 80 kW (kilowatt) capacity that powers 10 Level 2 Electric Vehicle (EV) Charging Stations next door to its office in San Rafael, California (a level 2 charging station takes a few hours to fully charge a nearly fully discharged batters system on a car). The station will generate about 120,000 kWh (kilowatt hour) of electric energy per year and power the 10 EV charging stations. When the sun is shining, the solar energy directly charges the battery electric vehicles, and at other times will receive power from MCE's other California's renewable energy sources (mainly wind and solar). If there is excess solar energy, it will flow back into the grid and be used to offset the energy use of its nearby office building. MCE contributed funds to make required infrastructure upgrades, and received some financial support from local area California governmental organizations. The effort complimented MCE's Electric Vehicle Program where it has funded and supported 644 charging ports at mainly multifamily dwelling and workplace locations in their service area.

*Community Choice Aggregation or CCA, is a method that is being used in California and other states of the US. These are covered in more detail in the California Plan, but here is a summary. A CCA is a not-for-profit organization that provides an alternative to investor owned utilities, where the CCA provides alternative renewable energy supply, but the utility still handles transmission, metering and billing. Marin Clean Energy is the first of about 19 Community Choice Aggregation organizations in California, and it began service in 2010 with the aim of providing stable electricity rates to customers and reducing greenhouse gas emissions.

CONCEPT OF GLOBAL SOLAR-ELECTRIC TRANSPORTATION SYSTEM

HIGHWAYS AND ROADWAYS

❏ The Global Plan proposes direct electrification of the world's highways and roadways.

❏ The Plan proposes solar-electric highways and roadways. So the plan here is to have solar panel systems with raised structures covering highways, or where the space along the highways is available, ground mounted solar systems.

❏ See the concept on the next page of such a Solar-Electric Charging Station.

❏ As is proposed elsewhere for power plants, the solar system will be accompanied by battery backup system, so there is power at times other than when the sun is shining.

❏ At each location, there will be electric vehicle charging stations, so battery electric vehicles can be charged, some directly from solar panels, and later directly from the battery system.

❏ At other times (like at night), the solar charging station can be on the transmission grid and powered by electric power from elsewhere.

❏ If the solar-electric charging station is stand-alone (not tied to the grid or connected to the utility), then its battery system will need to be much larger and be capable of charging vehicles when the sun is not shining.

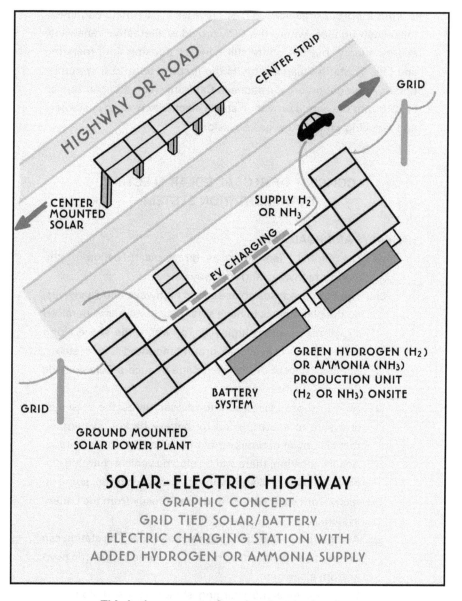

SOLAR-ELECTRIC HIGHWAY
GRAPHIC CONCEPT
GRID TIED SOLAR/BATTERY
ELECTRIC CHARGING STATION WITH
ADDED HYDROGEN OR AMMONIA SUPPLY

**This is the concept of a solar-electric charging
and refuelling station.**

RAIL TRANSPORTATION SYSTEMS

Similarly, light rail, bus systems and all railways will develop supporting systems for pure electric, battery and storage fuel use. Although the cost of adding pure electrification of mass transit type systems (such as electric trams) is high, wherever these make sense, these should be developed or expanded. For battery light rail vehicles, solar PV charging stations will be developed that charge these vehicles throughout the day, and at night from stationary batteries that have been charged. All rail vehicles, especially diesel-electric locomotives will be converted to hybrid battery electric and storage fuel turbine based engines. End-use engines, fuel cells and turbines that use storage fuels will need the RDD&D (Research, Development, Demonstration & Deployment) so that these achieve widespread use. The use of diesel fuel in railway locomotives and other types of light rail systems will be phased out after the whole system is electrified, or converted to storage fuel-based vehicles.

STORAGE FUEL OPTION FOR HIGHWAYS, ROADWAYS AND OTHER MODES

The storage fuel can be hydrogen that is produced and consumed quickly on-site, or ammonia, that is produced and stored and consumed over longer periods. The size of the storage fuel production unit can vary depending on local demand. The storage fuel production unit will only need water that is split to provide the hydrogen, and nitrogen that is drawn from the air – both resources that are available everywhere. Since these fuels can be produced locally, they do not need to be transported over large distances.

Electrification of Buildings and Homes

A significant number of homes and buildings globally use propane, fuel oil and natural gas for heating and other appliances (water heaters, clothes dryers, and cooking appliances). Parts of the developed world have piped natural gas, while many other parts of the world use gas cylinders for cooking (which is a big improvement over cooking with wood or coal).

So, here is the Plan for the Electrification
of Homes Buildings

1. **Require that all new structures of all kinds have no fossil fuel options (natural gas, fuel oil or propane), and that they be fully electrified**, have battery electric vehicle charging stations, have solar panels, and they meet mandated energy efficiency standards that are technically feasible. This has been done by the city of Berkeley California in 2019. (Berkeley's all-electric building ordinance requires that starting Jan 1, 2020, all new buildings be built all electric – no gas hook-ups – covers new houses, apartments and commercial buildings.)

2. **Change all laws and regulations, and building and energy codes** in order to make it easier for any retrofits of existing structures to switch to the all-electric modes.

3. For each nation to engage in a nation-wide program that is a combination of incentives, rebates, tax credits, and education in regard to the all-electric technologies needed. This should include the encouragement for solar thermal panels, solar ovens for cooking and electric heat pumps.

4. Starting 2035, the Plan proposes a mandatory electrification, helping users financially and physically to retrofit their homes and buildings, for electrification.

5. **Electrification Technologies:** Air conditioning is generally electric powered the world over. However wherever natural gas is used in homes and buildings, these need to be converted to electric powered units. So natural gas furnaces need be converted to electric heat pumps, and gas cooking stoves to electric (direct or induction) stoves – induction heating is where a frequency is used to heat steel cooking utensils. Also all other appliances like clothes dryers need to be converted to electric dryers.

6. **What Governments Need to Do:** It is important that the costs of new and retrofitted electric units be comparable with natural gas units, otherwise incentives or rebates must be offered by utilities or governments (or tax credits) to make it easier for home owners and building owners to electrify their homes. At the same time, training programs need to be put in place to educate owners and technicians of contractors on how to install new electric units, or retrofit

older natural gas units. Further, central governments need to put in place industrialization strategies for the volume production of these units.

Electrification of Industry

This is an area that is technically very challenging but needs to be addressed. There are several end-use electrical technologies that are already growth areas that can grow more. These are cryogenics, direct arc melting, induction heating, resistance heating and melting, ultraviolet curing and infrared processing and many other electric technologies.

The Plan for the direct use of Renewables and the electrification of Industry are as follows:

1. The expansion of known technologies and methods for electrification must be made universal. All industries will need to switch to these if they can use them. For this, all the encouragement, incentives and standards will be needed.

2. Locally, all of industry will maximize the use of renewable energy (mainly solar PV) to produce electricity for ALL of their electric needs (existing and expanded).

Photo by Author

Electric transmission lines bringing electric energy into the East Bay of San Francisco over the hills.

3. Produce storage fuels on-site – Governments need to help industries and companies with RDD&D on producing green storage fuels on site (or purchasing from elsewhere).

4. Develop end-use technologies that will enable them to substitute coal, oil and natural gas use with the use of either direct electric or the use of storage fuels.

5. The industrial sector will be invested in terms of all of the RDD&D (Research, Development, Demonstration and Deployment) needed for establishing new methods and technologies or improving on existing ones, or furthering either electrification or the use of storage fuels.

6. Improve the energy efficiency and material recycling and re-use efficiency of all industry.

7. Clean manufacturing should mean not only one that supports industrialization for renewable energy but also conversion of ALL existing industry to clean renewable energy and elimination of toxic and hazardous materials.

THE NEEDED EXPANSION AND UPGRADE OF THE GLOBAL ELECTRIC TRANSMISSION SYSTEM

THE ELECTRIC GRID – ENHANCEMENT OF THE SIZE AND SMARTNESS

The Plan calls for a total overhaul and modernization of the entire global electric power system. Electric power needs the supply of storage fuels, renewable energy power generation, transmission and distribution. Plus, modernizing the whole system will need smart and flexible grids that can make the system more efficient (conduct operations with less energy used), a flexible strategy to account for the variability of renewable energy (which only makes electricity when the sun shines or the wind blows, as the case may be), and begin to take account of the strategy of battery storage, as well as the production, storage, transport and use of storage fuels (to regenerate electricity).

Expansion and Enhancement of the Electric Grid

❏ Fossil Fuel to Renewable Energy Conversion: As per above, all fossil fuel based electricity generation will be converted to a combination of solar PV (or other renewable energy) plus battery system plus natural gas or storage fuels. If the storage fuels are produced and then used on-site to produce electricity, then no added expansion of transmission lines will be needed.

❏ Electrification: To the maximum attention possible, as per the previous section, the global economy will be electrified. For direct electric supply, this will mean a 3 to 5 times expansion of electrical energy and power.

❏ **Transmission Grid Expansion:**

❏ Option 1: If the new added renewable energy generation facility is located close to the usage center, or if there is more roof top solar, then only a local increase in the size of the transmission system (together with an interconnection point) will be necessary. This will minimize the cost of the transmission system upgrades and is preferred. Also, this will lead to greater energy democracy in that local entities can own and control these production units.

❏ Option 2: There is an expansion of local community micro-grids that are capable of operating independently (with combined solar PV and battery system), so these can disconnect and operate independently even if the larger grid fails.

❏ Option 3: If the added renewable energy electric power stations are far from the user locations, then a major expansion of the electric transmission system will be needed. This will need greater attention given to grid size, reliability and safety.

❏ All measures will be taken to enhance the smartness of the grid, both in order to manage the variability nature of renewable energy, and also to better manage the supply and demand sides of electric power, so that the use is more efficient and peak power problems are avoided. Smart grid as most people understand it today is where it may have something like automatic turn on and turn off capability of people's air conditioners, so that on a very hot day, when everyone wants to use air conditioners continuously, the utility company can rotate the turning on and off of air conditioners remotely, so that peak power does not go too high (which currently means turning on added generators to meet peak power – these are called *peaker power* plants).

As the overall plan indicates above, the electricity production and the accompanying transmission lines will need to grow 3 to 5 times to meet the needs of added electrification through renewable energy.
The Global Plan for expanding the global electric transmission grid is described on the previous page. Whenever one considers an electrical energy system, there is the generator, the spur transmission (that gets the electricity to the main or bulk transmission line), the Point of Interconnection (POI), that interconnects the spur to the bulk transmission line, and the main or bulk transmission line that carries electric energy far away. "Brownfield" sites are those where an existing power plant is simply being replaced. In such Brownfield cases, where say an existing coal, oil or natural gas generating station is being replaced by a solar PV plus battery generating station, one can use the existing transmission line if enough land is available locally for the solar PV plant. **Hence, in most cases where fossil fuel power plants are being replaced by renewable energy power plants (Brownfield Sites), little or no expansion of the spur transmission grid may be required. However, for grids to work reliably and be resilient, the whole transmission system globally needs to be modernized and upgraded.**
This chapter has covered mainly the energy aspects of the Global Plan. With the almost total replacement of fossil fuels, the high levels of pollution involved with them will be gone, and the carbon dioxide emissions from these will be nearly eliminated. The direct greenhouse gas emissions aspects are dealt with in a later chapter.

Plan for Bioenergy

Bioenergy mainly consists of the generation of electric power by the burning of fuels that are biological in origin. If it relies on crops then these must be grown on non-agricultural land. The increasing use of good farmland to produce ethanol is not a good or sustainable model. Other sources of bioenergy include the use of biomethane fuel from sewage treatment, manure treatment and landfills – either to combust directly or to convert to a fuel like hydrogen. The quantitative Plan is as it appears in the WEO2018 report.

We now turn to what is needed for make our global transportation systems green.

REDUCING THE CARBON FOOTPRINT OF TRANSPORTATION – INCLUDING AVIATION, SHIPPING AND TOURISM

Besides near total electrification, the electric and low carbon modes would be substituted for high carbon modes of transportation: So, mass transit, pedways and bikeways would replace much car traffic, for distances less than say 500 miles (or 800 kilometers) airline traffic would be replaced by high speed rail, and diesel trucks would be replaced by electric, battery-electric and storage fuel trucks.

Shipping – Transitioning Out of Fossil Fuels

When we talk of expanding world trade, all of that leads to more and more goods being shipped by sea and some by air. For goods to be made in one country and shipped all over the world takes a lot of ship travel (and some cargo by air), and as more of that has happened, the carbon emissions from shipping have increased. The more that goods need to be transported over longer distances, the more carbon emissions there are. Until recently, as shipping occurs between nations and did not count in the greenhouse gas emissions of nations, this had escaped attention. It is now important to make sure that we pay attention to this as these ships are emitting carbon dioxide in the ports and in all over their travels over the seas.

For shipping of goods, materials and fuels between nations, there are many ways in which the carbon footprint can be reduced. As a follow-up to the Paris Agreement, one of the committees of the International Maritime Organization (IMO) organized a meeting at which five options were considered: (1) Slow steaming the ships so they travel slowly and avoid unnecessary travel; (2) Improving design of ships like improvements in hull and propeller design, and waste heat recovery; (3) The use of renewable energy like wind power and kite systems; (4) The use of batteries to store excess energy, and the use of shoreside electrical power (powered by solar PV or wind) in ports; and (5) Switch to lower carbon fuels. Also, one of the immediate actions recommended was to begin reducing the use of high sulfur fuel oil that was giving high levels of pollution.

This Book proposes a plan for Shipping as follows:

1. Elimination of the use of high sulfur fuel oil and replacement with low sulfur fuels to begin with.

2. The use of sails and renewable energy kite systems, combined with solar PV technologies to provide energy and propulsion. Flettner Rotors and Kites are two wind based technologies that can considerably cut energy use.

3. The use of hybrid battery and electrical propulsion systems (batteries and motors) to reduce fuel consumption, much like used in cars today.

4. This should be combined with complete switch to electrical power from shoreside when in ports, with all that power being provided by renewable energy (solar PV and wind).

5. Replace all fuel oils and fossil fuels with storage fuels like hydrogen and ammonia, with these fuels being produced onshore using renewable energy (solar, wind and hydro). Ammonia as a fuel would be ideal with liquid ammonia being carried on board, and the use of a combination of internal combustion engine and fuel cell technologies would provide power. This area does need a significant amount of research and development, and hence needs investments in RDD&D. Projects are underway to develop compression ignition engines for ships that burn ammonia.

Research and development of ammonia as shipping fuel and the development of engines that burn ammonia is proceeding well and should be globally supported. The advisable strategy will be to begin with the small measures such as use of electrical power only in ports, and shutting down of engines, and the switch away from high sulfur fuel oil. However, all of the other activities need RDD&D (Research, Development, Demonstration and Deployment), so that the research, demonstration, economics, technologies, equipment, supply of storage fuels, etc. will be worked out in cooperation with the International Maritime Organization (IMO).

Aviation – Transitioning Out of Fossil Fuels

Aviation represents a really big challenge and needs to be tackled effectively. In response to the Paris Agreement, the International Civil Aviation Organization (ICAO) organized a scheme called the Carbon Offsetting and Reduction Scheme for International Aviation (CORSIA) that aims at reducing the emissions from the expansion in civil aviation from 2019-2035. CORSIA calls for increasing the fuel efficiency of aircraft, new technologies to select more efficient flightpaths and reduce delays, using lower carbon fuels (mainly bio-fuels), and investing in emissions offsets. Of the 73 nations that agreed to initially participate, implementing what they agreed to will cover about 77% of the projected increase in emissions from 2019 to 2035 (Ref: ICAO). There is NO talk of even beginning to address the greenhouse gas emissions that are already being emitted annually. Clearly, a bolder action plan is needed as aviation is a big contributor to greenhouse gas emissions.

The Book Plan for Aviation

❏　For ALL areas connected by land, for travel distances less than 200 miles, air travel should be replaced by electrified light rail and medium speed passenger rail powered by solar PV energy, supplemented by battery backup and storage fuels.

❏　For ALL areas connected by land on the same continents, travel should be switched to electric powered high speed rail supplied mainly by solar PV energy, supplemented by battery backup and storage fuels. For the Americas, this means connecting all the way from the northern tip of North America to the southern tip of South America, one each along the eastern and western shores. For Eurasia, this means high speed rail powered from the western end of Europe, all the way through Russia (for one route), another through China, and another through India and South-east Asia, all the way to Vietnam. Another route will be all the way around Australia.

❏　High speed stations will be linked to and integrated with medium speed rail, light rail, bus transit, bike and pedestrian travel.

❏　Aviation will be used only for cross ocean and cross water travel over long distances, using the above strategy as per CORSIA for ALL aviation emissions. Bio-fuels can only be produced from non-agricultural land and there must be no net deforestation.

❑   Rather than going to the final destination by air, the air travel will be organized so that the flight ends at the extreme ends of the medium and high speed rail network, and travel from there is by other rail, mass transit and autos either electric or fueled by storage fuels.

❑   An RDD&D program is needed to develop aircraft engines using storage fuels like ammonia. In the short term, these technologies can use mixed fuels that combine with jet fuel, until technologies are developed that use only storage fuels. Because of the long lead times, laboratory research on this must begin soon.

❑   Bio-fuels are being developed for jet engines, but care should be taken to ensure that these fuels come from biological sources that do not use fossil fuels.

DEVELOP AN INTERNATIONAL INTEGRATED LOW CARBON TRANSPORTATION SYSTEM

For the people of the world to continue to have a reasonable level of mobility, a transportation plan is proposed for the whole world that will integrate all the modes of low or zero carbon transportation, so that one can travel from one end to the other with little or no carbon emissions! That means starting with pedestrian, bike travel, electrified vehicles, light rail, buses and storage fuel autos, linking with major travel hubs or stations for rail and, only as needed, air travel. Then again, at the other end of a rail terminal or an airport, there will be direct links with all the other zero carbon transportation modes, all powered by solar PV, batteries and storage fuels. Here is a concept for such a system.

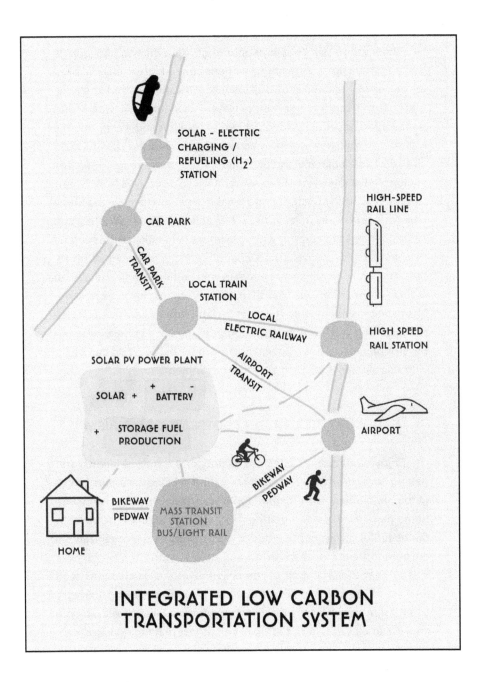

SOLAR - ELECTRIC CHARGING / REFUELING (H_2) STATION

CAR PARK

CAR PARK TRANSIT

HIGH-SPEED RAIL LINE

LOCAL TRAIN STATION

LOCAL ELECTRIC RAILWAY

HIGH SPEED RAIL STATION

SOLAR PV POWER PLANT

AIRPORT TRANSIT

SOLAR +   +   − BATTERY

+ STORAGE FUEL PRODUCTION

AIRPORT

BIKEWAY PEDWAY

BIKEWAY PEDWAY

HOME

BIKEWAY PEDWAY

MASS TRANSIT STATION BUS/LIGHT RAIL

INTEGRATED LOW CARBON TRANSPORTATION SYSTEM

CONCEPT OF A LINKED AND INTEGRATED LOW CARBON
TRANSPORTATION SYSTEM

This system will enable people to go on a bikeway (or human powered transportation with or without added battery electric power) or pedway (sidewalk of walkway) to a local mass transit station that links to a bus line or a light rail line. This in turn links with a local train station, an airport, a high speed rail station and a car park. The highway or roadway on which battery electric and storage fuel vehicles run has a solar-electric plus battery plus storage fuel refueling station. The whole system is powered by a solar PV plus battery plus storage fuel power plant. This will enable a person to leave the home and go from one system to the other and do all of that safely and emitting very little carbon, with maximum capability of elderly and disabled people to travel on it. Depending on the distances involved, bikeways and pedways can be maximized so that people are able to access all the hubs and park their bikes or trikes there, as needed. The aviation system which uses jet fuel or biofuels can then concentrate on long haul and cross-continental flights. ALL new cities or developments that are established anywhere in the world can begin with this system, making it very easy to implement.

REDUCING THE CARBON FOOTPRINT OF TOURISM

Enjoying nature, architecture, history and fun destinations, and getting away from a severe winter or hot weather are part of the global enjoyment of tourism. People who are rich, and even those of the middle class enjoy getting away for a vacation or for travel to the beautiful places of the world. Even environmental organizations encourage their members to go and enjoy nature. The problem is that all that travel and all of the activities at the destinations lead to a lot of greenhouse gas emissions that are damaging the very beautiful places that they (and we) are visiting. I visited Alaska on a cruise and all but two of the glaciers are fast melting. I visited Leh, Ladakh at the western end of the Himalayas in India, and later the same year the area was devastated by massive rains and mudslides during the monsoon season. I visited the garden isle Kawaii of Hawaii, but it was struck later that year with massive rains, mudslides and isolation of people. Many of the beautiful areas of Europe are being devastated by heavy floods and now heat waves, the like of which they have never known. **Our tourist destinations are fast deteriorating because of Climate Change and may not be worth visiting in the not too distant future.**

A recent study (*The Carbon Footprint of Global Tourism*, Nature – nature Climate Change) looked at the entire carbon footprint of tourism from travel to and within destinations (air and land travel) and all of the other aspects like food, accommodation, fuel, and shopping, and all of the activities that occur in other places in support of tourism. It showed that global tourism expenditures grew from US \$2.5 trillion in 2009 to about US \$4.7 trillion in 2013, with the greenhouse gas (GHG) footprint increasing from 3.9 to 4.5 Gt-COe (giga tons of carbon dioxide equivalent), or about 8% of all GHG emissions! The US ranks the highest in emissions, followed by China, Germany and India. [16]

So how does one go about making tourism a zero emissions activity? Recognizing that greenhouse emissions are a problem, the United Nations World Tourism Organization (which otherwise promotes increases in tourism), proposed two strategies – to encourage tourists to go to locations closer to home and use more public transportation and less aviation, and to provide incentives for operators to improve their energy and carbon efficiency. Neither of these strategies appear to be working. So here is the Plan.

Proposed Plan to Reduce Emissions
from Tourism to very Low Levels

1. The strategies proposed above for road transport and aviation must be adopted for tourist travel – low carbon, electric (energized by renewable energy) and high efficiency.

2. Laws and agreements have to be adopted that minimize aviation travel, requiring that travel distances be minimized and that all travel within nations be by low or zero carbon means. So, travel to Europe should be such as to travel by air only to the closest destination, and that all travel on land areas be by high speed rail, bus, and light rail, or zero carbon highway modes.

3. All local travel within tourist cities must be by electric vehicles, storage fuel vehicles, and all cities of the world must encourage all local travel to be by pedestrian, bike or bus

means. Walking and small electric vehicles, bikes, trikes and quad bikes should become the norm.

4. All food, materials and fuel must be local – locally grown food, locally produced energy (solar PV, wind, geothermal or hydro), and all accommodations must be totally turned into net zero energy establishments. Exotic food from far away locations must be discouraged by all means possible – luxury seafood, beef and meat from distant locations, or gourmet foods from other parts of the globe, must be shamed out of existence.

5. All cruise ships must be converted or replaced by ships that use the plan described in shipping, and must convert to use of storage fuels produced by use of solar PV energy.

6. All island nations that are distant tourist locations must be helped locally to be net zero energy nations, through use of solar PV and wind energy, through water harvesting, and making themselves into nations where only biking, walking or horse/animal buggies are allowed – taxi or hotel electric cars providing transport of people and goods as needed. That this can be a great deal of fun is demonstrated by the Mackinac Island in Michigan USA, where all cars are banned and one reaches there only by ferry. Travel by low carbon cruise ships to these distant island destinations, or by ferry if some mainland is close by, should be encouraged.

7. All tourist travel within nations, or within land masses not separated by sea or water, will be converted to a low carbon mode and aviation travel discouraged through taxes, and incentives for low carbon options – with high and medium speed rail invested in for all land travel.

INVESTMENTS IN ENERGY EFFICIENCY – DOING MORE WITH LESS

The whole economy would become much more efficient through deliberate efforts to increase energy efficiency in energy production and distribution, in homes, in buildings, in transportation and in agriculture, meaning that the same tasks should use much less energy. How do we do this? First let us look at the plans that are already out there that propose energy efficiency improvements.

The International Energy Agency (IEA), as per their WEO2018 report showed that the four areas of the economy where energy efficiency enhancements have already been done from 2000 to 2017 are in transport, industry, residential buildings and services buildings (business, municipal and organizational). Global energy efficiency policies because of extending existing energy efficiency standards to added products led to increases in the coverage of products from about 15% in the year 2000 to about 30-40% in 2017. In its Efficient World Scenario (EWS) the report projects the following energy efficiency improvements: (1) Transport: Road vehicles can use 40% less fuel per passenger mile or per vehicle-kilometers traveled in 2040 than today, and with hybridization and logistics improvements road freight would use 46% less energy per metric ton-kilometer; (2) In Industry, the energy needed to produce per ton of steel, and per unit of pulp and paper would decrease by about 25% mainly due to increased recycling rates and improved energy efficiency – with most of that coming from improvements in electric motors and use of heat pumps; and (3) In residential buildings, each unit of area would consume 26% less energy in 2040 than today, and in non-residential buildings 37% less than today. Their Sustainable Development Scenario (SDS), if adopted by governments would give even larger reductions in energy use.

In 2017, the world spent US $236 billion on energy efficiency, and if current policies are continued, the world will spend $300 billion per year in the 2018-2025 period, increasing to about $500 billion in the 2026-2040 period, with most of this being in the European Union, followed by the US, China and India. California has done an admirable job with energy efficiency also. In their Sustainable Development Scenario (SDS – highest efficiency, WEO2018), the world would need to invest about $500 billion per year in the 2018-2025 period, increasing to about $800 billion in the 2026-2040 period. As can be seen, the increased spending above what is already being planned is not much. As per IRENA (the International Renewable Energy Association) report GET 2018, according to their REMap case, a 40% reduction in carbon dioxide emissions can be achieved by 2050 compared with 2015 through energy efficiency base reductions in energy use.

Energy Savings and Greenhouse Gas Reductions by Switch in Meat Eating and Related Agriculture

There is also a great deal of evidence that overall energy consumption and greenhouse gas emissions will be reduced by a reduction in the production and consumption of meat. Agriculture causes about 25% of all greenhouse gas emissions and about 80% of that comes from animal agriculture. Transitioning to a more plant based or vegan diet is estimated to reduce food related greenhouse gas emissions by about 70%. In terms of land use, about 70% of agricultural land supports livestock farming, and this uses about 30% of all the land of planet Earth.

Livestock farming also generates about 37% of all human related emissions of methane that has 23 times more global warming potential than carbon dioxide. Also, the activities related to livestock farming generate about 64% of ammonia emissions which contribute to acid rain and acidification of ecosystems. Animal agriculture has also contributed the most to tropical deforestation, where 70% of previously forested tropical land has been converted to pastures, and 20% of all pastures have been degraded by livestock overgrazing, compaction and erosion. Switching from a red meat and dairy diet to eating poultry, fish and vegetarian diet has a big effect on reductions in related energy use and greenhouse gas emissions.

Someone who has spoken about this issue is Sailesh Rao who has argued for a switch from meat eating to veganism and the positive effect this will have on Climate Change, although he does take up more fundamental issues regarding our civilization. [17]

Plan for Energy Efficiency – More with Less

This Plan calls for energy efficiency growth or reduction in energy use to be about 14% of energy use by 2030 and about 25% by 2050 of the increased total energy levels. This would save the energy that would normally be consumed by end users, and hence reduce the need for this energy to be supplied. Hence, the same functions would be performed and the same benefits obtained but with less energy.

1. **Mandatory for Anything New**: All new buildings, cars, vehicles, industrial processes, and other activities from now on

must be the highest efficiency that is available at the time. Technologies, research, development, deployment, government energy regulations and company strategies must be aligned to make sure this happens! Any person, company, builder, developer, or organization must be required to meet high mandatory efficiency standards. All nations of the world should provide the incentives, investments and regulations to make sure this happens. From now on, the world cannot afford anything that is energy inefficient!

2. **Minimizing Transmission Losses:** To do this, the renewable energy production must be close to the building or industry – preferably on the property.

3. **Transportation:** All vehicles sold after 2020 must have higher and higher energy efficiency standards. A significant transition of all fossil fuel vehicles initially to plug-in hybridization (meaning smaller fossil fuel engine and larger than normal hybrid battery system). This will mean a more than doubling of fuel efficiency. This needs to be done for ALL vehicles. The second and third stages would be total electrification and the use of storage fuels. Inefficient and fossil fuel vehicles must be mothballed, scrapped, and recycled in a phased manner.

4. **Industry:** Electrification combined with the implementation of energy efficient methods of production that would reduce the energy requirements of all industry – metals, pulp paper, products and cement. This would lead to decreases in energy use of about 25%. All new industrial plants must be required to be net-zero or produce as much energy (by renewables) as they consume.

5. **Buildings and Homes:** Energy audits and total retrofits of residences and buildings will be implemented for existing structures, combined with mandatory high efficiency standards for all new homes, apartment buildings and services buildings. These will include heating ventilation and air conditioning (HVAC – more efficient heating and cooling units), lighting, better insulation, total electrification and use of more efficient appliances. The whole sector would use about 30% less energy by 2050 than today.

6. **New or Modified Cities and Habitats:** All cities must be

designed to be highly efficient, and low carbon, minimizing travel distances, maximizing transit, maximizing areas where people only walk, or bike or use larger human driven or small electric vehicles. First, the scope for stress free walking must be the highest priority, followed by human, electric and solar powered small vehicles. These will then be linked with bus and light rail mass transit stations, and parking lots for larger vehicles. **The concept of small eco-cities is presented in a later chapter.**

7. **The investments needed per year are projected to be about $1,100 billion per year for all three sectors, but this includes the money needed to electrify all three sectors.** This is higher than the $300-500 billion that is currently planned and $500-800 billion per year projected by the International Energy Association in their Sustainable Development Scenario.

8. **Global Reduction in Eating of Red Meat and Dairy Products:** the Plan proposes a phased reduction in the eating of red meat and dairy products of up to 50% globally, which will add to the energy savings of about 10% of total use and greenhouse gas emissions reductions of about 10% also. This will also enable a massive reforestation of the Earth, that will greatly add to the carbon sink capacity of forests, and help revive biodiversity and plant and animal species.

REDUCING THE CARBON FOOTPRINT
OF THE GLOBAL MILITARY

Finally, the militaries of the world also need to switch their operations to low carbon modes as Climate Change is already adversely affecting even their operations. This is true of all nations, and so it is in their interest to include military operations in their Climate Change solutions, **otherwise, besides adversely affecting their military operations, after the devastation of Climate Change, their nations may not be worth defending!** Again, each nation needs to come up with zero and low carbon operational modes, so that most of their ongoing military operations (transport, exercises, weapon systems, training, energy use in bases and by troops, etc.) are converted from high carbon fossil fuels to zero or low carbon modes.

In 2018, the world military expenditures rose to $1.82 trillion, about 76% higher than that in 1998. The top spending nations were: US ($649 billion), China ($250 billion), Saudi Arabia ($67.6 billion), India ($66.5 billion), France $63 billion), Russia ($61.4 billion) and the UK ($50 billion) (Figures from the Stockholm International Peace Research Institute). [18] In 2019 the US budget is about $700 billion and in 2020 it is projected to be more than $700 billion. The greenhouse gas emissions of the militaries of these nations are very significant, but seldom come up for scrutiny or discussion. **In 1997, it was requested that military emissions not be covered, and hence they were left out of the Kyoto Protocol. These have also been left out of the Paris Agreement discussions and accounting. But if the Climate Change problem is to be solved, the greenhouse gas emissions by the world's militaries also need to be significantly reduced.**

Also, Climate Change is damaging the locations, efforts and bases of the militaries. The Boston Institute of Brown University has documented its bad effect on the US military (*Pentagon Fuel Use, Climate Change & the Costs of War*, Boston University, June 2019). In 2014, the US Department of Defense (DOD) issued a "Climate Change Adaptation Roadmap" that stressed the importance of adapting to Climate Change. In 2018, DOD reported that the US was already suffering from Climate Change effects in terms of recurrent flooding (53 installations), drought (43 installations), wildfires (36 installations) and desertification (6 installations), and that the effects would worsen over the next 20 years if Climate Change was not solved. The US navy has expressed concerns about the effect of melting permafrost (in the Arctic area – this must be affecting Russian bases as well), and rising sea levels and coastal storms, that can have a bad effect on base infrastructures. The Norfolk Naval Base, Norfolk, Virginia and the Keesler Air Force Base have been badly affected by flooding.

As per the Watson Institute Report the US fuel use had been steadily declining, but was about 1,000 Trillion BTUs (British Thermal Units) for about the last 20 years, and among organizations, the organization that is the single largest user of petroleum is the military. Its fighting vehicles consume fuel at a very high rate, with its 60,000 Humvees consuming about 4-6 miles per gallon of diesel. After a spike during the Afghanistan and Iraq wars, the greenhouse gas emissions have been about 60 million tons per year of CO_2e

(carbon dioxide equivalent), which was more than the emissions of the Scandinavian nations of Finland, Sweden and Denmark, who emitted about 30-50 million metric tons each per year. Meanwhile, the US military industry emitted about 150 million tons of CO2e per year during its manufacturing operations. [19]

With the US economy and the US military so heavily dependent on oil for its functioning, it has focused its military capabilities a lot in terms of maintaining an assured supply globally and especially to its operational areas. Since domestic US and Canadian petroleum production has increased recently, the vulnerability of US economy to disruptions of oil supply from the middle east has decreased. However, supply lines to its military bases and operations around the world are very vulnerable to attack and disruption. Although the US military has installed solar PV at most of its installations, renewable energy is still only 1% of its total energy use. There is much scope for both the US and the other global militaries to reduce their consumption of fossil fuels. Hence the following plan is recommended for the global military.

Proposed Plan to Reduce Fossil Fuel Use
of the Global Military to Very Low Levels

1. Convert all of its vehicles for transport or fighting to the hybrid battery-electric mode, with much smaller engines. Convert the rest to be battery electric vehicles, with solar PV powered charging stations located at all suitable locations.
2. Establish solar PV battery backup plants to power all of its installations for direct energy supply. Initially use backup at nights with natural gas plants, and convert to storage fuel generators as soon as these become available.
3. Establish solar PV plants to produce large quantities of storage fuels like ammonia and transport these to its locations for use by mobile vehicles, or by electric generation plants nearby.
4. Power all of its industry with solar PV plants that are backed up by battery systems.
5. Develop non-carbon storage fuels for its jet aircraft that currently produce such large amounts of greenhouse gas emissions, and develop jet engine designs that maximize the use of these fuels.

The global energy transformation that has been proposed in this chapter covers all aspects of fossil fuel use and how we can transition out of these fuels to the solar and renewable energy age. It is the only way we will be *sure* that carbon emissions from fossil fuels (which are 87% of all emissions) are down far enough to cool our planet. We have to cover everything and leave no stone unturned in order to succeed.

Chapter 3

Massive Carbon Sinks – Forests and Coastal Ecosystems

The Energy and fossil fuel related carbon emissions plan was aimed at achieving the goal of keeping the global temperature rise below 1.5 degrees Celsius. The rejuvenation of carbon sink ecosystems is meant to supplement that, although some proponents think it should be the main plan. This chapter lays out a quantitative Global Plan for enhancing the carbon sinks of the planet. Significant deforestation, land degradation, coastal ecosystems degradation, coral reef bleaching and desertification actions over the last few centuries and the reduction of the productive and capacity of agricultural soils to absorb carbon, have been devastating the planet. The decreases and degradation of these major carbon sink ecosystems will be summarized. Then a plan will be proposed for a rejuvenation of these carbon sink ecosystems, globally, so that these areas of the planet not only become healthier and more biodiverse with increases in most forms of life, but also be rejuvenated as quantitatively effective carbon sinks. The implementation strategy will emphasize democratic control by local communities in cooperation with regional, state and national democracy, in a way so as to generate local business opportunities, jobs and the availability of local goods and services. This will be shown to lead to a much greener, hospitable and productive planet, with revitalized carbon sink ecosystems, and healthier and happier communities living near these ecosystems, controlling and making this happen.

So Where are the Forests Today?

Quantitatively carbon absorption by carbon sinks varies with the stage at which the ecosystem is and there are a variety of estimates available. In this chapter the main ecosystems that will be covered will be forests (including land based ecosystems) and coastal ecosystems. **A significant case will be made for the reforestation of all the regions of the earth and the restoration and addition of coastal ecosystems along all of the ocean coasts. Then plans will be proposed to make this happen.** Although the quantitative carbon absorption of these ecosystems may not be accurate, they are needed to provide an extra margin and to make sure that the average temperature rise is kept below 1.5 degrees Celsius, even if there is some small use of fossil fuels by 2050. While some attention will be paid to other carbon sinks like other vegetation, agricultural soils and grasslands, main attention is paid to forests, land based ecosystems and coastal ecosystems.

Young trees absorb more during the early times of growth (20-50 years) and mature trees absorb less, but cutting down mature trees or burning them releases the carbon in them. Different trees absorb different amounts of carbon in different regions of the world. A forest plantation on one hectare (2.47 acres) produces wood that is 4 cubic meters in eastern Canada, 10 cubic meters in southeastern US, and 40 cubic meters in the Amazon region of Brazil. Over the first 20-50 years of growth, per year a tree absorbs 13 Kg (about 29 lbs) of carbon in the temperate regions and about 50 Kg (about 110 lbs) in the tropics.

It has been estimated that the world has lost 3.9 million square miles (about 10 million square kilometers) or about 3.9 billion hectares, since the start of the 20th century (World Bank). The US has lost about 100 million hectares (247 million acres) since the year 1620. Recent deforestation figures differ whether it is based on satellite data (which says the deforestation is high, especially in the tropics), and that based on registered data from governments, which say that deforestation is low. One thing is certain – in 2019 the world lost a lot of its forest cover to wildfires – in North America, Europe, South America (especially the Amazon) and Australia (fires extending into 2020). With current business as usual, it is estimated that our Earth will lose about another 223 million hectares of forest by 2050.

The main causes of deforestation are mainly for all the products that we consume or that are used locally to make money. In all areas of the world trees are cut for wood pulp for paper – in Asia these are for timber and for palm oil plantations for fuel, in Latin America these are for soya bean and beef, in temperate regions for timber for construction, and in Africa for fuelwood and land clearing for agriculture. ALL of these causes of deforestation need to be stemmed. Of the human sources of carbon dioxide emissions, 87% is emitted by the burning of fossil fuels, 9% due to land use changes (mainly deforestation) and 4% due to mainly manufacturing (like producing cement). If deforestation was stopped we would prevent the 9% of the emissions coming from land use changes.[20] The plan of this book addresses what needs to be done here, while finding alternative sources of income to replace this with activities that do not put pressure on the forests.

Existing Global Reforestation Initiatives

Before we present the Book Plan, let us take a look at the major global reforestation plans that have been proposed so far. These are the Bonn Challenge and the New York Declaration on Forests. **The Bonn Challenge** was launched in 2011 by a joint effort of the Government of Germany and the International Union for the Conservation of Nature (IUCN). The aim of the plan is to restore 150 million hectares of deforested and degraded land into reforestation, and 350 million hectares by 2030. The aim of the Bonn Challenge is to use the Forest Landscape Restoration (FLR) approach which aims to restore ecology and create multi-use landscapes of benefit to humans. It was stated that achieving the 350 million hectares of reforested land will provide US $170 million of net benefits from improved crop yields, watershed protection and forest products, while absorbing about 1.7 gigatons (billion metric tons) of carbon dioxide equivalent per year. An example of its positive effects was that Pakistan committed to and surpassed its goal of restoring and planting trees in 350,000 hectares of degraded land in northern Pakistan. Since 2011, nations and organizations have committed to restoring about 60 million hectares. [21]

The **New York Declaration on Forests (NYDF)** was signed in September 2014 by governments, companies, indigenous people's organizations and non-governmental organizations, and endorsed by the UN Climate Summit later that year. It outlined ten goals which if achieved would reduce carbon emissions by an estimated 4.5-8.8 billion metric tons every year. A review of the New York Declaration on Forests in 2015 showed some measure of progress. Besides inclusion in in the Sustainable Development Goals to end deforestation by 2020, governments had pledged to restore about 60 million hectares of forest, the finance and application of efficient cookstoves had accelerated rapidly (that would reduce fuelwood use), large private investors had pledged to end deforestation caused by their agricultural supply chains, the Norwegian Pension Fund had decided to divest of investments in unsustainable palm oil production, and some progress had been made in improving forest governance and several grassroots organizations had launched a global initiative to map indigenous and community land. However, the natural forests still continue to be deforested at a high rate and the pressure from deforestation due to beef, soy, paper and palm oil production, and deforestation due the expansion of unsustainable urban areas, mining and infrastructural development is still too high. [22]

Global Plan for Reforestation and Afforestation

This book proposes a reforestation plan that will not only add to the carbon absorbing potential of the forests of the Earth, but also make the Earth much more beautiful, productive and beneficial for all. For global society the benefits will be in terms of adding to the strategy for solving the Climate Change problem, beautiful nearby areas to visit, a rejuvenation of biodiversity and wildlife ecosystems, and a much steadier stream of forest based products that are needed (together with a change in consumption and recycling patterns). For the people who are on the lower rungs of the economic ladder, this can mean better livelihoods, better local democratic control, more food and fiber from local forests on a sustainable extractive basis, and cleaner and healthier local living conditions. This is providing we follow the strategies of Energy Democracy (covered later in the book) and a restoration of the land rights of indigenous and local communities that live near these reforested areas. Crowther, et al., found through analysis that excluding urban and agricultural areas, about 0.9 billion hectares of land could be afforested and that they estimated that this would absorb 205 gigatons of carbon when these forest mature. [23]

The Plan Proposed for Global Reforestation and Afforestation is as follows:

1. **Existing global efforts:** The **Bonn Challenge** aims to restore 300 million hectares of deforested and degraded land by 2030. The New York Declaration on Forests (NYDF) has similar goals, and is being followed up through the United Nations.

2. The UNFCCC (United Nations Climate Change) based activity **REDD+ (Reduce Emissions from Deforestation and Degradation, REDD+,** with financing for tropical nations) is a good place to start, but it needs to be massively expanded.

3. Halt ALL deforestation by 2030, and find reforestation strategies that include strategies to reduce, reuse and recycle the products that cause this deforestation. All forest cutting must be accompanied by planting more trees than one cuts.

4. **Reforest and afforest all areas of the Earth, but especially the high carbon absorption potential areas by 1 billion hectares by 2050. This is an expanded version of the plan proposed by Crowther.** This is equivalent to what has been proposed by IPCC (the Intergovernmental Panel on Climate Change), as part of the strategy to keep temperature rise below 1.5 degrees Celsius.

5. In ecology, two approaches have been proposed: the "wilderness approach" (establishing wilderness areas and leaving them totally alone – but with tourism), and the "garden approach" (establishing forests, gardens and land base ecosystems but allowing local communities to extract products on a sustainable basis, leaving the ecosystems intact). The Plan proposes about a 50:50 strategy.

6. For the garden approach, we should provide local community or small local business control to all newly afforested areas, so they can own, control and use these for extractive purposes for their vital needs, but on a sustainable basis, so that the forests and land ecosystems stay intact.

This is what logging patches look like (*see right*) when there is clear cutting in the old growth forests in Northern California. This area is in Lassen County, California, near Mount Lassen. Each of the brown patches in this photo is about 20 acres in size and amounts to clear cutting or deforestation. These clear cutting plans have been approved by California State Government agencies such as the California State Board of Forestry and Cal Fire (California Department of Forestry). These clear-cutting forests or timber harvesting was

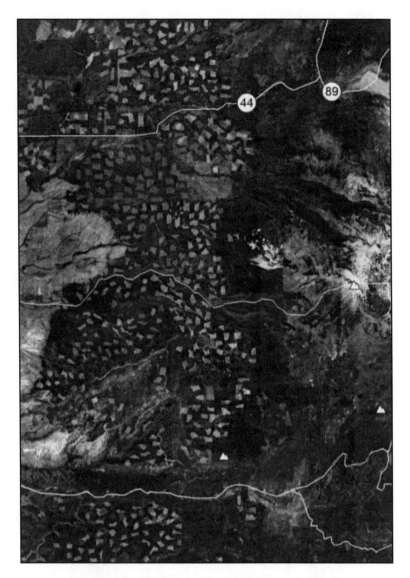

What clear-cutting looks like in Northern California
Battle Creek Watershed west of Mount Lassen.

approved by Cal Fire without regard for water, air, climate and biodiversity. The US Federal Government is encouraging logging in federal forests in California. [24]

Clear cutting of forests is really destructive and absolutely not the way to do it. Most old growth forests in California are gone and most is 80-100 year old second growth. When they clear cut fully grown trees, it takes newly planted trees many decades to grow, and if these are replaced by monoculture plantations (all the trees of one species), this releases soil carbon and we lose the carbon stored in mature trees. This also increases the fire danger and the severity of wildfires for many decades until the trees are mature. There are also bad effects on all of the ecosystems in the forests including streams.

PROPOSED REFORESTATION AND AFFORESTATION GOALS BY NATION

It is important that the increase in forest cover help in five ways: (a) Help absorb carbon for Climate Change solutions; (b) Maximize biodiversity of all types (not only animals and birds, but trees and plants, enabling grasslands and savannahs to be managed alongside forests – this will help some of the massive extinction of species that is occurring; (c) Provide income and consumption benefits to hundreds of millions of people through extractive ways (but with more trees planted than are cut down) – also urban forestry and agroforestry; (d) The reforested and afforested areas need to be designed and managed so that wildfires are easy to control (see accompanying concept sketch); (e) Help with the restoration of degraded and arid lands that have been increasingly suffering from desertification (where the land has begun to turn into a degraded desert – happening globally); and (f) Encourage other land ecosystems, such as savnnahs and grasslands.

The photo (*right*) of a forest show that it can be very dense and contain and absorb vast amounts of carbon in the trees and the accompanying vegetation.

FOREST WILDFIRE DISASTER RISK REDUCTION AND MANAGEMENT

It has become clear that forest wildfires have reached a very serious stage globally. In fact, many people are claiming that it is a sign that we are already in a runaway greenhouse effect, where global warming itself is leading to effects that are increasing carbon dioxide emissions, and adding to these emissions in such a big way, that

Photo by Author

A Forest in Costa Rica.

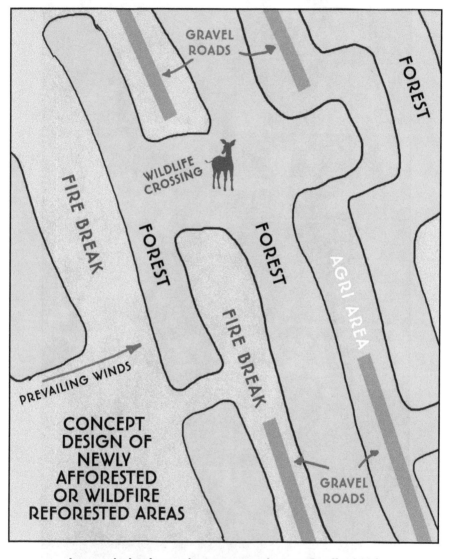

Layout design is very important so that newly afforested
areas support biodeversity and other uses, but the wildfires
are easy to control.

it we have no hope of reversing it. If such a case has to be avoided, and if they are to become big absorbers of carbon, then we need to design, manage, afforest, and reforest in ways that make this happen. A concept sketch (*left*) here provides a feel of the kinds of layout design that may have to be done.

Goals by Nation – Millions of hectares

The following land areas are proposed in order to meet the goal of 1 billion hectares (2.47 billion acres) added by 2050.

TROPICAL FORESTS

Brazil	50
China	40
India	30
Indonesia	40
Venezuela	10
Mexico and C. America	50
Australia	30
Sub-Saharan Africa	80
S. Africa and Madagascar	60
SE Asia, Incl. Vietnam	60
N. Africa and Middle East	60

TEMPERATE FORESTS

Russia	90
USA	60
China	40
Australia	30
India-Nepal-Bhutan	20
Europe	40
Central Asia	50

BOREAL FORESTS

Canada	80
Russia	60
USA	20
TOTAL	1,000 Million hectares

There is adequate land globally that this afforestation can be done without reducing the amount of agricultural lands, or without disturbing other ecosystems like savannahs, chapparals and grass-lands, which also absorb carbon and support different species.

Agroforestry, Urban Forestry and Rejuvenation of Desertified Land

Agroforestry

There are many places in the world where trees are near agri-cultural areas. However, this Book Plan proposes agroforestry for all forms of agriculture. Design of the farms with trees, either in rows or in various combinations provides many benefits – less wind and soil erosion, better moisture retention, more biodiversity of plants and animal species, organic fertilizer falling from the trees, nitrogen fixing trees, and multiple products available from the trees them-selves: fuelwood, fruit, coffee, nuts, vegetables, etc. The **Association of Temperate Agroforestry** says that agroforestry must have four components: the combination of crops, trees and (possibly) ani-mals must be intentional, intensive, interactive and integrated. The respective layout of crops and trees must be intentional, intensive (to closely manage cultivation, fertilization and irrigation), interac-tive (designed so that the trees and crops complement each other), and integrative (so that the whole agroforestry farm is combined into one unit with trees and crops benefitting each other). [25]

To implement agroforestry on a large scale will require a glob-al program of research, education and extension to reach potential farmer/foresters and teach them well established methods, and even have demonstration plots established where they can go and look and learn. As of 2015, the world's cropland was 1.7 billion hectares, the pastures were 1.8 billon hectares and the shrub covered areas were 1.7 billion hectares. The Plan calls for 5% of all cropland to be covered by trees grown using the principles of agroforestry.

Urban Forestry

In most regions of the world, urban forestry has been embraced as a way of improvement and beautification of cities, as well as a way of adding greenery, minimizing pollution and the heat island effect. Examples abound in China, the US, India and other nations. There are ways of making sure that there are not significant costs to the cities involved, by enabling the planting and harvesting of trees in urban areas but with the requirement that more trees are planted than harvested, and park areas remain intact so that wildlife can flourish. Urban forestry strategy can be combined with the concepts of eco-cities where the trees not only provide increased carbon sinks, but provide employment, products and material for composting, and can generate incomes so that after the programs are established, they do not cost the city anything to maintain.

In keeping with the principles of energy democracy, that enable local businesses and people to benefit from incomes and the availability of goods and services, such alternative ways of doing things may help local people to earn a livelihood, while helping the community with a standing tree resource that absorbs carbon. Small towns, suburban areas and cities, instead of having to spend out of their budget to plant and maintain and prune trees, can set up a program to plant different hardwood species based on their carbon sequestration potential, hardiness, disease resistance, native species appropriateness, diversity, shading properties, and water retention potential, with three trees planted for every two extracted. At the end of a significant period, the urban forest would be 150% of the previous urban forest, and be more suitable for the region. The planting and extraction sequences can be arrived at through mutual agreement between the city residents, city government and the tree contractors, whose economic and financial structure satisfies energy democracy principles (local residents, worker cooperatives, etc.). Besides the carbon absorption benefit, the benefits will include the development of local people (education, training and skills development), improvement in the urban environment, and better local incomes and less dependence on spending out of the local government budget.

We next address the fruitful area of coastal ecosystems.

Plan for the Massive Expansion of Blue Carbon – Coastal Ecosystems

The surprising fact is that coastal ecosystems can absorb more carbon per area than even mature rainforests. So much so, that people have begun to call it "Blue Carbon". In terms of total quantity, next to land based forests, coastal ecosystems provide the next greatest potential for absorbing carbon. They also support the fisheries and ocean life as they provide crucial habitats and spawning locations that enable many of these species to grow and flourish. Overfishing, and the growth of fish and shrimp farms along the coasts, has also been a major cause of the collapse of fisheries.

The three main types of coastal ecosystems are mangroves, tidal marshes and sea grasses. As of now, however, it is estimated that these coastal systems are being destroyed at the rate of about 340,000 to 980,000 hectares each year. So far, it is estimated that we have lost 67% of the mangroves, 35% of the tidal marshes and 29% of the seagrasses, and that if this destruction continues, we will lose another 30-40% of the last two, and nearly all of the mangroves in a hundred years. All the while, these ecosystems, instead of absorbing carbon are big emitters of carbon. Here is a description of some of these ecosystems.

Mangroves

Mangroves look like forests on the coast, are more on land that is regularly flooded with tidal water, and they have an ability to absorb carbon that is between 6-8 tons of CO_2 equivalent per hectare (megagrams, Mg of CO_2e), which is about 2-4 times greater than mature tropical forests. Besides absorbing carbon, mangroves provide spawning areas for fish species, they filter pollutants and contaminants from the water, and protect coastal areas from storms, floods and erosion. Mangroves continue to be lost at a rate of about 2% every year due to deforestation for aquaculture ponds and other types of coastal "development". Although they are only 0.7% of the forested area of the Earth, this destruction is estimated to cause carbon emissions that are about 10% of those from global deforestation.

NOAA: (https://oceanservice.noaa.gov/facts/bluecarbon.html)

Tidal Salt marshes

Tidal marshes grow in coastal wetland soils that are sometimes several meters (or yards) deep. They are coastal wetlands that grow through the accumulation of mineral sediment and organic matter that is then flooded by salty water during high tides. They absorb carbon at about the same rate as mangroves, and their destruction releases carbon at a similar rate. They filter pollutants from coastal areas, provide critical habitats for fish and other sea species and they help provide a buffer against storm and floods, that protects coastal areas from erosion. The main destruction of these is being caused by coastal "development" and their draining and conversion to agriculture. Rising sea levels will also cause problems unless these marshes can grow and shift.

Sea Grasses

Seagrasses grow offshore under water and they have deep roots in soils that are often up to four meters (about four yards) deep that store carbon in the underwater soil. They are less than 0.2% of the sea area but absorb about 10% of the carbon in ocean sediments each year. The entire global storage of carbon on seagrasses is about 20 billion metric tons. In addition, seagrasses are important habitats for fishes, sea turtles and manatees, and continue to filter and secure sediment. In recent years, we have been losing seagrasses at the rate of about 1.5% annually due to decreasing water quality (pollution), deforestation and dredging.

Combined, at the current rates of destruction of these three coastal ecosystems, it is estimated is leading to global carbon emissions of 0.15-1.02 billion tons of CO_2. With area that is only 2-6% of

Photo by author.

Coastal ecosystem in San Francisco Bay.

the total tropical forest area (even a smaller percentage of total forested area), these systems lead to about 3-19% of the carbon emissions from all deforestation, and recent estimates show that the total carbon emissions from this damage is about equivalent to the emissions from the United Kingdom (ranked 9th in emissions by nation).

The accompanying photo shows a coastal ecosystem in the San Francisco Bay of California.

The International Blue Carbon Initiative: A significant program that was formed in 2011 is this initiative by a partnership of Conservation International, IUCN (International Union for the Conservation of Nature) and IOC-UNESCO (part of the UN Economic Social and Cultural Organization). This program seeks to coordinate global efforts in this area, promotes international action on this, and works with national governments such as Indonesia, Philippines, Ecuador and Costa Rica. This Blue Carbon Initiative is developing monitoring methods, encouraging research, and promoting blue carbon demonstration and development projects. (https://www.conservation.org/projects/blue-carbon)

The Plan for Coastal Ecosystems

Considering the importance of Mangroves, tidal marshes and seagrasses for absorbing carbon and the many other benefits they provide it makes sense to propose a global program for their rejuvenation and new expansion. Some good programs already exist, such as the Blue Carbon Initiative – this plan will build on those. So a plan is proposed as follows:

1. Stopping all of the destruction of all of these coastal ecosystems by 2030.
2. Simultaneous rejuvenation of all existing coastal ecosystems in all continents except Antarctica. The estimate of the global length of coasts varies from 1.2 to 1.6 million kilometers (0.75 to 1 million miles). **Along this ENTIRE length, the introduction, growth and management of coastal ecosystems from a few hundred meters (or yards) to as much as 10 kilometers (or about 6 miles) off shore along ALL coasts – about an average of 1 kilometer. This will give us about 1.2 to 1.6 million square kilometers (0.5 to 0.65 million square miles). This will be accomplished by 2050, although the**

activity will be firmly established and continued in an organized fashion beyond. See the accompanying sketches that
provide some idea of these ecosystems.

3. A reduction of beaches to a few small ones as needed for
    tourism, while developing the visits and tourism of these
    new and beautiful ecosystems along every mile of coasts.

4. The removal of all destructive aquaculture activities along
    the coasts, and whatever ocean farming is conducted
    should be organic and support habitats for ocean species.

5. Although the three main ecosystems have been described,
    other areas that can receive attention for restoration in-
    clude near shore corals, estuaries, river deltas, deep water
    swamps, maritime and riverine forests, kelp, oyster reefs,
    and shell fish beds.

6. Each nation or regional groups of nations will need to take
    up the rejuvenation or introduction of coastal ecosystems in
    a systematic way, engaging in proper planning, financing,
    implementation (construction of supporting structures and
    beds and planting of species of trees or plants), adaptive
    management and monitoring and reporting.

7. Rather than a simple hand waving about employment to
    be created by these activities, all activities will be defined,
    planned and financed in such a way that the local commu-
    nities will be included, enabled and empowered to have
    democratic involvement and control of these activities,
    and receive the major share of the benefits from the prod-
    ucts, services, income and food that become available from
    them.

8. An absolute control of all land based pollution that gets
    washed down rivers, including hard materials (like plastics)
    as well as run off of chemicals and biological waste.

9. Last, but not least, a massive accompanying program for the
    revival of all fisheries that globally are dependent on these
    ecosystems to provide the habitats for all fish, plant and
    crustacean species. This will lead to a revival of all fisheries,
    many of which are collapsing, and will revive fishing and
    other economic activities, with all involved to make sure they
    work to grow the carbon absorbing potential of all coastal
    ecosystems, create and maintain habitats for species, and

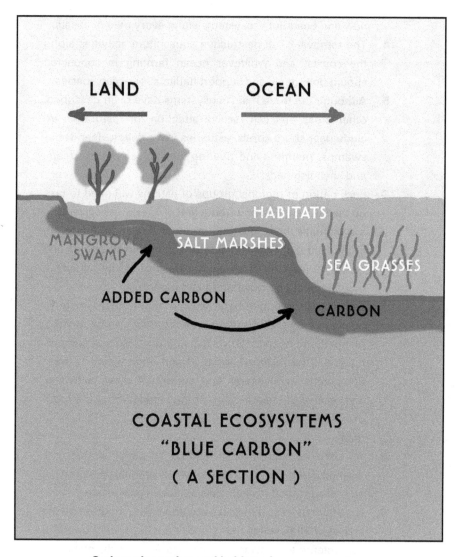

Carbon absorption and habitats for ocean species.

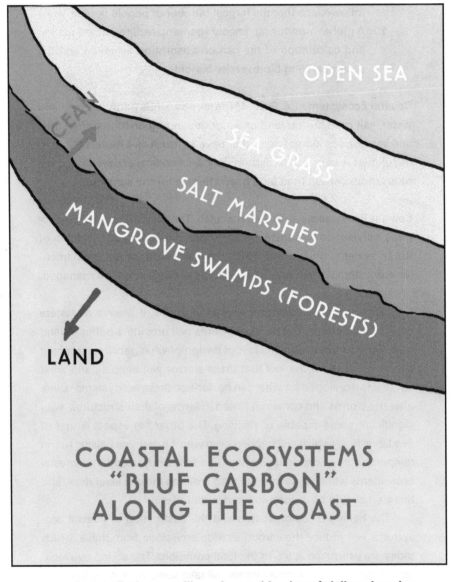

Arial Sketch: Each area will need a combination of civil engineering construction and ocean planting.

only extract (e.g. fish catches), that enables the ecosystems and species to thrive and grow. All coastal communities, and fisherman should be democratically involved, and the principles of energy democracy and just transition should be followed, so that the largest number of people benefit.

10. A global monitoring, encouragement, facilitation, education and calculation of the carbon absorption achieved and the accompanying biodiversity benefits.

Coastal Ecosystems – A Slice. Mangrove swamps partly on land and water, salt marshes on land or water depending on high or low tide, and sea grasses like eel grass that have as much as 4 meters (13 feet) of soil that is very rich in carbon. Bay area coastal ecosystems have much more carbon than land based forests for the same area.

Coastal Ecosystems – An Aerial sketch. The civil engineering structures will need to be constructed offshore, depending on the depth of the seawater at the location. Then, the plants or trees for that particular ecosystem will need to be planted as needed, and then managed.

Hurricanes, cyclones and coastal storms will always devastate coastal ecosystems, but the ecosystems will provide a buffer to land areas, and as for forests, the layout design of what gets implemented should account for the fact that these storms will happen, and what strategies developed for what can be done so these ecosystems revive after the storms and come out ahead in terms of their structures, with significant areas capable of reviving. The other big aspect is that of Sea Level Rise (which will happen even with 1.5 degrees Celsius rise in temperature), where again it should be fully understood that coastal ecosystems will shift up into the land areas as the sea level rises, and this shift should be accommodated in their design.

The halting of deforestation and the destruction of coastal ecosystems will reduce the carbon dioxide emissions from these, which today are estimated at 9% of the total emissions. The added rejuvenation of land and ocean ecosystems will take some time to mature over the next few decades as these are planted and grow. However, good management will help to absorb larger amounts of carbon in ecosystems once they mature, and can be a big part of the strategy to restore biodiversity and begin to stem the massive extinction of the species.

CHAPTER 4

Advanced Disaster Management for Climate Change

The aim of this chapter is to propose a Global Plan that will help the world better prepare for Climate Change related disasters to help minimize their damage and deaths, make it easier to provide rescue and evacuation, be more organized ahead of time to provide relief, temporary housing and medical services and recovery of electrical power, and plan better for recovery and reconstruction so that the communities where disaster had struck are better prepared to deal with future disasters and suffer even less damage the next time around. Climate Change is making it essential that the world engage in continuous year round large scale preparation and organization of resources aimed at doing this.

Already, natural disasters have been getting worse and more devastating because of Climate Change. There is very little uncertainty about this now and we are only at about 1 degree Celsius (1.8 degrees Fahrenheit) average global temperature rise. **Even if we follow the entire plan outlined in this book we will still only reach 1.5 degrees Celsius temperature rise, and even then, things will be worse, but hopefully still manageable. If we allow the temperature rise to go higher, we will end up with catastrophic situations.** So it is best that we get with it and work in every way possible to restrict the temperature rise to no more than 1.5 degrees Celsius. After we have achieved that, we can then proceed to bring the temperature rise further down by reducing the concentrations of greenhouse gases.

As is already happening and even for the 1.5 degrees Celsius rise, land areas will be increasingly devastated by heavy rains, flooding, wildfires, mudslides and tornadoes of increasing severity. Coastal areas will be increasingly devastated by hurricanes, cyclones, rising water temperatures, ocean acidification (carbon dioxide dissolved in water gives carbonic acid), retreating arctic sea ice, sea level rise, high tide flooding, higher storm surges (walls of water several feet or meters high), the possible collapse of high altitude glacial lakes (e.g. Himalayas), and extremely heavy rain events. These disasters have become much more predictable. So, this chapter proposes a plan for disaster management for all the different kinds of disasters – before, during and after disasters.

What the World Has Already Started to Do – Disaster Risk Reduction (DRR)

The world has started the process of coming to grips with how it can reduce the risks from natural disasters through formally starting to talk about **Disaster Risk Reduction (DRR)**, which aims to reduce the damage caused by ALL disasters (not just those caused by Climate Change) caused by earthquakes, floods, droughts and cyclones, through actions done before the disaster strikes and then later in recovery, rehabilitation and reconstruction. **The United Nations Office for Disaster Risk Reduction (UNDRR) based in Geneva, Switzerland**, is coordinating a global effort that had previously been managed under the Hyogo Framework, but as of March 2015, transitioned to the Sendai Framework for 2015-2030, which is a non-binding agreement intended to coordinate and facilitate nation states who have the primary responsibility.

The seven global targets of the Sendai Framework for DRR are aimed at substantially achieving the following goals: (1) Reduce the global deaths from disasters by 2030, compared to the period 2005-2015; (2) Reduce the number of people affected by disasters by 2030, again compared to the period 2005-2015; (3) Reduce disaster economic loss as percent of GDP (Gross Domestic Product – or nation's economic activity); (4) Reduce the damage to critical infrastructure and basic services (Water, health, education, etc.); (5) Increase the number of nations with local and national disaster risk reduction strategies; (6) Enhance global cooperation with developing nations through sufficient support; and (7) Increase the availability and access to early warning systems and disaster risk reduction information to people and populations at risk by 2030.

The Sendai Framework for DRR has Four Priorities for Action: (1) Understanding disaster risk in terms of the people and assets that are at risk, and the types of hazards, so that one can better define how to do risk assessment, prevention, reduction, preparedness and response, (2) Strengthening governance at the local, national, regional and global levels, so that in addition to these there is better response for recovery and rehabilitation, (3) Encouraging public and private investment to implement measures that people need for themselves and their environment, and (4) For recovery, rehabilitation and reconstruction, adopting a "Build Back Better" strategy, so that people and assets are better protected when the next disaster strikes.

So where is this global Sendai Framework based effort as of the time of this book? On the plus side, about 116 nations have started reporting though the Sendai Framework Monitor in terms of providing information and 91 nations have stated that they have begun the development of disaster risk reduction strategies. However, the place of implementation is very slow, there is not much awareness in populations about DRR, strategies to protect the really vulnerable groups have not evolved, it does not appear that the goals set for 2020 will be met, and which further reduces the probability that the goals set for 2030 will be met. A parallel global effort is that of the Global Facility for Disaster Reduction and Recovery (GFDRR) that works with some nations but the funding is channeled through the World Bank. This organization has funded some projects around the world and cooperates with the UNDRR which is described above. The financing aspect of the Disaster and Risk Reduction activities will be taken up in the next chapter on global action plans.

So, now we have to see what we can do, both to encourage global actions and to plan and implement actions robustly for the risk reduction of Climate Change caused disasters.

The Plan for Disaster Risk Reduction
for Climate Change Caused Disasters

The world needs to be planning year round in preparing areas, methods, organizations and resources for disasters. Each type of disaster will need the most likely areas to be prepared to attempt to minimize the damage caused by the disaster, so that when expert people come to help contain (for example firefighters containing a wildfire), their job is made much easier and the effect of the disaster is minimized. Also, before the disaster strikes, the months and years before that need to be spent organizing the resources, equipment and organization that will be needed to help people before, during and after the disaster. Also, the months and years before the disaster need to be spent making the homes, buildings and communities more resilient, and putting in place protective structures (like sea walls) and ecosystems (like the coastal ecosystems described in the previous chapter).

Then, during the disaster, the plans proposed will need organization and resources in place that help people during a disaster (survival, evacuation, search and rescue, etc.). Then after the disaster, organization and resources will need to be ready and properly placed to provide temporary housing, food, medical services and on site energy production for the displaced people. The final stage will be that of organization, resources and actual implementation of the tasks of rebuilding the areas damaged by the disasters in such a way that they get back to semblance of decent living and are better prepared for the next disaster. This can benefit from the "Build Back Better" approach defined globally above. This can be followed by reporting that helps others at other places in the world better understand and use their experience to better prepare their location for future disasters.

Here we cover what is needed globally and by national governments to better prepare themselves and their populations for Climate Change related disasters. Although we are not covering other natural disasters such as earthquakes and tsunamis, the same strategies as outlined below can help with those types of disasters as well. We now address what is needed for four major categories of Climate Change related disasters: (1) hurricane, cyclones and coastal storms; (2) land based tornadoes and floods; (3) forest wildfires; and (4) mudslides in hills and mountains.

The Plan for Coastal Disasters – Hurricanes, Cyclones, Coastal Storms and Floods

Hurricanes or cyclones are increasing in ferocity and severity as global temperatures rise, causing increasing disruption and damage. These and coastal storms not only cause damage and deaths along the coast but often many hundreds of miles inland through severe flooding and high winds. The global organizations described above and some nations have taken up seriously the task of reducing damge from disasters and planning for recovery. Here we propose a global plan to deal with this activity.

1. Building coastal ecosystems all along the whole world's non-ice coastline (as per the plan in Chapter 4) is the best beginning that the world can make to start protecting its coastal areas, for this activity will not only absorb significant amounts of carbon but help reduce the severity of coastal storms by absorbing some of the damage, and also reduce the height of the storm surge (or height of water surging inland).

2. All nations that can have storms of these types should analyze and build storm protection barriers along with their coastal ecosystems, like sea walls, levees, and offshore rock barriers that minimize the onshore movement of waves and water.

3. All nations subject to hurricanes and cyclones need to analyze new home and building designs as well as retrofitting designs on how buildings can be designed to withstand floods, storm surges and winds, and begin implementing this process. Example: GFDRR has helped Mozambique design and provide recommendations on how school buildings can be built or retrofitted so as to seal and strengthen foundations, walls, windows, roofs, doorframes, and general structure in order to withstand these disasters – some of which have begun to be implemented. [26]

4. By now, most nations provide early warnings, starting a few days in advance once a hurricane or cyclone has been observed from space. Efforts should be made to ensure that all citizens in the affected coastal areas know sufficiently in advance in order to prepare themselves for these, in terms of what to do to protect their houses in case they have to evacuate.

5. Although earthquake related tsunamis are not covered here, in the event of tsunamis, as the time is very short, the only measure that will be effective in terms of early warning will be sirens located about every mile or kilometer along the entire coastline of potential tsunami locations. This system could then also be effectively used in case of hurricanes, cyclones and storms.

6. All nations should implement themselves or be assisted to prepare resources, equipment and people in advance for storms. This should include mobile equipment carriers that can create living facilities for large numbers of displaced people, that consist of temporary housing, medical, sanitary and energy facilities.

7. All nations that are prone to such storms should put in place organization, teams and forces (even paramilitary type forces that are multi-skilled, high-tech and standalone – but not armed) to be able to direct or assist the population in tasks of providing specialized response during disasters, deploy before a disaster, be able to review and provide feedback to disaster management control centers, have the equipment and resources to perform search and rescue (including evacuation boats), and work with citizen volunteers that have trained in emergency response actions (before disasters) distributed in all villages and small towns – along the coast and inland to the extent needed. Example: India reported in its UNDRR Disaster Risk Reduction Report that it has taken measures to establish such a force consisting of former paramilitary personnel who receive new and upgraded training. [27]

8. After a disaster has passed, and search and rescue, and emergency medical relief has been provided, and fatalities taken care of, there needs to be immediate wheeling in of adequate temporary housing, medical, sanitary and energy equipment and supplies of food, water, medicine and sanitary supplies, to the affected people.

9. In recovery and reconstruction, after equipment has been hauled in and the debris cleared there must be strict rules enforced in terms of building back: (1) All homes and building that are at a certain distance from the coast must be

built or retrofitted to withstand future storms (water storm surges, and high winds – see example of Mozambique above), or they must not be allowed to be built at all; (2) All hospitals, electric supply, schools and water supply facilities must have all equipment such as electrical panels, air conditioners, furnaces, emergency generators and pumps located at least one floor up from ground, and the building and protective structure built or retrofitted so that they survive a future storm.

10. For sea level rise areas, thoughts should be given to preventing the infiltration of salt water into freshwater groundwater. Also, where sea level rise cannot be contained, cities and communities should design their living areas so that water areas and land areas live together such as in cities like Venice, Italy, with boats being used instead of cars, and walkways and bikeways constructed along the waterways. Highways, airports and city zones that are predicted to be under water should be relocated or raised.

Plan for Tornadoes

Tornadoes are funnel clouds that can develop in a storm when a rotating mass of air at higher wind speeds touches down on the ground and then moves along the ground. The wind speed can be such that it can pull off roofs, demolish entire homes and buildings, pick up and drop cars and other vehicles hundreds of meters or yards away, and have some of this debris flying around and dropping down. This results in much damage to communities and possible loss of life. These disasters are similar to hurricanes and cyclones except that they occur inland, and become more similar if accompanied by heavy rain and flooding. Global warming is leading to an increase in the thermal energy in the atmosphere and it has been observed that the number of tornadoes in a tornado "cell" have been increasing – this means many more tornadoes occurring together for the same storm. The whole central part of the United States has been experiencing an increase in the severity of these storms and tornados, along with heavy flooding.

Early warning systems in the US authorities usually first send out a Tornado Watch, meaning that there is a high probability that tornados may occur. Then if actual tornados are sighted or if the probability increases, they send out a Tornado Warning. Most city locations have siren based systems that warn residents, so that they often have time to seek shelter. The main disaster risk reduction plan needs to prepare communities better to provide safe houses, shelters and tornado proof home and building designs, so that damage is minimized and lives are saved. So here is the Book Plan.

1. All nations and communities that can have tornadoes should have good early warning systems in place that provide enough notification to people and communities of the Tornado Warning type.

2. It's not just the wind velocity in kilometers or miles per hour that is a problem, but the differences that develop in air pressures between the insides and outsides of structures, especially if windows are blown in or broken, which cause walls and roofs to be pulled off their moorings and blown away.

3. All nations and communities need to put programs in place that implement building designs, standards, and codes that will provide safe shelter locations for homes, buildings, schools, hospitals and shopping centers, as well as lead to construction more likely to survive a tornado.

4. Safe room shelters in homes need to be properly designed according to professional guidelines and advice given by emergency management agencies. In the US, people need to use the FEMA P-320 Safe Room Construction Plans (Federal Emergency Management Agency). These will normally be located in the middle of the house, or in a basement if a house has one.

5. All public and business buildings such as schools, hospitals, business and government buildings, airports and train stations need to be built or retrofitted with safe shelters. All nations, states and communities that are at risk for tornadoes should begin to mandate that ALL new structures (including newly built homes) have this and that programs be put in place to retrofit existing buildings with safe structures.

6. Finally, all the aspects of disaster management, from early warning to search and rescue and relief and rehabilitation be put in place so as to help communities hit by tornadoes

survive and recover from these disasters.

7. During reconstruction, laws and programs be put into place, and enough financing be provided so that all new re-constructed structures follow the guidelines of plan Item 5 above – so that all homes and buildings have safe shelters as well as design features that enable them to better survive future tornadoes.

Plan for Forest Wildfires

As dry and hot weather has intensified with Climate Change, wildfires are becoming more and more frequent, damaging and dead-ly. At the same time, they are turning a carbon sink, the forests, into a carbon emitter. The wildfires have raged in recent years in western United States and Alaska, western Canada, southeast Australia and Europe. The year 2017 saw major wildfires in Portugal, Spain and Italy, and in 2018 in Greece and Sweden. Till August of 2019, there were additional fires in the Siberian region of Russia (Arctic circle), Canary Islands (Spain), southern France, the Hawaiian island of Maui, and British Columbia. Greenland is seeing massive wildfires, which to-gether with Siberian Arctic Circle wildfires are not only releasing large amounts of carbon dioxide, but are thawing the permafrost, which can release methane, and the black soot from the fires reduces the ability of snow to reflect sunlight (so less heat escapes to space).

In 2018, the town of Paradise in California was devastated by the "Camp" wildfire that moved so fast that people were not able to escape quickly enough, leaving over 80 people dead and 11,862 structures destroyed, including 9,700 single family homes and 118 multi-family buildings. In the same year, a fast moving wildfire in Greece left about 100 people dead, and nearly destroyed all of the tourist resort towns of Mati and Kokkino Limanaki, on the east coast of Greece, 18 miles from Athens. The Paradise, California fire released smoke that caused toxic breathing conditions in even far away com-munities like the San Francisco area for nearly 7-10 days. The toxic chemicals, lead batteries (from burnt out vehicles) and toxic electron-ics, and the volume of debris created special challenges for cleanup.

It must be realized that the greatly increasing forest wildfires in the temperate and boreal forests (mainly in the "developed" nations), are the beginnings of a **Runaway Greenhouse Effec**t, and must be contained and minimized if the strategy of rejuvenating carbon sinks like forests is to succeed. Because, with these exploding wildfires and deforestation in the tropics, the forests are currently increasing carbon emissions, and not absorbing carbon as they should.

It is now obvious that we need stronger global and national responses to wildfires so they stop becoming massive emitters of carbon. All forested areas need attention so that steps can be taken to minimize the wildfires, make it easier to control them, and engage in disaster risk reduction. So, here is the Book Plan for disaster risk reduction for wildfires.

1. **Fire containment zones in major forests** – fire suppression: In the past, in the US there have been attempts at fire suppression or creating zones by controlled burns, and currently for any major fire, firefighters are dispatched to the scene and fight and contain the fires. In order to make the fires easier to contain the plan proposes creating forest gaps that run perpendicular to the prevailing winds, so that fire cannot jump from one forest area to the next. This can be done by small contractors or by timber logging contractors who then should plant a greater number of trees elsewhere.

2. **Fire containment zones in all new forests and tree plantations**: In Chapter 3 the plan proposed a billion hectares of added forests, about half of which would be in areas of the Earth where the current forest fires have become frequent. All of these newly reforested or afforested areas should be planted in segments designed so that if fire occurs in one of the segments, it does not spread to another segment. The same methods as used in Item 1 will be adopted. Fire containment and fire-fighting aspects must be part of the design of any afforested areas or new tree plantations.

3. **Fire defensible spaces around homes, buildings and communities**: Currently, in California there is an effort to establish fire defensible spaces around homes, buildings and communities by clearing ground level brush, low tree branches, and dead trees for a certain distance away from the structures. This procedure will be adopted globally, so that in future, it will be harder for fires to reach the structures and be easier for firefighters to contain the blaze and protect communities.

4. **Goats and other natural controllers of brush**: Surprisingly,

in areas where the rainy season leaves a lot of ground brush that can spread a fire, goats are being used a very low cost way of getting rid of the brush. Goats should be used only in temperate and boreal forests and not in arid areas, where they can worsen desertification.

5. **Resources and organization before fire season:** As with the hurricanes and cyclones plan above, globally and within nations, resources and equipment, and people and organizations must be put in place in advance, not only to make it easier to contain fires, as in items 1 and 2 above, but also to help with evacuation, search and rescue and relief. Equipment and resources should be prepared in advance and stored nearby but in non-forested locations, so that they can be quickly sent to provide help in parallel to the efforts of firefighters whose main job is to try and contain the fires.

6. **Better evacuation routes and communications:** In both the cases of the wildfires in 2018 in Paradise, California, and in Mati, Greece, the evacuation routes were not well established and not properly communicated, so that the population could not evacuate in an orderly manner. Better evacuation routes and wider roads need to be constructed (this is being done in Paradise, California), so that all of the population can evacuate faster than the movement of the fire.

7. **Relief and temporary housing:** The resources and equipment organized in Item 5, should quickly be activated and brought into use for the rescue, relief and temporary housing areas for evacuees. The housing areas should create temporary housing communities for living quarters, sanitation, energy supply (mobile solar panels and battery backup units), and medical help, in addition to adequate food and supplies.

8. **Reconstruction, location and building rules:** Efforts will be made to move people out of forested areas, create fire defensible spaces around living areas, and establish new rules for reconstruction. First, there must not be ANY homes approved for new construction inside forested areas. Then, all construction in new or wildfire devastated areas must be of fire resistant construction, and the use of materials that can create toxic fumes on burning be banned. The construction of consolidated building complexes of fire resistant housing, rather than isolat-

ed single family homes will be encouraged.

9. **Preparation for next forest fire season:** After the dry sum-
    mer months are over, the cycle of preparing for the next
    wildfire season should begin, as outlined above – preparing
    fire containment zones, fire defensible spaces, fire resistant
    reconstruction, better fire evacuation routes, and resources
    and equipment for relief and temporary housing. As newly
    afforested and reforested areas are added, the same needs
    to be put in place aggressively for those areas as well – with
    firm rules that control the location and building of new com-
    munities and housing near these areas.

Plan for Landslides in Hills and Mountains

The excessively high rains caused by global warming means
that hill and mountain sides that are normally stable when dry, become unstable and start flowing downhill as rivers of mud that bury
whatever comes in their path – cities, communities, people and farm
fields. Normally, trees and vegetation that cover the ground often
hold the soil together and prevent it from getting washed down.
However, when a wildfire burns away the trees and brush, the land
is now bare and if heavy rains come later, the result is mudslides. As
if the devastation of the wildfires was not enough!

Hill and mountain areas, from the Himalayas to the Alps, and
from the Sierra to the Andes, need special attention to make sure
that there is some ground cover and that there is proper drainage in
case of heavy rain. The reservoirs that are developed to hold excess
water along the watershed should not be too large otherwise they
will cause problems of their own. Glacial lakes that are developing
because of the melting of the Himalayan glaciers, if they get too big,
and if all of the ground areas around them get too wet in the rains,
are bound to collapse and flood the downstream areas with mud
and waters in ways that can be catastrophic.

A good example of pro-active work to reduce landslides is the
case of Hong Kong. After a heavy landslide in 1972 that killed over
a hundred people, in 1977, their Geotechnical Engineering Office
(GEO) established a Slope Safety System that led a comprehensive
enforcement of geotechnical safety standards, community participation for slope safety, systems of early warning and emergency
response, good information on landslide events, and implemented

measure to mitigate landslide risk. This led to reduction in fatalities and then no fatalities for a decade. [28]

So here is the Plan:

1. All hill and mountain areas that are deemed to be at risk should be evaluated globally and by national governments to see if there need to be measures put in place to reduce the probability of landslides.

2. A program similar to Hong Kong's Slope Safety System should be put in place that establishes geotechnical standards for early warning systems, regulates development on the slopes, and implements measures that reduce the probability of landslides and mud slides.

3. Areas that should receive special attention are those that are subject to heavy rains, or ones that get wildfires and then have a high probability of getting heavy rains. Burnt out zones should get immediate attention after the wildfire to begin programs for establishing structures, land contouring and planting vegetation, together with monitoring and early warning systems to alert downstream communities of increasing danger and possible need for evacuation.

Finally, although earthquakes are not related to Climate Change, there needs to be disaster risk reduction and preparation for disasters in all communities that lie along earthquake faults. First, all houses and buildings should be evaluated for possible collapse from earthquake and be seismically retrofitted to withstand them. For different types of construction (wood frame, concrete, mud houses, etc.) a good deal of knowledge exists about this and globally and within nations, such programs should be implemented. Next, there needs to be a system of training of citizens who can perform some of the tasks of taking care of themselves and their communities if fire and police personnel are unable to come immediately to their aid, or are overwhelmed by an earthquake disaster. Such a program has been implemented in the US and is called Community Emergency Response Team (CERT), put in place by the US Federal Emergency Management Agency (FEMA) that has trained citizen volunteers on tasks such as earthquake safety, search and rescue, provision emergency supplies (food, water and medicine), provide medical assistance and evaluation, and help the neighborhood community cope with the disaster.

The Plan calls for keeping greenhouse gas emissions below what is needed to keep the global average temperature rise below 1.5 degrees Celsius. However, as the temperature rises from the current 1 degree Celsius to that level, there will be a need to handle disasters in an organized fashion. The case of wildfire mitigation is especially important, if carbon emissions from wildfires are to be kept in check, and the global program for afforestation and reforestation is to succeed in absorbing carbon.

Chapter 5

Adapting to the Consequences of Climate Change and A Regenerative Agriculture

This book outlines a Climate Change plan that aims to restrict the global average temperature rise to 1.5 degrees Celsius. However, even with this temperature rise, the consequences of Climate Change will need to be faced so that global society and nations adapt many aspects of their activities and land areas so as to try and minimize the impact, or make changes to how they do things. Adaptation here means deliberate actions that are taken in advance in any sphere of activity to prepare for changes.

So in agriculture, crops may need to be moved from one region to another, crop varieties may need to change, and irrigation practices may need to change for flood or drought conditions. Fisheries have already started adjusting to changing practices and restrictions on the catches when areas are getting overfished – now there may need to be changes in fisheries resulting from rising water temperatures or storms. Rising temperatures are leading to heat waves, which means that cooling shelters may need to be built for use in those parts of the year when temperatures get so hot that people die, especially people without access to air conditioning or even water coolers. Adapting to floods may require that houses be built on stilts, or people may need to increasingly live in houseboats. Adapting to rising sea levels may need the construction of dikes or levees, or coastal zones prone to sea storms or flooding may need to ban the building of homes there, or mandate a change of location or design of homes, buildings and highways. Establishing coastal ecosystems will help the coastal areas adapt better to these effects.

Here we address the adaptation of human populations (us), on the aspects of the planet that we depend on and to try and minimize the damaging effect of Climate Change. Here we deal with four main aspects:

a. Adapting to the rising temperature – heat waves and droughts.

b. Adapting to the increasing floods and storms, and rising sea levels – changing habitats and productive activity locations.

c. Adapting agriculture, fishery and forest strategies for extreme temperatures, heavy rains and weather disasters of increasing severity.

d. Adapting infrastructure to better withstand Climate Change.

The consequences of Climate Change are already getting quite challenging. If these are not to get much worse, we need to restrict the global average temperature rise to less than 1.5 degrees Celsius. Hence it is important that we proceed with the plans as outlined in Chapter 3 and 4 that deal with both carbon sources and sinks. However, we still need to prepare for what has already put in motion, and prepare our global population in a systematic manner to help them cope with the consequences.

Globally, adaptation has been part of the discussions. At the COP16 (Conference of Parties to the UNFCCC – United Nations Framework Convention on Climate Change), meeting in Cancun US $100 billion were promised by the richer industrialized countries to developing countries through a Green Climate Fund, but these funds have not been forthcoming. The UNFCCC estimated that about $49-171 billion would be needed by 2030 for adaptation actions by developing nations. This does not include the massive adaptation that will be needed by the richer nations also that are beginning to be devastated by Climate Change. Another path for funding in smaller amounts has been through the World Bank's Global Environment Facility (GEF) intended to provide loans to developing nations. An Adaptation Fund was set up that is funded through the Clean Development Mechanism (CDM) that was part of the Kyoto Protocol. It has been based on a 2% levy that was supposed to have been funded for a few hundred million dollars that was dependent on a supposed carbon price. The most hopeful sign that things may be moving in the right direction and there might be some funding coming forward was the formation in October of 2018 of a "Global Commission on Adaptation" with a commitment of $200 billion by the World Bank and its partners. In what follows, we try to describe a Plan about what needs to be done.

Adapting to Heat and Drought

Heat waves are striking most of the world on an annual basis, with each year being recorded as hotter than most previous ones. This is often being accompanied by multi-year droughts that are leading to severe water shortages. The entire global population will have to adapt to the rising temperatures, heat waves, droughts and water shortages. The large masses of people living in developing nations, most of whom live closer to the equator need strategies on how to cope with the higher levels of heat.

ALL of the governments of the world need to develop and implement heat preparedness plans, that educate and empower all of their populations about what to do when extreme heat events and high temperatures occur, which are more likely than ever. Every village, small town and large city needs to construct and define cooling centers for humans, and if needed, for animals. These cooling centers can also serve as Climate Change resource centers. Where insulated cooling centers have air conditioning, this added electricity must all be powered by increased local solar PV power, which at other times can provide electric power for other energy needs. Until such time as these become available, lower cost open sheds that provide some shade from the intense heat of the midday sun for people and animals should be constructed. This needs to be enabled globally, so that all governments define and implement their plans.

Climate Change is leading to multi-year droughts at many locations. This is having a bad effect on agriculture (dealt with below), and water shortages for rural areas and cities. Many big cities are running out of water. In April 2018, the large city of Capetown, near the southern tip of South Africa ran out of water on a day it called "Day zero". In June 2019, the large city of Chennai (formerly called Madras) in the southern Indian state of Tamilnadu, on the east coast of India, ran out of water before the monsoons came. In both cases the reservoirs that they were relying on went dry. In most cities of the world, the disregard for wetlands, water harvesting, heavy wasteful water use, the heavy heat island effect caused by too much concrete and paved surfaces, and fewer trees and nearby forested areas, have worsened the situation. **Climate Change is being particularly unforgiving to these cities and all human habitats that are ignoring natural and environmental cycles and affairs and proceeding along heavy technical and housing development and high levels of fossil fuel use.** The situation in the areas of the countryside around the cities is even worse and does not hit the news until there is famine or large scale migration as people abandon their farms and homes since they do not have even a minimum level of water to live, and even less to irrigate their farms (which in the past used wasteful agricultural practices and water use).

Plan for Heat and Drought Adaptation

The Plan proposes the following actions for adaptation:

1. All nations, regions and cities establish heat preparedness plans and set up cooling centers in all villages, small towns and large cities that will be ready to be activated when a heat emergency arrives.

2. In most cases, especially in developing nations, this means new construction of low cost sheds, open or enclosed, that provide shade to people and animals.

3. Solar PV power should be added in case the cooling centers have air-conditioning or water coolers, so that the electricity use does not cause added fossil fuel use.

4. Both human habitats and immediate surrounding areas benefit from urban forestry (as covered in the previous chapter), but must be supplemented by added trees near or surrounding the cooling centers – again tied to local democratic control and livelihoods. This is true of ALL nations.

5. Homes, buildings and cities need to develop strong features for insulation and ventilation that provide cooling and energy efficiency (see Chapter 2).

6. All built up areas establish green roofs, reduce concrete and paved areas, and require shaded and ventilated roofs to reduce the albedo effect and reflect the sun's energy back out

to space (black surfaces are bad as they absorb heat) reducing the heat island effect as concrete and solid surfaces absorb heat during the day and emit it at night.

7. All villages, small towns and cities to develop strong water harvesting plans combined with the development of local wetlands that absorb and retain water during the rainy season. Cities that do not have it need to be reconstructed to add these features. See the concept of eco-cities shown later in the book.

8. Strong measures be taken to ensure the water harvested be used to replenish the ground water that is being used, but with strict controls that do not allow contaminated water (e.g. from pesticide and herbicide laced farm fields) to get to the ground water. **Ground water use must from now on be subject to strong regulations and control and only allowed as needed and along with strong actions for ground water replenishment. All ground water aquifers come under strict control that does not allow withdrawals unless there is an equal to or greater recharging.** All developed nation areas that have been experiencing drought must now implement strong water harvesting plans.

9. Reforestation and afforestation plans (Chapter 4) must be strongly implemented to improve the local climate and to absorb carbon, including agroforestry and urban forestry.

10. Regions and nations that are dependent on melting snow to provide them with their water supply should start developing plans for when the snow cover will be gone due to global warming – this is an URGENT task. This may need the development of new reservoirs constructed with the needs of the environment and local people strongly safeguarded or accounted for. For example, areas of California that are dependent on snow melt from the Sierra Nevada mountains need to start thinking of alternatives. At the same time, parts of northern India that rely on snow melt from the Himalayas need to prepare for the times when there will be no snow melt, and the rivers will run dry all summer if water is not stored during the rainy season.

11. Although this will be dealt with in the next section on flooding, when floods do come, construction features like lakes

and ground water replenishment will be implemented that store the excess flood waters and use these to maintain flow in the river at other times as well as supply water for the dry season. These require major reconstruction projects that are part of flood control measures. This is the only action that can break the cycle of areas where floods are followed by droughts.

Adapting to Heavy Rains, Floods, Storms and Rising Sea Levels

The byproduct of rising temperatures is that there is more evaporation from all the water masses of the Earth, especially the oceans. All of this extra moisture has to go somewhere and it has been coming down as more rain, but the problem that has developed is that this comes down as heavy rain often in a very concentrated way. Previously, if a place may have gotten 1-2 inches (25-50 millimeters) of rain in 24 hours, now it often gets 10-20 inches (250-500 millimeters) or more in 24 hours. This is producing heavier and heavier flooding by the way of flash floods, urban floods, river and rural flooding, and coastal flooding. Flash floods can occur anywhere and these just overwhelm whatever natural features there may be to cope with the high volume of rain. In hilly and mountainous regions this can lead to the catastrophic washing away of entire communities.

Urban floods occur when the heavy rains overwhelm the capacity of storm water sewers or other urban drainage systems, and which can overwhelm water facilities, sewage treatment plants and transportation infrastructure, like below ground transit train systems, as happened in New York city with Superstorm Sandy. River and rural floods occur when the heavier than normal rains are causing rivers to crest higher than normal, flooding the rural areas, villages and cities that come along the river's path. Coastal flooding has been occurring with higher frequency and increasing ferocity, as hurricanes get stronger, often not only giving storm surges due to high winds but high levels of rain that increase the flooding. In most cases, depending on nation and location, in addition to loss of life there is usually damage to homes, buildings, city infrastructure (electric, sewage treatment, water supply, transportation, roads, rail lines, etc.). In addition, there can be contamination of the mixing of flood waters with toxic chemicals or untreated sewage. **In rural areas, and especially those that have seen forest fires in hilly and mountainous areas, there can be mudslides from heavy rains as the land is now without cover and cannot hold the soil and hillsides together. Then, after the floods pass, there can be drought, fires and high temperatures.**

We deal with the disaster management aspect of these events in the next chapter, but here we cover the longer term activity of how we can adapt the land areas, coastal areas, hill or mountain areas, and villages or cities so as to be able to minimize the consequences of these extreme water related events.

Plan for Adaptation to Floods and Coastal Storms

1. **Storing Flood Waters For Future Use:** With the long term consequences posed by drought and water shortages that can make land areas uninhabitable, the plan proposes flood control measures that store the flood waters for future use. Freshwater that falls as rain is preciously needed by humans, agriculture, land areas and animals. Hence, land areas that have any probability of flooding should develop water storage structures (ponds, lakes, reservoirs, etc.) that store water when the floods come, so that as the excess water flows away, some water is left for future use. If the water is not contaminated (by chemicals or pesticides), then it may be stored as surface water, or used to replenish ground waters through recharging points.

2. **Storing Flood Waters Along Rivers:** All rivers that are prone to flooding will develop storage structures for flood control and water storage, that are used when floods come. For example, a channel may divert water to a system of two lakes, one that stores the water for local use, and another that slowly releases the water to the river to regulate flow during the dry season. These structures can be built all along the river's length so as to provide flood control and water storage measures. See the following concept layout of twin lakes that provides an idea of some of the things that can

be done. This will especially help those rivers that currently rely on snow melt from mountains to maintain flow in the summer.

3. **Water Harvesting:** All areas that have any kind of water shortages must develop water harvesting from homes and land areas so that excess rains can be harvested and used, with care taken to avoid water contamination. These may also help to reduce the water runoff that can make floods worse.

4. **Coastal Areas** that are subject to coastal storms and sea level rise will need to implement a host of measures: (a) Building onshore (levees, dykes, etc.) and off shore structures (storm control barriers, etc.); (b) Implement coastal ecosystems all along the coasts as described in detail in Chapter 4; (c) Regulate and relocate all home, building and other structures away from the coast so they are not subject to damage; (d) Require all homes and buildings that are located at or near the coast to have elevated design so they can withstand storm surges and high winds; (e) Model what areas will be submerged by sea level rise and put in place time bound plans of relocating these to higher ground – these may be highways, rail lines, airports, electric transmission lines, housing areas, etc.; (f) Coastal areas that are subject to hurricanes, cyclones, tsunamis and storm surges must have detailed evacuation plans and routes, with the local communities trained to evacuate if there are dangers from these storms that cannot be avoided. Florida has such detailed plans and communities evacuate on highways that are open only in one direction before the arrival of a storm or hurricane.

5. **Floods Adaptation for Cities:** Large metropolitan areas need special measures for flood control and water harvesting: (a) Relocate all infrastructure and facilities in buildings to higher levels or stories in homes and buildings – furnaces, air conditioners, electrical power generators, electrical panels, etc.; (b) Redesign all transportation structures, especially

ones that are subways so they are not prone to flood or have significant drainage methods (this happened for the New York subway system during Superstorm Sandy); (c) Raise the pumps of all water treatment plants so they are above flood stage; (d) Redesign all storm water drainage systems for a much higher capacity – in most cities in the US these are designed to drain 1 inch of rain in 24 hours – the capacity of these needs to be increased by ten times; (e) All storm water drainage systems should design some level of water harvesting so that the water can be stored for future use (taking care that the water is relatively free of contamination); (d) Establish area wide evacuation plans with local communities fully trained and educated on how and when to evacuate areas where flooding cannot be avoided; and (e) Make all essential services like supply of fuel and hospitals, and fire-fighting and police services resilient to floods by elevating as much of their facilities above flood waters (second floors of buildings).

CONCEPT OF LAYOUT OF TWIN LAKES THAT STORE FLOOD WATERS

When the river floods, locks # 1 and 2 are opened and lock # 3 is closed so that flood waters fill up both lakes. When the lakes are full, all three locks are closed. When the flood waters recede, lock # 3 is opened a little to allow the waters to fill the river so some river flow is maintained (good for river wildlife) and river ecology. In the dry season, the first "store & use" lake is used by nearby communities to provide a water supply. The sizes and depths of the lakes can be increased or decreased depending on the land area available. Also, there can be hundreds of these Twin Lakes along the length of a river. These can also serve as wetlands and have recharging points for ground water.

Adapting Agriculture and Fisheries

Just as I was starting to write this section came news of the United Nations report that Climate Change threatens the world's food supply. This report, titled "Climate Change and Land – IPCC Special

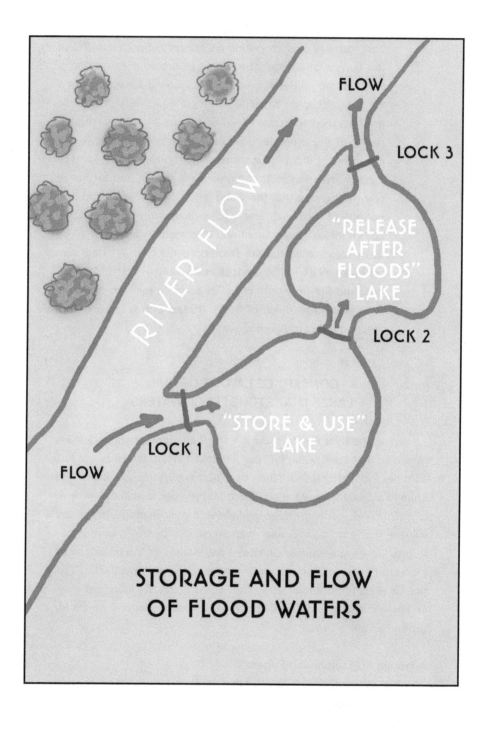

FLOW

LOCK 3

RIVER FLOW

"RELEASE AFTER FLOODS" LAKE

LOCK 2

"STORE & USE" LAKE

LOCK 1

FLOW

STORAGE AND FLOW OF FLOOD WATERS

Report on Climate Change, Desertification, sustainable land management, food security, and greenhouse gas fluxes in terrestrial ecosystems," released August 8, 2019, Geneva, Switzerland at a meeting of the United Nations. This was published by the Intergovernmental Panel on Climate Change (IPCC). [29]

The main causes are severe and rapid land degradation and even desertification to drying and unsustainable land use (pastures, deforestation, excessive tillage, etc.), extreme weather (like droughts, flooding, storms, hurricanes, and cyclones), high temperatures that are too high for crops and orchards, freshwater shortages, unsustainable agricultural practices (too much dependent on tillage, fossil fuels, chemical fertilizers and pesticides/herbicides) that degrade soil quality, excessive monocultures of crops that lack diversity and resilience, and the extremely high levels of beef consumption that divert land to meat production and cause massive deforestation.

The IPCC report on Climate Change and Land states that the estimated mitigation potential (that of reducing greenhouse gas emissions by better ways) from crop, livestock and agroforestry activities is 2.3-9.6 GtCO2e/year (giga metric tons of carbon dioxide equivalent) by 2050, and that from dietary changes (mainly beef consumption) is estimated at 0.7-8.0 GtCO2e per year. That is significant when compared to the current greenhouse gas emissions of about 45 GtCO2e per year. So there is some potential for these activities serving as a carbon sink in addition to those recommended in Chapter 4. They state that, "Practices that contribute to Climate Change adaptation and mitigation in cropland include increasing soil organic matter, erosion control, improved fertilizer management, improved crop management, for example, paddy rice management, and use of varieties and genetic improvements for heat and drought tolerance. For livestock, options include better grazing land management, improved manure management, higher-quality feed, and use of breeds and genetic improvement. Different farming and pastoral systems can achieve reductions in the emissions".

In addition, in relation to dietary changes where the consumption of beef is reduced, "Balanced diets, featuring plant-based foods, such as those based on coarse grains, legumes, fruits and vegetables, nuts and seeds, and animal-sourced food produced in resilient, sustainable and low-GHG emission systems, present major opportunities for adaptation and mitigation while generating significant co-benefits in terms of human health. By 2050, dietary changes could free several Mkm2 (million square kilometers) of land and provide a technical mitigation potential of 0.7 to 8.0 GtCO2e yr-1, or per year, relative to business as usual projections. (They think that there is high level of confidence that this is true)."

They stated that about 25-30% of food is currently wasted, which contributes as much as 8-10% of human caused greenhouse gas emissions. Besides directly not wasting the food we eat, they recommend education and implementation of improved harvesting techniques, on-farm storage, infrastructure improvement, and lower losses in transport, packaging and retail. In relation to the democratic and distribution of benefits aspects they recommend that there should be improved access to markets, more secure land tenure, adding environmental costs to food, making payments for ecosystem services and enhancing local and community collective action. In relation to all this, we now turn to what we should actually do in this regard.

An Agriculture Plan that Provides Adequate
Food and Adapts to Climate Change

Besides the air that we need to breathe, without which any human would not last more than a few minutes, we need water and food for our nourishment and survival. We presented the adaptation plan for water in the last section. Here we present the plan for adaptation of agriculture that provides us with our food, and other materials.

Agriculture practices (including "modern" ones) have been on an unsustainable path for many decades now, and now with increased heat, floods, drought and natural disasters, the threats to our agriculture and food supply have become more severe. First, if the temperatures get high enough, crops stop producing food or materials altogether. Then, if they get flooded, most crops are destroyed. Since most of the crops are dependent on rain (80% of global agriculture) for their watering, prolonged drought means they will not be able to produce an output. Then, along come massive natural disasters (coastal storms, hurricanes, cyclones, tornadoes, etc.) that can damage standing crops.

The United Nations has started several small efforts in this direction and nations have started developing National Adaptation Plans. But the whole global effort needs to be much bigger, with a transformation of agricultural methods, crop varieties, dietary changes and geographic locations to ensure that we have enough food to eat for the whole global population.

Problems with "Green Revolution" Agriculture

To understand the massive nature of the change in agriculture that is needed, especially to make it better adapted to Climate Change, it is important to understand the basic problems with the current agricultural methods. The "Green Revolution" agriculture that was developed in the US and then introduced to developing nations in the 1950s and the 1960s was sold as a strategy for agricultural abundance. The basics of the method were that hybrid seeds for wheat and rice (and other large crops), when combined with high levels of fertilizer, pesticides, herbicides, mechanical tillage (diesel fuel) and water gave higher yields per acre. Although production levels did increase, these replaced mixed farming methods that used more diverse crops (of higher nutritional value for local populations) that cost less and gave the farmers a higher profit. The new "miracle" seeds replaced thousands of indigenous and traditional varieties of seeds that were better for local populations.

Since now large areas were comprised of only a few varieties of each crop, insects and weeds that could not establish themselves in mixed farming crop rotation method now became "pests" and problem "weeds". This kind of agriculture led to increased wind and water erosion due to higher tillage, exhausted the organic fertility of soil essentially reducing it to inert materials that responded only to chemical fertilizer, high levels of chemical fertilizers that led to pollution of water – rivers and lakes, high levels of chemical pollution by pesticides and herbicides contaminating surface and ground water and causing cancer, and leading to more vulnerability to pests high levels of energy use (diesel fuel in tillage and harvesting), and high levels of water use as these "high yielding varieties" of crops needed more water than before. When these methods were introduced around the world, and especially in nations such as India, the seeds, fertilizer, water, diesel fuel and biocides were subsidized to create the artificial appearance of profitability. But over time, these subsidies were reduced or removed and led to massive financial losses for farmers and contributed to numerous farmer suicides. In developed nations like the US loss of subsidies has led to the disappearance of small family farms and their replacement with large farmer or agribusiness owned farms. The genetically modified crop varieties are making these problems much worse.

Now, many decades after these methods were first used, there are severe problems: losses in soil fertility; decreasing carbon in the soils; wind and water soil erosion; worsening insect "pest" and "weed" problems as these become resistant to one or more pesticides or herbicides; high levels of surrounding pollution (by fertilizer, herbicide and pesticide runoffs causing the deaths of lakes due to algae blooms caused by nitrogenous fertilizer; economics that do not suit local farmers but operate for the benefit of large agribusiness that sells all these inputs; and an unfavorable energy ratio where large amounts of energy including fossil fuels are spent and the energy output, either as bio-fuels or as food calories, are low. These methods provide high yields per acre for a few decades until the soil is exhausted, but the output per unit inputs of energy and water are much less than other types of agriculture.

Progressing Towards Regenerative Agriculture

At this time we need more agriculture methods that regenerate the soil, increase its fertility, increase its carbon absorption capacity, and are able to produce food outputs with less dependence on chemicals, water and diesel fuel. Two of these methods are organic farming and natural farming. **Organic farming** starts with making the soil with a higher level of organic matter, uses more of a larger variety of crops and seed varieties, uses only organic fertilizer obtained mostly from composting, has no use for pesticides, herbicides and fungicides, uses much less water, and can use intensive planting techniques combined with companion planting of crop varieties that like each other or complement each other. An earlier version of companion planting was to plant nitrogen fixing legume crops in rows between the main crop. Organic farming can be quite intensive and provides higher yields. The advantages are that this type of farming results in food that is higher in nutritional value, has no herbicide or pesticide residues on it, is often tastier and better liked by local populations, is not prone to large pest and weed infestations because the plants are healthier, and continues to improve the fertility of the soil that absorbs more and more carbon, and retains moisture better. It is also more efficient than "green revolution" agriculture in terms of food output per unit input of fertilizer and water. This type of farming has already become quite obvious at most grocery stores and markets where organically grown produce has become more valuable and fetches a higher price.

Natural Farming

Natural farming, which had been used in the past, was popularized much by Masanobu Fukuoka in his book *The One Straw Revolution*.[30] In this type of farming, there is no tillage whatsoever, the previous crop residues and other plants are simply pruned back, the crops are planted each time by broadcasted mud covered seeds (in one variation of the method) or inserted by tools into the ground. The plants grow among the pre-existing plants, and the crop grows with only limited watering. This type of farming is ideally suited to dry and arid areas as there is no soil erosion whatsoever, the land retains its moisture much better so less watering is needed, there is no diesel fuel used at all, compost fertilizer is often used, and the remaining crop residues are added as organic matter to the soil to improve its fertility. This is the best method of reclaiming arid and degraded lands and turning them into reasonably productive farm fields, with a lot of local greenery added all around. This type of agriculture is also suited better when combined with agroforestry, where trees provide shade and retain moisture, protect the crops from high temperatures, and add their leaves as compost to the crops. Even small sandy areas can be stabilized by biodegradable netting and then converted to this type of agriculture, with small inputs of water.

"Green Revolution" agriculture was introduced when the knowledge from research done at agricultural universities was spread to farmers by the way of government demonstration plots, extension agents visiting farmers and financial and marketing support for governments. **The next stage of agriculture needs the same method, with agricultural universities switched to research, demonstration and extension on the newer refined methods of more organic and natural methods of agriculture.**

So, here is the Plan for the Adaptation and Rejuvenation of Agriculture.

Enhancing Agriculture as a Carbon Sink

1. New global programs at all agricultural universities and agricultural research stations (local, national or United Nations), that refocus their research to all of the areas listed below, and then follow this up with demonstration plots, farmer education, farmer visits by extension agents to educate farmers about the new or modified methods, and support of the new or modified strategies for seeds, implements, and the financial aspects of new or modified methods. This would be followed by support for large scale deployment in nations, and regions, and the changes to trade rules to favor the export and handling of these crops, if needed. (Research, Demonstration and Deployment).

2. Transition away from large monocultures to a much greater diversity of each crop using many of the pre-existing traditional seed varieties, with marketing systems and locations where farmers bring their harvest for sale which accommodate and have expertise in evaluating the quality and establishing pricing for many varieties of the same crop. For each crop, the number of seed varieties need to increase, with a greater use of traditional varieties and the discouragement of genetically modified seeds, unless there is clear value in terms of drought resistance.

3. Identify and switch to drought resistant varieties of crops that require less water. At the same time, begin to secure and improve all water sources (water harvesting, storage of flood waters, increase in the groundwater table, etc.).

4. Switch to greater organic methods of farming where there is a reduction of the use of chemical fertilizers, herbicides and pesticides, water and tillage, and a greater use of composted fertilizer and organic pesticides like simple detergent solutions that are sometimes used in organic cherry farms. Encourage the growth of micro-organisms and worms in the soil, that otherwise get killed by pesticides and herbicides, as they add their own fertilizer.

5. **In areas that have seen land degradation and desertification (where the lands appears on its way to become desert),** the use of natural farming techniques are suitable as they stabilize the soil and ensure that the land is always covered by green plants that retain moisture. Tillage here is to be totally avoided unless needed to get a resilient species of plant or

tree permanently established.

6. Also, in areas that have seen land degradation, the greater use of agroforestry where there is a design pattern of rows of trees and crops or other patterns that shade the crops, add additional output or use from the trees, and help shade the crop in case of higher temperatures. The greater use of trees that provide fruits and fuelwood will help rural areas much for food and cooking fuel, unless electric cooking and solar cookers are introduced. This should be combined with the existing UN program for introducing more efficient cook-stoves.

7. A massive effort in all crop lands to increase the fertility of the soil and its carbon sink aspects by organic methods, green manuring (growing a green crop and plowing it under to add to organic matter), compost fertilizer, composted manure, and mulch (small pieces of leaves and wood). This will not only increase crop yields but will also add to the carbon buried in the soil, the potential for which has been calculated to be significant.

8. Switch to multiple cropping where nitrogen fixing crops alternate with nitrogen using crops. This is already done, but should be combined with leaving the field fallow (no crop) or green manuring it to improve fertility.

9. An expansion of efficient irrigation methods like trickle irrigation and irrigation through pipes that delivers water only where needed. The amount of flood irrigation needs to be reduced, especially switching to rice production and seed varieties that do not need flooded fields.

10. **The total discouragement of the use of ground water for irrigation, or strict controls on it so that water withdrawals from ground water are balanced by groundwater recharge from clean water locations** (pesticide and herbicide runoff locations to be avoided). This is URGENT otherwise these areas will quickly become desert with NO food production.

11. The total change of crop locations or the change of crop types if these are damaging or unsuitable. For example, the Indian state of Punjab needs to stop the growing of field flooding varieties of rice that have unsustainable water use and encourage pesticide and herbicide poisoning.

12. The change in locations (for example Ethiopia) or quantity of export cash crops like cotton and coffee. A switch to a greater quantity of food crops to feed the local and global population. This must be combined with foreign debt relief if cash crops are being used to repay debts.

13. A major reduction in livestock farming, especially of pigs and cattle that have severe pollution effects through untreated manure, the emission of methane from cows and the associated deforestation they cause, especially in the Amazon.

14. A major reduction in the growing of soybean and corn as feed for livestock and for the making of ethanol from crop lands. Significant tax and incentive changes that divert those land areas to other food crops for direct human consumption and reforested areas.

15. The shift of ALL bioenergy growing for bio-fuels away from croplands and onto barren lands or ones that were degrading and needed to be revived. The palm oil plantations that are on land that was deforested need to revert back to either forests or into agroforestry, where some sustainable extractive use may be encouraged for livelihoods.

16. The shift of all pastures and ranches for beef cattle that were created by deforestation back to forests – again where some extractive use from the forests is enabled.

17. A major global program for the growth of food and agricultural products in urban areas on as much land adjacent to living areas and the development of "urban farmers markets" for folks to sell their excess produce.

18. A major program to help farmers and their families and those living in rural areas or small towns get added employment through the processing of produce they grow, and more local non-agricultural income activities (small industry, service businesses, etc.) and help in local marketing so they can add to their incomes if farming alone is not enough. Transforming their communities as shown in the concept on eco-cities will help.

19. A big improvement of storage techniques by farmers themselves so they can store their produce on the farm and sell it later when they can get a better price.

20. A major change in agricultural pricing and price support methods, as well as crop insurance nationally and globally, so that farmers are not adversely affected by crop surpluses or crop failures.

21. The start of a global program with the Food and Agriculture Organization (FAO) and the World Food Program (WFP) of the storage of food products to take care of food emergencies that happen because of Climate Change. These will consist of food warehouses owned and operated by the international organizations with the permission of the host nations for storage and transport.

22. Within nations and globally, the agrarian economy needs to change to enable the above with support for the local markets where the farmers bring their crops or produce for sale, with suitable quality evaluations for the diversity of crops and the financing and crop insurance for farmers modified accordingly.

23. A big change from mechanized farming involving tillage and harvesting with greater skill and labor intensive and semi-automated methods that favor small farmers. It's not productivity per worker but employment per acre that needs to be increased.

With such an adaptation process, the world will be better prepared to withstand the adversity that will come even with a 1.5 degrees Celsius average temperature rise, agriculture globally will become a bigger carbon sink, and better local and global food security will be achieved.

Chapter 6

National Energy, Climate and Ecosystem Plan for the US and California, Including the Green New Deal

The US gross domestic product (GDP or size of its economy) in 2018 was about $20 trillion, or about 24% of the whole world's GDP of $84 trillion. In comparison, China's GDP in 2018 was about $15 trillion, making it the second largest national economy in the world. If one could count all the nations of the European Union together, their GDP was about $18 trillion. Out of the global military spending of $1.8 trillion in 2018, with the US increasing its spending to $649 billion and China to $250 billion, the twenty nine NATO (North Atlantic Treaty Organization) nations, including the US, spent $963 billion in 2018 or more than 50% of global spending.

As of January 2020, the US was by far the biggest economy in the world with the strongest military. If one takes its own spending and that of its allies, it is militarily the most powerful. The US has been a leader in the past two centuries along with the European nations in fossil fuel development and in fueling its industrial and other growth by the use of fossil fuels. So much so that along with teaching the rest of the world how to base their "development" on fossil fuels, the US has a very powerful lobby that dominates the political landscape, and has been effective in slowing the growth of alternative energy – especially clean renewable energy. Not only has this lobby been effective in stalling development of renewable energy in a big way, it is also not doing as much as other nations in the Research and Development of the technologies of the future – whether it's renewable energy, "storage" fuels, or clean transportation like high speed rail. Currently, Japan, Australia and some Scandinavian countries are showing more interest than the US in research in these areas.

In 1991, when I was in the Chicago area, I came to know about the Earth Summit. This was the United Nations Conference on Environment and Development (UNCED) that was scheduled for June 1992 in Rio de Janeiro, Brazil, to address the problems of environment and development faced by the world. In order to understand the process and to participate actively, we formed an informal group in Chicago called the Earth Summit Network (ESN), of which I was one of the founders and one of two main coordinators. The other coordinator was Tom Spaulding of the YMCA (Young Men's Christian Association). For about the period of the year, we organized several teleconferences and public events to educate the Chicago public about the issues at the Earth Summit. At the first teleconference that we held in Chicago, Al Gore, later vice-president of the US and author of the book *An Inconvenient Truth* who was then a young senator, spoke about the issues. We also tried to apply pressure on the senior US Bush administration to be more flexible at the global warming negotiations and sign the Climate Change treaty. We were certainly small so our effect was not much, but the US president George H. W. Bush did sign the global warming treaty, the United Nations Framework Convention on Climate Change, UNFCCC, which was described in Chapter 1. Thereafter, I began a process of self-education through reading and writing that culminated in a book titled *Rethinking Progress – Towards A Creative Transformation of Global Society*, which is about the global environment and development crises (problems and solutions), about which more may be found in the section about the author at the end of the book. [53]

So, what is the effect of Climate Change on the US?

Global Warming Is Already Devastating the USA

Global warming is not some distant future problem. It has already begun to devastate the US and the world. To understand that, one needs to understand that one of the key things that happens is when air temperature rises, there is greater evaporation from the sea, and the air has more energy. This leads to two effects. It increases the energy and hence the wind velocity of weather related phenomenon like hurricanes, tornados and coastal storms, while increasing the amount of rain most of the time. We have seen both. The hurricanes are getting stronger and more devastating. Katrina ($120 billion losses), Superstorm Sandy ($75 billion losses), etc., the list continues to grow. Each time the devastation is greater and the hurricane leaves more damage and grief. Caused by a coastal storm, the catastrophic floods in South Carolina (October 2015) are now known to have given one of the highest levels of rainfall in US history, 15-19 inches of rain in a 24 hour period. It was called a "one in a 1,000 year storm." Out of 59 sites recording rainfall, six sites set all-time records (NOAA data – U.S. National Oceanic & Atmospheric Administration). In recent years, many rainfall events in the Chicago area have led to very high levels of rainfall – some to flash flooding. More and deadlier tornadoes, and severe rainfall events are likely to damage the region. **Global warming is not some future problem – its devastation has arrived!**

Some of the other symptoms in the US are that glaciers are melting and disappearing. All but a few of Alaska's more than a hundred glaciers are melting and receding. California is facing a persistent and prolonged drought. The dry conditions are leading to worse and worse wildfires every year which could lead to a runaway greenhouse effect – more wild fires, more carbon dioxide in the atmosphere. With the mountainsides denuded of vegetation, any rain that follows can cause massive landslides, burying entire communities. This has already happened in the western US. The Mississippi Floods of 2005 with high levels of precipitation and a stationary weather front dumped so much rain that it led to massive flooding of the Mississippi River.

What the future holds for the US is that the hurricanes and coastal storms will get stronger and stronger devastating coastal areas. Tornadoes will get more severe and frequent, and will be felt further north as weather patterns shift causing untold misery in America's heartland. What is now known is that with Climate Change tornado cells are showing up with an increase in the number of tornadoes per cell. Floods will go from bad to worse leading to massive inundations as seen in Texas and South Carolina in 2017-2018.

US National Climate Assessments

The US Global Change Research Program (USGCRP) is legally required to look at the issue of Climate Change, and every four years publish its finding in a National Climate Assessment (NCA), which is an interagency ongoing effort of the United States Government. The first NCA report was released in 2000. Between 2002 and 2009 they published several Synthesis and Assessment Products (SAPs), a second report in 2010, and a third report in 2014.

The Fourth National Climate Assessment (NCA4) Report was published in two volumes, the first in October 2017 (477 pages), and the second in November 2018 (1,524 pages). The US National Oceanic and Atmospheric Administration (NOAA) was the lead agency for this assessment in which a total of 13 US Federal Government agencies, 1,000 people, and about 300 scientists were involved, with about half of the scientists were from outside governments. **So, the fourth National Climate Assessment is a very thorough scientific assessment of the best scientific minds of the United States. Here is a summary of their findings from the November 2018 Report, some of which have been paraphrased to make them easier to understand. Some examples have been added. [31]**

Communities across the country are already experiencing the impacts of Climate Change with more frequent and intense extreme weather and climate related events, and changes in average climate conditions, which are affecting and are expected to continue to damage infrastructure, ecosystems, and their social situations. This is placing increasing challenges to human health and safety, quality of life and the rate of economic growth. Without significant reductions in global emissions and adaptation, extreme events will cause substantial losses to American infrastructure, labor productivity, reduction of the efficiency of power generation, and occurrences abroad will affect trade, and all of these will overall act to reduce economic growth. Climate Change is affecting the quality and quantity of water available for use and is increasing risks and costs to agriculture, energy production, industry, recreation and natural areas. Power plants that rely on a good supply of cooling water will be adversely affected, and water supply and drainage infrastructure, designed for past conditions, may not be adequate for the future.

In terms of health, extreme events are affecting air quality, and increasing the transmission of disease through insects and pests, food quality and water are threatening the health of Americans. Indigenous peoples (native Americans), the original dwellers of America are being increasingly affected by Climate Change as it threatens their livelihoods, economies, heath and cultural identities. The degradation of American ecosystems, and those on the continent, are having an adverse impact on the benefits and services these ecosystems provide. Coral reef, sea ice, coastal, water, mountain, glacier and forest ecosystems are already experiencing degradation. Agriculture is being hammered by rising temperatures, extreme heat, wildfires on rangelands and heavier than normal downpours. These are affecting and will increasingly affect livestock health, declines in crop yields and quality and lead to degradation of the lives of rural and small town folks throughout the country.

America's infrastructure has been aging and deteriorating because of poor investments. However, Climate Change will further stress the infrastructure, by heavy rains, flooding, wildfires, mudslides and other extreme events, leading to adverse impacts on the economy, national security, essential services and health. Climate Change will adversely affect energy and transportation systems, threatening fuel shortages, and power outages. Many coastal areas will be submerged or adversely affected by rising sea levels and increasing storm surges. The coastal areas are being threatened by rising water temperatures, ocean acidification (carbon dioxide dissolved in water gives carbonic acid), retreating arctic sea ice, sea level rise, high tide flooding, higher storm surges and extremely heavy rain events.

As it is for the rest of the world, the situation for the US is grim, unless this Plan is acted upon.

History of US Actions and Plans Proposed by Others

The US did sign the global warming treaty in 1992, and was then quite active in bringing about the Kyoto Protocol in Kyoto, Japan in 1997, which was an agreement to take some actions. However, because of opposition in the US legislatures (Congress and Senate) by the Republican Party, US never ratified the protocol. Again, US leadership brought the world together to sign the Paris Agreement, in Paris, December 2015, which has been described in Chapter 1.

Each nation who signed the agreement and the US also submitted its Intended Nationally Determined Contribution (INDC) plan, which was a voluntary submittal by each nation as to what it would do as its share of Climate Change solutions.

The INDC (Intended Nationally Determined Contribution), submitted by the United States agreed to reduce greenhouse emissions by 26-28% from 2005 to 2025 (from about 6,300 million metric tons of carbon dioxide equivalent in 2005). This was along with the intended effort (uncommitted) to reduce emissions by about 80% by 2050. This target included all gases covered in the US 2014 inventory of greenhouse gases and sinks: carbon dioxide (CO_2), methane (CH_4), nitrous oxide (N_2O), and other man-made chemicals. The US INDC included commitments to increase vehicle fuel efficiencies, building efficiencies, reduction in man-made chemicals used as refrigerants, the reduction of methane gas emissions from landfills and oil production facilities, and the Clean Power Plan (CPP).

The CPP aimed to reduce US carbon dioxide emissions from electrical power generation by 32 percent by 2030 from 2005 levels. The main focus of the CPP was on reducing emissions from coal-burning power plants, as well as increasing the use of renewable energy and energy conservation. It required individual states in the country to reduce their carbon dioxide emissions to given levels by various means, and the states had to submit emissions reduction plans by September 2016, extendable if approved to September 2018. If a state did not submit a plan, then the US EPA (Environmental Protection Agency) would impose their own plan on the state. However, the Trump Administration, besides announcing that it was going to withdraw the US from the Paris Agreement, in October 2017 began the process of repealing the Clean Power Plan, although it takes two years to formally repeal a regulation. In 2013, the Obama Administration defined a national Climate Action Plan that laid out a number of domestic initiatives (including the CPP) and encouraged the other nations of the world to follow suit. It was this action that encouraged the other nations of the world to come up with their voluntary contributions at the Paris Agreement.

Then, in addition, politicians electioneering as candidates for the US 2020 presidential election came up with their own plans. The first one that was noteworthy was by the **Governor of the State of Washington, Jay Inslee,** that proposed that for the next ten years

(2020-2029) about $9 trillion of investment, with about $300 billion per year in federal government spending that would encourage $600 billion per year in private investment, with a claim that this would create 8 million good jobs. His proposed "Evergreen Economy Plan" proposed five main strategies: renewable energy and electrification development; infrastructure and community resilience; clean manufacturing; research and development; and job growth.

Plan Proposed by Senator Bernie Sanders for the US

Another plan put forward by US presidential candidate Bernie Sanders is much more ambitious and comprehensive. It proposed converting all electricity generation and transportation to renewable energy by 2030, and complete decarbonization of the rest of the entire economy by 2050. His plan further proposed a direct public investment of $16.3 trillion during this period, and the creation of 20 million good paying union new jobs in renewable energy, energy efficiency, construction, transportation and industry. Also, the creation of a new Civilian Conservation Corps in agriculture, engineering and in preserving public lands. He would provide a just transition to all fossil fuel workers in terms of five years of salary, benefits and retraining or early retirement benefits so that these workers come out ahead after the transition. The plan proposes to save all families money by investing in energy efficiency, modern low carbon transportation, reduce the cost of changing to high efficiency electric vehicles and rebuilding the crumbling infrastructure. His plan would support the transition of agriculture to smaller family farms, to more regenerative and sustainable agriculture and maximize the growing of local foods, and free farmers and ranchers from the strangle hold of corporate interests.

A major part of his plan has to do with a transformation of the energy sector. He proposes the replacement of all private electric utility companies with Power Marketing Administrations or PMAs – some of which exist already, and get all PMAs to build enough wind, solar, energy storage and geothermal power plants to replace all fossil fuels in electric power. He proposes spending $1.52 trillion on renewable energy and $852 billion to build energy storage capacity. In order for this to happen reliably, he feels that the entire utility model for producing and delivering electricity needs to be changed from mainly corporate private ownership to mainly publicly owned utilities that behave responsibly, with a good combination of championing energy solutions to Climate Change, and responsiveness to electrical customer needs. He proposes that the renewable energy generation sources will be publicly owned, managed by federal PMAs, the Bureau of Reclamation and the Tennessee Valley Authority. This electricity will be sold to utilities that will distribute this electricity to consumers, with preference given to publicly, municipally or cooperatively owned utilities with democratically controlled pubic ownership.

Besides that, he proposes a modern smart electric transmission and distribution grid that is resilient to disasters, manages and transmits large amounts of renewable energy, has the capacity to rapidly charge electric vehicles, and is energy efficient. He proposes spending $526 billion on a smart, high voltage, underground, and direct current smart grid, that makes the transition to renewable energy smooth, safe and timely. At the same time, he proposes an investment of $2.18 trillion on vastly improving the energy efficiency of homes, business, organizational, and industrial buildings, and lowering their energy bills. The energy efficiency efforts would focus first on the leakiest and most energy inefficient structures, and housing for seniors, people with disabilities and low income families. The money would be invested as sliding scale grants for low and middle income families and small businesses. Federally mandated standards will ensure that new and existing buildings and wealthy landowners meet the same energy efficiency goals. A similar investment of $964 billion would help all homes and buildings to transition to electrification, and end the use of fossil fuels for these needs. This would enable the added electricity to be met by expanded generation of renewable energy. In addition, he proposes to slowly get rid of unsustainable source of electricity like nuclear power, geoengineering, carbon capture and sequestration, and trash incinerators.

From the financing end he proposes ending all fossil fuel subsidies, and making the fossil fuel industry pay through litigation, fees and taxes. Revenues will be collected for certain periods of time, and thereafter only to cover operations and maintenance costs. He proposes scaling back military spending that currently is spent in protecting oil supplies. Then there will be the income tax revenue from the new 20 million jobs created, as well as reduced spending on providing safety nets for people as more will be having good paying union jobs. In addition he proposes that wealthy and large corporations pay more in taxes. He claims that the US economy will lose $34.5 trillion in economic activity by the end of the century, while on the other hand, the benefits of his plan will be to save $2.9 trillion over 10 years, $21 trillion over 30 years and $70.4 trillion over 80 years.

The United States of America having been in the forefront of the Industrial Revolution, along with European nations and later Japan, based almost of all of its economy on fossil fuels. First coal, then oil and then natural gas. Because of its emphasis on fossil fuels and discouragement of renewable energy and low carbon technologies, with the exception of the state of California (described later), the US has fallen behind other nations in the application of green technologies. The US has now the opportunity to demonstrate in a big a way that it can transform its economy totally with renewable energy and green low carbon technologies. The overall plan that is described next shows how to do exactly that.

The Proposed Energy and Climate Plan for the US

The pie chart following shows the current energy use by source, then the projected energy use by 2050, and then what the Plan proposes for 2050. According to the AEO2018 Report (Annual Energy Outlook) by the US Energy Information Agency (EIA), the US consumed about 28.8 PWH (petawatt hours) of energy in 2017. The following pie chart shows the details. One can see that the three fossil fuels provided 81 % of US total energy needs, while the four renewable energies (Bio energy, Hydro-electric, wind and solar) only produced about 8%. These three fossil fuels produced about 5 million Metric Tons of carbon dioxide, which is most of the US greenhouse gas emissions. Updated versions of the AEO2018 report have been published in the AEO2019 and the AEO2020 reports. [33, 34, 35]

In June 2020, the US Congress's Select Committee on the Climate Crisis published its congressional action plan for the USA's contribution to solving the climate crisis. The proposed plan aims at reducing net US gas emissions 37% below 2010 levels by 2030 and 88% below 2010 levels by 2050. Including other sectors, the aim is to make the US reach net zero carbon dioxide emissions before 2050. The plan is truly comprehensive and covers infrastructure, clean energy, clean energy technologies and manufacturing, just transition for fossil fuel workers, managing climate risks to health, and reforming agriculture. [32]

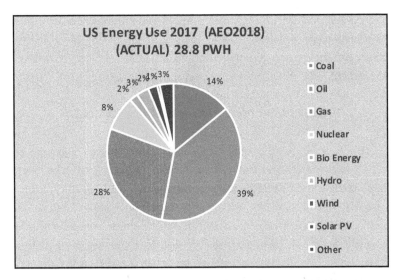

ENERGY ACTUALLY CONSUMED BY THE US IN 2017

In 2017, the US consumed about 18% of the world's energy (162 PWH), but its reliance on fossil fuels was very high at 81%, with 14% of that being from coal.

The same AEO2018 Report makes the following projection for 2050 if current policies continue. Energy use in the US is projected to grow very little in about 30 years.

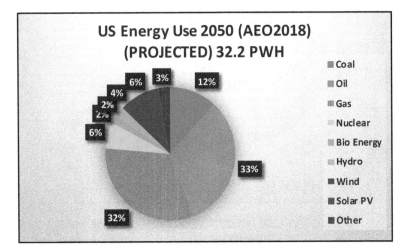

US ENERGY USE PROJECTED FOR 2050 BY THE US EIA (AEO2018) – BUSINESS AS USUAL

US Senergy use is projected to grow only about 12% from 2017 to 2050. However, the US Energy Information Agency projects that the US will still be 77% reliant on fossil fuels (about 12% on coal). Wind will have grown to 4% and solar PV to 6% of the total. Clearly, this is not the path to climate solutions. So, here we present the Plan for the US.

Proposed Energy and Climate Plan for the US

Because of its emphasis on fossil fuels and discouragement of renewable energy and low carbon technologies, the US has fallen behind other nations in the development and use of green technologies. The US has now the opportunity to demonstrate in a big a way that it can transform its economy totally with renewable energy and green low carbon technologies. The overall plan that is described next shows how to do exactly that, and then the rest of the chapter provides details on how to do it.

Basically, the US Plan goes along with the Global Plan described in Chapter 3, so many of the parts will not be repeated here.

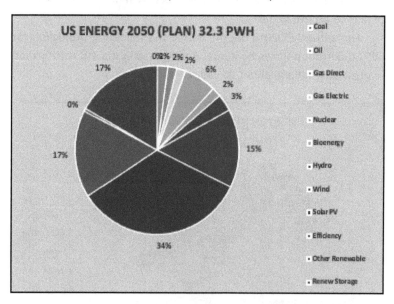

US ENERGY USE PROJECTED FOR 2050 BY THE PLAN

The Book Plan for 2050 reduces fossil fuel consumption down to about 5% of the total (down from 77% of the total in the above Business As Usual scenario as projected in AEO2018 report). Coal is totally gone, oil is there in a small way, and most of the remaining small amount is natural gas. A small push for wind energy increases it to 15% of total, solar PV to 34% of total, Energy Efficiency saves 17% of the total, and renewable energy based storage fuels at 17% of the total. The extent to which energy efficiency goals are not met, will need to be met with an expansion of solar PV and storage fuels.

Here's a list of the Plan. Again RDD&D means Research, Development, Demonstration and Deployment, meaning the technology or hardware is taken from laboratory to prototype, to demonstration size project (means a large enough project that fully confirms that the technology succeeds on a big scale and establishes the numbers for the economics), and finally to all aspects of deployment (meaning production plants, storage, transportation, infrastructure, and use). In the case of end use technologies, this means the same thing, except that the fuel is simply taken and then the technology is used to power the machine or engine that uses it – so the technology RDD&D is centered around the machine or engine and its demonstration and final production, distribution and support.

1. **Overall – Transitioning Out of Coal and Natural Gas**
   a. Coal and natural gas power plants REPLACED by solar PV + Battery + Natural gas for evenings and nights – latter replaced by replaced by storage fuel generators.
2. **Overall – Transitioning Out of Oil – Solar-Electric Highways of the type described above to replace use of gasoline and diesel fuels**
   a. Solar-Electric vehicle charging stations that also supply storage fuels like hydrogen and ammonia to fuel cell vehicles.
3. **Storage fuels RDD&D (Research, Development, Demonstration & Deployment)**
   a. US to join other nations to do the RDD&D for the Green Production of non-carbon fuels that store renewable energy (production process powered by renewable energy) – storage and distribution of fuels.
   b. Storage and Distribution of these fuels on a massive scale.
   c. Also, RDD&D in regard to end user technologies for storage fuels used in vehicle internal combustion engines, gas turbines and Fuel Cells.
4. **Electrification of buildings, homes and industry**
   a. Apply existing technologies, and do RDD&D to develop

the rest – incentives.

b. What cannot be electrified, develop methods using storage fuels (RDD&D).

5. Electrical Transmission Upgrades

a. Increased Capacity (3-5 times) with more local location of solar PV power plants near users (to reduce transmission costs), and democratic control by local governments, organizations and companies.

b. Smart Grid features that enable the grid to manage the variability of renewable energy, as well as the demand and supply aspects to manage peak power and increase reliability of the grid's ability to satisfy demand reliably under all conditions.

6. Expanded Carbon Sinks – reforestation and coastal ecosystems

a. In all regions, add 80 Million hectares of forests – with all of the aspects described in Chapter 4, including agroforestry and urban forestry.

b. All designed so as to properly manage forest fires and their consequences.

c. Enhanced carbon sink coastal ecosystems – Atlantic, Pacific and Gulf coasts – entire coastline – Mangrove swamps, salt marshes, sea grasses, coral reefs and other ecosystems.

7. Rejuvenated Agriculture

a. From agricultural universities to farmers and marketing, transform US agriculture to the regenerative agriculture and agroforestry described in Chapter 5.

b. Increased soil fertility and carbon absorption, by deliberate processes to increase the organic and carbon content of the soils.

8. Advanced Disaster Management – Disaster Risk Reduction

a. Wildfires, hurricanes, tornados, coastal storms – before, during and after disasters.

b. Massive organization infrastructure to do disaster risk reduction, prepare for disaster relief, and proper reconstruction (Build Back Better).

9. Implementation of all of the Mobilization Goals of the Green New Deal – described in detail below.

Overall for US – Transitioning Out of Coal

US coal consumption was at about 14 Quads (Quadrillion BTU) or about 4,110 billion KWH in electrical energy terms in 2017, as per the AEO2018 report of the US Energy Information Agency. Then it was projected to be essentially flat at about 13 Quads or about 3,820 billion KWH till 2050. For electric power, the capacity of coal power plants fell by about 60 Giga Watts (GW) mainly due to the US EPA enforcement of Mercury and Toxics standards. However, coal fired electric capacity is projected to further decrease by about 65 GW between 2017 and 2030, before leveling off at 190 GW by 2050. Coal is mainly used for electric power production, but is also used by the steel industry as coking coal, by the cement industry and in the making of many products. The US also has the world's largest proven reserves of coal, and according to the US EIA in 2008 had about 260.5 billion short tons of coal.

When one burns a million BTU (British Thermal Units) of a fuel the amount of carbon dioxide emitted are about 215 pounds (98 kilograms) for coal (an average for the different types of coal), about 160 pounds (73 kilograms) for either gasoline or diesel, and about 117 pounds (53.2 kilograms) for natural gas. Clearly, the case for eliminating coal from its use as for electric power and heat by burning it has come. It needs to be the first to go.

The Plan will eliminate most coal fired power plants by 2030, and ALL by 2050. The overall plan needs replacing all of the coal fired power plants with a combination of solar PV and Battery power plants – as described in Chapter 3. Where coal use cannot be electrified in the rest of the economy (as in industry), the RDD&D will be needed up front to replace coal with storage fuel based technologies. The Plan is projecting that by 2050, all of the mining, use and export of coal will be gone.

Overall for US – Transitioning Out of Oil

As of early 2019, in terms of the daily production of oil (petroleum), out of the world's production of about 80 million barrels per day (mbl/day) the US was producing about 15 million barrels per day, Saudi Arabia about 12 mbl/day, Russia about 11 mbl/day, and the four nations of Iraq, Iran, China and Canada near about 4 mbl/day each. By 2022, the US is forecast to become a net exporter of oil. The natural gas liquids production (liquids separated from natural gas during gas production) is growing and will increase to about 5 million barrels per day by 2023. The natural gas liquids consist of mainly ethane, propane, isobutane, normal butane and natural gasoline. For what the US Energy Information Agency calls its Reference Case (AEO2018 Report), crude oil production could vary from 10 to 19 million barrels per day, and natural gas plant liquids production to about 5.5 million barrels per day, by 2050.

As of 2018, in terms of proportions, US oil consumption use was 46% for motor gasoline, 20% for distillate fuel (heating oil and diesel fuel), and 8% for jet fuel. Besides transportation fuels, oil or petroleum is used for fuel oils for heating and electricity generation, asphalt and road oil, and materials that are used in making chemicals, plastics and synthetic materials that are in most products people use and consume. Most of the greenhouse gas emissions from fossil fuels come from burning them, and about 45% of the emissions come from oil or petroleum.

Clearly, for Climate Change solutions, we need to get out of this scenario. Here is how we can do it. We need to transition ALL highway transportation to electric and storage fuels. For transitioning out of gasoline and diesel use, the details for this are described in the section on Solar-Electric Highways. There will be a parallel program similar to a "cash for clunkers" program that the US has used in the past that will then be used to get all fossil fuel cars off the roads by 2050 (that includes any added due to increase in the number of vehicles), and replace them with battery electric and storage fuel cars. For the aviation segment, besides the use of bio-fuels, aviation will be replaced by a network of high speed rail crisscrossing the country from north to south along each of the west and east coasts, and for east-west – one northerly route going through Chicago, and the other going from Southern California to Florida. The Plan proposes that all of the US be covered by a transformed transportation policy that emphasizes low carbon transportation between regions, and in cities and local areas. For this see the section in Chapter 2 on reducing the carbon footprint of transportation, including aviation, shipping and tourism.

Overall for US – Transitioning Out of Natural Gas

US natural gas is about 28% of US energy use and contributes to about 28% of US carbon dioxide emissions. In 2017, the US produced about 28 trillion cubic feet of Natural gas and as per the AEO2018 Report the production is projected to grow to about 42 trillion cubic feet by 2050 for what it calls the Reference Case. The actual use of natural gas is projected to grow from about 28 trillion cubic feet in 2017 to about 34 trillion cubic feet in 2050. The excess of production over consumption will lead to significant exports of natural gas from the US. The carbon dioxide (CO_2) emissions from the burning of natural gas in the US are projected to grow from about 14 million metric tons of CO_2 in 2017 to about 18 million metric tons of CO_2 by 2050 for the Reference Case.

Natural gas produces less carbon emission than other fuels and is also cleaner burning and emits negligible amounts of sulfur, mercury and particulates (which cause smoke) when it is burned. Because of this, the US and many other nations have used this as an argument to substitute natural gas for coal or oil based fuels.

However, there are many damaging aspects resulting from the production and consumption of natural gas. During the drilling and extraction of natural gas from wells, methane gas leaks which is 34 times stronger than carbon dioxide in trapping heat over 100 years, and 86 times stronger over 20 years. Methane leakage needs to be no more than 1-2% for there to be any greenhouse gas emissions benefits of using natural gas. Although the burning of natural gas is cleaner, within about a half mile of drilling sites there are increased emissions of particulates and ozone – both of which are not good for health. Hydraulic fracturing (*fracking*) has been known to cause the contamination of ground water with the liquid used in fracking, and in poorly constructed wells to cause ground water to get contaminated with naturally occurring radioactive materials, methane and other gases, and volatile organic compounds. The large amount of water used in production can also result in local water shortages. The US Environmental Protection Agency (EPA) has identified about 1,000 chemical additives used in fracking, although a particular well may use only about a dozen of these. Lastly, fracking has been linked significantly with the increased incidence of earthquakes. So, if we have to get to zero greenhouse gas emissions and avoid they above negative effects of natural gas production, we need to transition out of natural gas.

For electric power, the Plan proposes replacing natural gas power plants with a combination of solar PV and battery storage. For industrial use, all technologies will transition to all electric energy and the increased electricity will again be met by a combination of solar PV and battery power plants, and solar PV (or other renewable) producing and using non-carbon storage fuels. As per above, all transportation will be transitioned to solar-electric highways and use of storage fuels. Generally, all commercial properties use natural gas for heating, cooling, cooking, and all appliances. These will all be switched to all-electric. The general strategy is to mandate and enable all new construction for power plants, industry, commercial and residential uses to a combination of all electric and storage fuels, and support this with all the research, development, demonstration and deployment actions needed. After successful demonstrations, all the technologies will then be applied and all sectors mandated to switch to the new energy sources by 2050.

The Development and use of Non-Carbon Storage Fuels in the US

In 1970, at a talk he gave at the General Motors Technical Center at Detroit, Michigan, John Bockris coined the term **"Hydrogen Economy"**. The concept of a "Hydrogen Economy" was popularized by a 1970 technical Report by Lawrence Jones of the University of Michigan. It was proposed to popularize the concept of generating non-carbon fuels that emit no carbon when burned. As described in Chapter 2, hydrogen has made its entry mainly in California and is even being supplied at refueling stations.

The Proposed Plan for Storage Fuels for the US

The US has usually been a leader in innovation and in showing the way to the future. However, it needs to stop its leadership in fossil fuels innovation and expansion and start to look at how it can be one of the leader nations in innovating for Climate Change solutions. Otherwise, it will get left behind. Other nations are pushing ahead with innovation in storage fuels – fuels that store the sun's and the wind's energy in a non-carbon way. Japan is leading the research in close cooperation with Australia, and the Scandinavian nations are proceeding too.

The biggest challenge here is to do the research to develop "Green" ways of producing storage fuels, or how to produce these using solar and wind or other renewable energy on an economical and commercial scale. The next big challenge is to do the research that will develop technologies (engines, fuel cells, turbines, etc.) that will consume these fuels and burn them without any carbon emissions. All aspects are important in RDD&D – Research, Development, Demonstration and Deployment.

The proposed plan is as follows:

1. Concentrate and expand its energy **research** in Universities and research laboratories into the technologies that succeed in producing storage fuels by green methods. Cooperate in this research with other nations that have a similar capability, or are leading the charge.

2. For the technologies that show promise through success in research, invest in **developing** them further and solving any technical problems that show up.

3. For the technologies that have succeeded in both the research and development phases, invest in larger scale **demonstration** sites that demonstrate all aspects of the technology on a mini-plant scale. This is where all involved can go and witness that all aspects of a particular technology will work on a reasonable scale, and to establish the information needed about the technical feasibility and economics of the technologies.

4. For the technologies that have been successfully demonstrated, take the steps to **deploy** these technologies on a nationwide basis, and cooperate with other nations in terms of imports, exports and funding of technologies and plants in all nations that will enable the global strategy to succeed.

For successful deployment of green storage fuel technologies, the US needs to take the following steps in the widespread deployment in terms of Regulations, Production, Transport, Storage and End-Use of these fuels:

1. Develop and Establish the **regulations** and standards for the safe production, storage, transport and end use of these fuels.

2. Invest in and establish the **production** facilities that will produce storage fuels for all applications: electric power, industry, buildings, agriculture and transportation.

3. If the Fuels have to be transported over large distances, establish the pipelines and tankers and ships to **transport** these fuels safely and economically.

4. For the **storage** of these fuels, invest in and develop the storage tanks that will safely store these until they can be used and consumed.

5. For the **end use** of these storage fuels (engines, fuel-cells, turbines, etc.), deploy the large scale electric power technologies, technologies for vehicle engines, and technologies for their use in buildings and homes, and in industry – replacing all fossil fuel technologies with either electric technologies or storage fuel technologies.

There will need to be special attention paid to the production, supply and end use of storage fuels that are produced in a distributed way using renewable energy (mainly solar) on all of the roadways and highways of the US (and globally), **so as to totally replace gasoline (petrol) and diesel in entire US and global transportation.** At the same time, there will need to be all of the efforts as per above RDD&D and actions needed for safe deployment of fuel cells, engines and turbines (end use) in vehicles. There can also be hybrid systems that combine battery systems with storage fuel prime movers (fuel cells and engines). Efforts on this front need to start in 2020. So, all investments in RDD&D on fossil fuels should stop and be diverted to efforts on storage fuels.

Solar-Electric Highways, Roadways and Trainways – Plan for the US

The entire US transportation system needs to be electrified, directly or indirectly. Direct electrification that seems feasible but will still require a significant effort is for most cars to become battery electric. Two forms of indirect electrification are to use storage fuels such as hydrogen or ammonia as fuel in fuel-cell cars, and the other indirect electrification is that of the direct use of storage fuels in engines (either internal combustion engines or turbines) to burn these fuels in vehicles. All of these non-Carbon storage fuels must be produced by renewable energy.

First, direct electrification. The Plan proposes solar-electric highways and roadways. So there can be solar panel systems with raised structures covering highways, or where the space along the highways is available, ground mounted solar systems. As is proposed for power plants, the solar system will be accompanied by a battery backup system so there is power at times other than when the sun is shining. At each location there will be electric vehicle charging stations so battery electric vehicles can be charged, some directly from solar panels, and later directly from the battery system. At other times (like at night), the solar charging station can be on the transmission grid and powered by electricity from elsewhere.

The US consumed 27 quads (quadrillion BTUs) of energy in transportation in 2017. The quads of energy used in transportation are projected to stay about the same even up to 2050. Assuming that all of these 27 quads are used in burning oil or petroleum based fluids, the energy used in electric energy terms is 7,930 billion KWH (or terrawatt hours). Since on average, internal combustion engines used in vehicles are only about 40% efficient, only about 40% of this is actually used in operating the vehicles, or about 3,172 billion KWH per year. To generate this much electricity every year would take solar PV installations of a total of 2,115,000 MW of electric capacity. Assuming that all of the distributed solar charging stations are 10MW (megawatt) stations, it will take 211,500 of these stations. These will replace the current 111,000 gas stations (providing both gasoline and sometimes diesel). Just like the gas stations, each of these locations could be locations where other commerce could flourish in terms of restaurants, shops, etc., where people can be while their cars are being charged.

Each 10 MW electric charging station could have its solar panels distributed along the length of the highways. For the 47,000 miles of interstate highways throughout the US, one station every 20 miles will mean 2,350 of these stations on the Interstate highways alone. The rest could be distributed throughout the rural areas where most of the roads are and near or in town areas. Each of these 10 MW charging stations (which produce in the US 1,500 MWH (megawatt hours) for every MW), would produce 15,000 MWH of energy every year or about an average of 41 MWH daily. Since 100kW solar system is known to be able to charge 12 electric cars at a time, a 10 MW solar station could charge about 1,200 cars at a time, although the number of charging stations may actually depend on the number of parking spots created. Each 10 MW station will either have its solar panels distributed along the length of the highway or roadway, or use a square area about 400 meters by 400 meters or 430 yards by 430 yards. If the solar panels are elevated (what is called a built-up environment or on an elevated structure), the cars will be parked underneath the panels while charging.

Similarly, light rail, bus systems and all railways will develop supporting systems for pure electric, battery and storage fuel-cell use. Although the cost of adding pure electrification of mass transit type systems such as electric trams is high, wherever these make sense, these should be developed or expanded. For battery light rail vehicles, solar PV charging stations will be developed that charge these vehicles throughout the day, and at night from stationary batteries that have been charged. All rail vehicles, especially diesel-electric locomotives will be converted to hybrid battery electric and storage fuel turbine based engines. End-use engines, fuel cells and turbines that use storage fuels will need the RDD&D so that these achieve widespread use. The use of diesel fuel in railway locomotives and other types of light rail systems will slowly be phased out.

Each solar charging station for road vehicles can also perform the following added functions:

1. Store and sell a storage fuel to cars, trucks and other vehicles (mainly hydrogen).
2. Have an on-site storage fuel production unit, powered by extra energy from the same solar panels, that produces and stores the fuel during the day, and sells it to vehicles.

The storage fuel can be hydrogen that is produced and consumed quickly on-site, or ammonia that is produced and stored and consumed over longer periods. The size of the storage fuel production unit can vary depending on local demand. The storage fuel production unit will only need water that is split to provide the hydrogen, and nitrogen that is drawn from the air – both resources that are available everywhere – although water will need to be supplied. Since these fuels can be produced locally, they do not need to be transported over large distances. However, globally, if some nations that specialize in producing large quantities of storage fuels, produce these fuels, then these can be transported in ships and tankers that use the same fuels they transport!

Electrification of Buildings and Homes and Supply With Renewable

A significant number of homes and buildings in the US use propane, fuel oil and natural gas for heating and other appliances (water heaters, clothes dryers, cooking stoves, and cooking ovens). There seems to be general agreement that for new homes and buildings, especially if the cost of infrastructure for the supply of natural gas is eliminated, that the structures can be fully electrified and that this will be totally economical. In July of 2019, the city of Berkeley, which is on the East Bay area of San Francisco, adopted an ordinance that there be no gas hook ups in new homes, apartments and commercial buildings. This will essentially require all of these new buildings to be all-electric. For the US, and for California, this is a great beginning! However, new buildings are only about 1% of the buildings and this does not affect the rest of the existing stock to begin with. California now also requires all new homes to have solar PV systems (essentially solar panels on the roof). This is a good beginning.

If the US has to be able to reduce its greenhouse gas emissions from homes, apartments and all buildings, besides having a plan for new structures, *the nation needs a strategy for full electrification of all new and existing structures*. Currently, where natural gas infrastructure is already in place and gas is being provided and at low prices, the costs of electrification can be high. For a home, replacing an existing gas furnace with a higher efficiency gas furnace is much easier and saves much money. But replacing it with, say an air source heat pump or even with a ground source heat pump, or one that exchanges heat with the ground, requires a much higher capital cost. Even though less energy is used, and the excess electricity is offset with the home getting solar panels (solar PV system), the high capital cost and the absence of rebates and incentives for switching to the electric mode make that a difficult choice for home owners. The same is currently true for most apartments and buildings.

So, Here is the Plan for the Electrification
of Homes and Buildings:

1. Require that all new structures of all kinds have no fossil fuel options (natural gas, fuel oil or propane), and that they be fully electrified, have battery electric vehicle charging stations, have solar panels, and they meet mandated efficiency standards that are technically feasible.

2. Change all laws, regulations and building codes in order to make it easier for any retrofits of existing structures to switch to the all-electric modes.

3. Engage in a nation-wide program that is a combination of incentives, rebates, tax credits, and education in regard to the all-electric technologies needed. These should include heating, clothes drying, water heating and cooking modes. This should include the encouragement and rebates for solar thermal panels for water and space heating that help reduce the energy load. In addition to air source heat pumps that can be used in milder climate regions like California, there will be encouragement for ground source heat pumps that use the fact that the ground temperatures below about 10 feet or three meters remain constant throughout the year.

Electrification of Industry and Supply with Renewable Energy

Studies have indicated that there is considerable potential for electrification in industry, but that this is a very specialized area that needs individual attention. Studies indicate that the potential for electrification is high in manufacture of metal products, machinery production, iron and steel mills, wood products, and plastic and rubber products, just because of the processes they use. The potential is medium or low in industries for food and beverages, chemicals, paper, non-metallic minerals, and in the making of petroleum and coal based products. It is assumed that the last of these will be eliminated, although petroleum and coal products not involving the burning of these (and hence high emissions) would still continue.

There are several end-use electrical technologies that are already growth areas that can grow more. These are cryogenics, direct arc melting, induction heating, resistance heating and melting, ultraviolet curing and infrared processing. Other promising areas are water supply reverse osmosis (desalination), induction melting, membrane processes, and electro-slag, vacuum and plasma (combined). All of these areas have grown much in the 2015-2020 period and will need to grow further up to 2050.

The Plan for the Direct Use of Renewables and the Electrification of Industry are as Follows:

1. The expansion of known technologies and methods for electrification must be made universal. All industries will need to switch to these if they can use them. For this, all the encouragement, incentives and standards will be needed.
2. Locally, on industrial sites, all of industry will maximize the use of renewable energy (mainly solar PV) to produce electricity for all of their electric needs (existing and expanded).
3. Produce and use storage fuels – help them with RDD&D on end use technologies for this.
4. Develop end-use technologies that will enable them to substitute coal, oil and natural gas use with the use of either direct electric or the use of storage fuels.
5. The industrial sector will be invested in terms of all of the RDD&D needed for establishing new methods and technologies or improving on existing ones, or furthering either electrification or the use of storage fuels.
6. All industry will produce as much of their own storage fuels as they need, or for other nearby industries. If no solar PV space is available then they can import the storage fuel.

ENHANCEMENT OF THE SIZE, QUALITY, RELIABILITY, SMARTNESS AND EFFICIENCY OF THE US ELECTRIC GRID

Transmission System Expansion and Upgrade

As the overall plan for the US above indicates, the electricity production will need to grow from the current 12% to at least 60%. This means a fivefold increase in the size of the transmission grid (60/12) at least, if the storage fuels (17%) are produced locally right next to the solar PV (or other renewable energy source). If not, then the size of the transmission grid will grow to be more than six times the size (77/12).

The Global Plan for expanding the global electric transmission grid was described in Chapter 2. Whenever one considers an electrical energy system, there is the generator, the spur transmission that gets the electricity to the main or bulk transmission line, and the Point of Interconnection (POI) that interconnects the spur to the bulk transmission line. "Brownfield" sites are those where an existing power plant is simply being replaced. In such Brownfield cases, where say an existing coal, oil or natural gas generating station is being replaced by a solar PV plus battery generating station, one can use the existing transmission line if enough land is available locally for the solar PV plant. **Hence, in most cases where fossil fuel power plants are being replaced by renewable energy power plants (Brownfield sites), little or no expansion of the spur transmission grid may be required.**

However, in case of expanded electrification, where additional renewable energy generating capacity is being added (these new ones are called Greenfield Sites), there will be need for new spur lines, points of interconnection and a large expansion of the bulk transmission lines. Many substations will also be needed at the points where the electricity is distributed at the end of a bulk transmission line to a consumer location, whether it be an urban area, a transportation hub (solar electric charging station) or an industrial location. The size of the expansion of the bulk transmission hub will be reduced by locating the solar PV plus battery generating station near or at the end-user locations.

The cost of bulk transmission expansions are affected by land and construction costs, overhead versus buried cable transmission, extent of transmission upgrade on the spur line, the length of the upgrades or expansion needed, and the economies of scale. In the transmission study by the University of Texas at Austin compared the transmission upgrade costs of an upgrade in Texas and California, and found that the costs were much higher in California because of the higher land and construction costs and the need to bury the cables in California because of environmental impact aspects. Greenfield sites may need new or upgraded lines in order to get the electric power to the load centers, which will either be urban or industrial sites that are recently electrified. The length of new transmission lines will be higher for wind generation if it is far from load centers, but can be very short for solar PV stations as these can be located right next to the load centers. [36]

The overall structure, organization and economics of the whole electricity system needs to be revisited. It is crucial that this meet the following criteria:

1. It should enable a fast transition from fossil fuels to renewable energy based electricity and storage fuels

2. It should represent the joint interests of consumers (for savings and convenience), the need of city and state governments (for sustainability) the federal government to meet the transition goals, and the interests of those who operate the transmission grid, electricity generators and storage fuel providers.

3. In terms of income, control, jobs, and community owned or cooperative businesses, it should produce the widest possible distribution of earning benefits, and meet the criteria of energy democracy and a just transition.

4. In terms of the financing aspects, it should make sure that there are enough finances through various forms of taxes as described in Chapter 9, and public investment through government budgets, and that the rest of the unfulfilled needs be met through private financing, with a maximum empowerment of community banks through the accumulated savings of all actors in the whole system.

US presidential candidate Bernie Sanders, in his own version of the US Green New Deal, has made some sweeping recommendations of his own. He points out that already four federal Power Marketing Administrations (PMAs) and the Tennessee Valley Authority generate power and distribute it to 33 states. He proposes to create one more PMA to cover the remaining states and expand the existing PMAs and empower them to add as much renewable energy as is needed. He proposes investing $1.52 trillion on renewable energy electricity production and $852 billion on the accompanying battery storage capacity.

He further indicates that rather than a private utility system that only responds to shareholder returns and profits for financiers, he proposed a system as follows, "The renewable energy generated by the Green New Deal will be publicly owned, managed by the Federal

Power Marketing Administrations, the Bureau of Reclamation and the Tennessee Valley Authority and sold to distribution utilities with a preference for public power districts, municipally and cooperatively-owned utilities with democratic, public ownership, and other existing utilities that demonstrate a commitment to the public interest. The Department of Energy will provide technical assistance to states and municipalities that would like to establish publicly owned distribution utilities or community choice aggregation programs in their communities. Electricity will be sold at current rates to keep the cost of electricity stable during this transition."

An example of a utility that meets these criteria is Arizona's Salt River Project (SRP), because it is a public utility company with elected boards, and it operates with minimal supervision by the state's public utilities commission that allows it to itself prioritize based on long term (like sustainability) and short term (like savings) needs of residents. Since there are no shareholders to satisfy, all of the revenue is reinvested in the grid.

The Role of Community Microgrids in Transitioning to Local Renewable Energy

One of the ways that solar PV plus battery energy can be added within a community without increasing the size of the large external transmission grid is to use something like community microgrids. For most rooftop and building solar PV systems, the grid tied inverter shuts down when there is a power failure and a user has no power unless they have a behind the meter battery system that provides backup power to some parts of their home or building. A mainline transmission grid (towers with cables), usually has a substation where the high voltage from the mainline grid is stepped down to the voltage used by the community. When the power failure occurs (no power coming from the mainline grid), if there is switch that disconnects, and if there is a large battery system that supplies power to the whole community (in front of all the meters, for some parts of the community loads), then the solar PV units at home or building will not shut down and will continue to provide power during the mainline power failure or shut down.

So, although local generators that can fire up in case of a power failure include diesel or natural gas generators, a community micro-grid is a good way for local renewable energy within the community to provide partial power, especially for critical loads. For parts of California that are prone to earthquakes, wildfires and mudslides (read disaster risk reduction chapter), this can be crucial to providing backup power. In California, an organization called the Clean Coalition is advocating the establishment of community microgrids as a way of increasing the supply of energy from renewable energy sources located within communities. Clean Coalition's analysis shows that for an added 200 MW (megawatt) of solar PV power and a 400 MWH (megawatt hour) battery system would provide a $346 million economic stimulus over 20 years, while creating about 3,100 construction job years and about 1,000 operation and maintenance job years, while providing backup up power to a whole community for critical loads in case of a power failure.[37] The Plan is proposing that to begin with solar PV based renewable energy plus battery systems be established to be sized as to provide 25% of the power for a community all the time, to begin with on a net basis (so that there may at times be power flowing in or out of the community through the mainline transmission grid – as happens for a rooftop system), functioning as an enlarged community microgrid.

Another major innovation that has come recently in the US is **Community Choice Aggregation** (CCA), although it goes by some other names too. This provides electricity consumers with an alternative to investor owned electric utilities, in which local not-for-profit organizations provide alternative energy supply, but the transmission and billing is still done by the investor owned utilities who still own the transmission and distribution infrastructure, metering and billing. **CCAs are capable of being a big part of the solution to Climate Change, providing their mandate is to supply only green renewable energy, with little or no greenhouse gas emissions.** The CCA can then go and develop contracts with renewable energy suppliers, including new projects, and supply it to the customers in the jurisdiction or areas the CCA serves. Customers in that area then have the option of getting part or all of their electricity from green sources.

The government entity setting up the CCA sets up a governing board, usually consisting of local elected politicians, who often lack the expertise and often hire consultants that advise them on the complex technical and contractual issues. Because of their not-for-profit status they are often challenged in terms of ability to access credit. Nonetheless, CCAs throughout the US have set records in terms of their performance in providing green power and climate protections, while providing renewable energy power at electricity rates that are competitive with fossil fuel and nuclear power plants. Only 13% of CCAs in the US offer green power, although all CCAs in California offer it as they are required by law to do so, although in California they are not called utilities by electric service providers.

CCAs can only be set up in US states where legislation allows them to operate, and the electricity market is deregulated in terms of separating the functions of electricity generation from transmission and distribution. At this time, only 17 states and the District of Columbia have deregulated markets, and in the remaining 33 states, the utilities have a monopoly of generation, transmission and distribution. If the new Plan proposed in this book is to succeed, deregulation should be legislated at the national level, so that in all the state's electricity generation is deregulated. Only such legislation will enable everything to be electrified, and the three or five fold growth of electrical energy, all powered by renewable energy, will be empowered.

The first generation of CCAs were simple ones. The second generation of CCAs are prevalent today in the US and involve about 1,500 cities. In this mode, the CCAs are mandated to provide green energy, and they purchase renewable energy from small organizations and companies through Power Purchase Agreements (PPAs) that contract for the purchase of power at certain rates for a certain number of years, so that the CCA can turn around and supply this power to the user. In this mode, an electricity customer is automatically enrolled in an agreement with the CCA to purchase, say, 50% of their energy from green sources, with the options to either have the option to get 100% renewable energy, or to opt out of the program altogether. A third generation of CCA that is being proposed would lead to a much greater level of involvement of the municipalities and customers, and lead to a bigger development of renewable energy with the principles of energy democracy locally owned and operated, and financed through Green Bonds. [38]

Based on the criteria listed above and the need to expand the transmission grid and account for the renewable production of non-carbon storage fuels and create a smart and reliable transmission grid that minimizes losses, **here is the proposed Plan for the US:**

1. Up front, the situation the US faces is that because of the worn out and aging condition of the US power plants and grid, the University of Texas at Austin study estimated that the needed replacements of aging power plants already need an investment of $2.7 trillion and the replacements of the transmission infrastructure about $2.1 trillion, for a total of about $4.8 trillion. That's before we start talking about Climate Change solutions as per this book. [36]

2. Brownfield sites where all the fossil fuel generating plants are replaced by solar PV plus battery storage generators located close by, will need little or no expansion, can use most of the existing grid, and be modernized and replace the aging parts as per Item 1.

3. Renewable Energy resources that are far from load centers (like wind and geothermal) have two options: (a) Lay long new greenfield lines to the load centers; or (b) Locate substantial production facilities for making storage fuels close to these sources, but then replace storage and transport facilities to carry the fuels to other use centers.

4. Renewable energy sources that can be located close to load centers (like solar PV plus battery storage) also have two options: (a) They will need very short spur transmission lines, but will need to be interconnected with the build big transmission grid, to carry the energy to the load center; or (b) They can also have storage fuel production facilities on-site, so the transmission line can be very short, but again there will need to be facilities for the storage and transport of these fuels to use centers.

5. As has been emphasized by others, the whole US electrical system from generators to transmission lines to users needs to be made smart, which for the overall system means "a grid with digital technology that allows and enables two way communications between utilities or electricity providers and customers. It involves using this information in an automated

way so that supply and demand are regulated so as improve reliability, availability and economics." A simple example may be a home air conditioner unit that can be cycled on and off remotely by the utility company on very hot days in order to manage peak demand and not lead to a failure of the system with a brownout or blackout.

6. For the Plan, there needs to be an overall Smart Grid that can manage the variable energy flows coming from renewable energy (Variable Renewable Energy or VRE). For this, the Green Smart Grid needs the following additions: (a) At the solar power plant, in case of cloud cover, the battery system with a four hour energy capacity will need to automatically kick in, and when the sunlight returns be recharged by the solar system; (2) When the wind power or solar system are producing excess energy, redirect this energy to the production of storage fuels and store these for later electricity generation; (3) When wind power and solar PV are producing less than needed power, the power plant will fire up storage fuel electricity generators, or in the short term before this technology is fully developed, import electric energy from other parts of the grid or fire up small natural gas generators; and (4) When roof top solar is generating full power in a given area, cut back on other parts of the system.

7. **Community Choice Aggregation (CCA) is a powerful model** for the existing electrical energy to be provided by them, but by law they should be mandated to provide green power, and then should receive preferential finance from the public sector and community banks, so they can better access private finance. In their efforts to encourage and develop renewable energy projects, they should favor the principles of energy democracy, and favor community and worker cooperative owned renewable energy providers.

8. The Financial and economic aspects of the whole electricity system will need to be revisited. Investor and shareholder controlled private corporations have a role to play, but they should also favor the principles of energy democracy, and favor local community and worker owned cooperative type enterprises in their selections of vendors for goods and services, and in renewable energy providers.

A Beautiful Carbon Sink –
Reforesting and Afforesting the US

In about the year 1600, at the start of European settlement, it is estimated that the US had about 46% forest cover. By about the year 1907, the forest cover had reduced to about 33%, due to is use as fuel, and timber for housing, industry, railroads, and clearing the land for farming. As of 2010, the US had about 304 million hectares (about 750 million acres) of forest cover, of which 25% was old growth forest, 67% is secondary forest, and 8% is tree farms and plantations. In terms of regions the northeast had 42%, the southeast had 40% and the west had 28%. In the 20 years (1990-2010), the US lost 0.4 million hectares, but added about 7.7 million hectares due to reforestation. So, for the last century or so, the US forest cover had mostly stabilized. However, since the start of European migration, the nation has lost about 120 million hectares (about 300 million acres) of forest cover.

In the Global Plan described in Chapter 4, the reforestation and afforestation target for the world is one billion hectares (1,000 Million hectares). **The part of this Plan for the US is to reforest and afforest the US with 80 million hectares. This is only reforesting 60% of what was lost since the year 1600.** It will need reforesting and afforesting of temperate areas (continental US), boreal areas (Alaska) and tropical areas (Hawaii and Puerto Rico). In the New Deal in 1933, the Civilian Conservation Corps planted 3 billion trees and employed 3 million people. This plan is similar to that but can be conducted a lot differently.

First, it is important to point out that there are many organizations who have been doing this activity or encouraging it. Most of the reforestation in the 1990-2010 period of about 7.7 million hectares (about 19 million acres) has been done by organizations such as the US Forest Service and Arbor Day Foundation. Other organizations that have been active trying to encourage reforestation are Nature Conservancy and American Forests. However, most of these organizations advocate reforestation and afforestation on like 40-50 million acres (16-20 million hectares). However, the Book Plan is proposing the much larger area of 80 million hectares (175 million acres), which considering the US total land area of 983 million hectares (2,430 million acres), is only about 7% of the land area. Over a 31 year period (2020-2050) this amounts to only 2.3 million hectares (or about 5.7

million acres added every year). If, on the average, a hectare has 1,800 trees (an approximate average, which will vary with the type of tree) this means a little over about 4 billion trees per year or about 128 billion trees in a 31 year period.

The main criteria that this reforestation and afforestation effort need to meet are:

1. That they provide the needed carbon sink.
2. That they provide the needed habitats for all forms of species.
3. That they provide livelihoods, incomes and products on a distributive basis.

The first criteria means that the total tree area continuously expand. The second criteria means that there be certain areas that are not disturbed (like old growth forests), or that when activities are done, they account for the health of all species and they provide them with enough habitat. The third criteria means that people have to have a central role in owning, managing and using a major part of the expanded forests for their livelihoods based on sustainable forestry extractive methods, that allows them to use enough of the forests for their livelihoods, businesses and usable products – with the central rule that they plant more than they harvest, and that they pay attention to the first two criteria. Monoculture tree plantations (all trees of the same type) and clear cutting timber harvesting practices are to be discouraged.

Plan for The US – Blue Carbon Rejuvenation of US Coastal Ecosystems Along Entire Non-Ice Coastline

As documented and described in the Global Plan for coastal ecosystems in Chapter 4, these ecosystems have a very large potential for absorbing carbon, comparable to forests. Out of the global non-ice coastline of 1.2 to 1.6 million kilometers (0.75 to 1 million miles), the US has about 95,000 miles (or about 153,00 kilometers) according to the US National Oceanic and Atmospheric Administration (NOAA), although this includes the northern shoreline of Alaska and the shores of the freshwater Great Lakes in the middle of the country.

So what has happened with coastal ecosystems or wetlands

as they are sometimes called? The US has lost more than half of its coastal wetlands, or about 110 million acres (about 45 million hectares), since the early settlers came from Europe. California lost about 91% of its coastal wetlands since 1780. American Samoa has lost 25% of its coastal wetlands to development and most of the wetlands of the Commonwealth of the Northern Mariana Islands are gone. Most mangrove forests, seagrass beds and coral reefs have not done well. Shallow water reefs have been damaged by hurricanes, fishing, coastal development, runoff and sedimentation (soil from water erosion of soils). Seagrass cover has been lost in Tampa Bay (more than 50%), Mississippi Sound (76%), and Galveston Bay (90%). This has also happened in Chesapeake Bay, Puget Sound, San Francisco Bay, and Florida's coast. Global temperature rise and sea level rise have also been degrading coastal habitats. [39]

However, there have been many US government agencies and organizations that have engaged in preserving and restoring coastal ecosystems and wetlands. Significant efforts exist in the US Department of the Interior, the NOAA, the US Fish and Wildlife Service, the US Environmental Protection Agency, the US Department of Agriculture and the US Army Corps of Engineers. Significant actions have taken place at coastal Louisiana, and in the Florida Everglades (which are actually an example of a very large assembly of coastal type ecosystems). **The administration of US president George H. W. Bush (about 1990) put forward significant wetlands protections for all inland wetlands, so much so that in many states of the US, no inland wetland can be destroyed, on public or private lands.**

The American Recovery and Reinvestment Act (ARRA) of 2009 was signed by the US president Barack Obama, which included the restoration of 50 coastal areas through the US National Oceanic and Atmospheric Administration (NOAA). Three of these restoration efforts that were evaluated were the oyster reef and seagrass areas of the Seaside Bays of Virginia, the oyster reef project in Mobile Alabama and the salt marsh restoration in the San Francisco Bay, California. **A study that was done by Abt Associates of Cambridge Massachusetts and reported on by the Center for American Progress and Oxfam America, showed that the economic and environmental benefits of the Virginia and California projects by far exceeded the amounts spend on them.** In the San Francisco Bay project the $8 million spent provided and estimated lifetime benefit of more than $69 million and the $2.5 million spent on the Virginia project yielded and estimated lifetime benefit of more than $35 million. The Mobile, Alabama project could not be fully evaluated, and it was hard hit by the financial crisis of 2009 and the British Petroleum Deepwater Oil Spill of 2010, but it provided significant employment to low-income, natural resource dependent workers. The study showed that overall, the total benefits including the ecosystem benefits exceeded the initial investments in a ratio of 15 to 1. [40]

Because of the crucial aspect of their ability to absorb large amounts of carbon and the need to restore habitats, and provide some increased protection against coastal storms, the Book Plan proposes a massive rejuvenation of coastal ecosystems, that will be part of the Global Plan described in Chapter 4. The plan for the US is as follows:

1. The US plan will go beyond just restoration to a national program to introduce coastal ecosystems along its entire coastline.
2. For the 95,500 miles (about 153,000 kilometers) of US coastline, the coastal ecosystems will be introduced an average or 1 kilometer (0.625 miles) width, that will give a total coastal ecosystem growth of about 38 million acres (or about 15 million hectares), about 38% of what has been lost since about the year 1620.
3. Finally, the plan includes a national level inventory of carbon absorption and evaluation, to estimate and evaluate the entire coastline of projects and activities in terms of the carbon absorbed. This will estimate the greenhouse gas sequestration taking place in these ecosystems.

Besides the main benefit of acting as a massive carbon sink, and all of the benefits that this will provide in terms of environment and economics, the addition and restoration of US coastal ecosystems will create a beautiful coastline the likes of which many have never seen. It will add to the beauty and wildlife of coastal areas.

Advanced Climate Change Disaster Management for the US

To begin with, it is important to point out that FEMA (the Federal

Emergency Management Agency) has excellent resources on their website and provide very good information in regard to all kinds of disasters. They also have a high level of experience and expertise in managing all kinds of disasters. However, the US needs to increase its Disaster Risk Reduction activities and preparedness manyfold and work with all of the local states, communities and people in regard to resources, training, awareness and implementation. **Because of the increasing probability and devastation that can be caused by Climate Change, the resources, efforts and visibility of these efforts needs to be many multiples greater.**

Common to all the major disaster types covered below are that

1. The US needs to prepare in advance to reduce the damage caused by disasters.
2. To prepare resources in advance for the evacuation of people
3. To prepare in advance for the relief of displaced people
4. To prepare in advance for the recovery and reconstruction
5. To continue to improve capabilities, resources, and organization to better respond to and recover from Climate Change disasters.

The major Climate Change related disasters that the US needs to prepare for are hurricanes and coastal storms, flooding, tornadoes and wildfires.

Hurricanes and Coastal Storms

First and foremost, it will really help all coastal areas if the action plan in regard to coastal ecosystems is implemented. The coastal ecosystems will help better withstand the effects of hurricanes, coastal storms and storm surges, although in each case the damage to the ecosystems may need some restoration. Then, nationally, the US needs to organize and prepare resources in advance, and store them at inland locations that will escape the wind and water effects of the storms, and which can be quickly pulled in after the disaster has passed to provide rescue, and relief. These will include resources as follows:

1. Mobile housing units that can provide temporary housing for the displaced population.
2. Food, medicine and water supply for the displaced people.

3. Mobile solar PV energy supply stations that provide energy for lighting, cooking and for operating facilities.

4. Mobile medical units that help provide medical relief as well as act to contain any diseases and medical problems (diarrhea, infectious diseases, etc.

5. Build better back.

6. Build only where there is less damage and then whatever is built must be resilient.

Mobile housing units should be assembled, with perhaps ten mini-houses per truck trailer, complete with solar panels. If a hundred of these are ready, they will be able to travel to a location needed and be able to set up temporary housing for about a thousand people in a matter of days. Other truck trailers can be medical units, sanitary units, supplies units and water purification units. Prior to a disaster, locations near a disaster zone should be selected and the land either purchased or rented in advance, so that it can be used speedily. If possible, these land locations can already be equipped with electrical and sewer connections. The provision and preparation of such materials and resources in advance, and located near expected disaster zones will make the tasks of relief and restoration much easier for the displaced people and emergency management organizations like FEMA.

Tornadoes

It has been found that with Climate Change, the number of tornadoes in a cell have been increasing. So, in all areas which have a high probability of tornadoes, the following actions should be taken in advance:

1. ALL NEW housing and buildings will need to be built to withstand the higher wind velocities of tornadoes (both in terms of shape and structure), and it should be mandatory that they still have tornado proof shelters.

2. All homes and buildings will construct a tornado shelter that will survive the tornado, or there should be enough in a community where people can rush to. All schools, medical facilities and government buildings will be retrofitted to have these shelters as well as retrofits to make them more resilient to high winds.

Wildfires

These are becoming more and more frequent and devastating, especially in the western US and Colorado. These regions and states need, with federal help, to begin making their forest areas less prone to wildfires, and there be measures in place, such as breaks in the forest, that make the wildfires easier to control. Then, after the wildfires have burnt an area, there needs to be advance preparation for stabilizing the burnt out hillsides, to ensure that there are no mudslides caused by the rains that follow, and that they begin to prepare to reforest these areas with suitable and diverse tree varieties. In the recovery and reconstruction part of this, new codes and regulations are needed to ensure that homes not be built adjacent to reforested areas, and that there be fire defensible spaces around any home developments that are constructed.

Eco-Cities and Low Carbon Transportation

It has become quite obvious that the mode of highway and urban development is not very energy efficient, and has contributed in a big way to high energy consumption and high emissions from fossil fuels. Urban sprawl in particular, with far flung suburbs with single family homes force everyone to use a car, and even the homes are designed for cars (car garages). **To make them energy efficient and low carbon, cities need to be designed to reduce transportation distances, so that there is much more thought given to the collocation of homes, businesses (where people work), grocery stores, shopping centers, entertainment locations, etc.** So, new housing developments must be required to be denser; and laws, regulations and codes changed to make urban sprawl very difficult.

Next, the forms of transportation that will need to be encouraged are all the low carbon modes, so that people have a lot more choices. Entire communities should be redesigned to make walking and biking and mass transit easier, and local travel by car more expensive and difficult. Then, all of the transportation modes will need to be inter-connected so that one can easily go from walking and biking to taking the train, to taking a high speed train, to taking a flight, to taking a bus, to taking a taxi, to renting a car (the last inter-connecting mode is the only one available today – that is not enough).

The Energy, Climate and Ecosystem Plan for California

Impact of Climate Change on California

California has taken good steps in the areas of car fuel emissions, battery electric cars, renewable energy electricity generation, and tighter standards on environmental and pollution regulations. However, California also has been suffering from the effects of Climate Change through droughts and wildfires, and some effects of heat waves, increased air pollution, ocean acidification and sea level rise. There was an extreme drought in 2014 that covered almost all of California, and in 2015 the drought cost agriculture about $2.7 billion and more than 20,000 jobs, and in 2016 was followed by heavy rains that led to flooding that damaged highways, threatened rural areas and isolated coastal communities.

California has become increasingly subject to wildfires due to increased temperatures, and drought (dry times), often accompanied by high winds. From 1979-2013, the length of the fire season increased by about 19%, and since 1985, more than 50% of the wildfires have been thought to have been caused by Climate Change. Since 1990, the average annual number of homes lost to wildfires has increased by 300%, and the number of homes at risk from wildfires was estimated to be about 900,000 in 2017. About 35% of the wildfires have started in high risk areas. Matters have been made worse by people building homes in forested areas. In 2017, 2018 and 2019 California has suffered from catastrophic wildfires in many of its forests. In 2017 there was a catastrophic wildfire in Sonoma County and in 2018 another one that essentially burned down the town of Paradise. Both were in Northern California. In 2019, the northern Kincade wildfire, again in Northern California, has been devastating. In 2019, till early November there were about 6,400 wildfires, that burned about 250,000 acres and about $163 million was spent in fire suppression.

The other bad news in relation to California wildfires is that in 2018 the estimated carbon dioxide emissions were 45 million metric tons. This wiped out some of the benefits of decreasing emissions down to 424 MMTCO2e (hence doing better than the 431 MMTCO2e goal for 2020), that were being tracked and are described above. This is also bad, because it points to one of the possible scenarios of a runaway greenhouse effect that Climate Change makes things happen that increase carbon dioxide emissions.

Status of Energy and Climate Change Efforts in California

While there has been foot dragging and often outright opposition at the national or federal level for solutions to Climate Change, the state of California located on the west coast of the US has forged ahead. There are three aspects of California's Energy and Climate situation: (a) California has achieved much in the past decades, both in energy and emissions; (b) There is much the world can learn from California (as it has led in many actions); (c) California still faces immense challenges, especially in transportation, electrification, high jet fuel use and in fossil fuel based electric power generation. Because of the energy and emissions challenges that remain, and challenges in the forestation/wildfire and coastal ecosystems front, a Plan is proposed for California that will help it in achieving the ambitious goals it has set for itself, which parallel what we are trying to do globally here.

California Achievements and State Government Goals

- ❑ If California was a country, it would be the fifth largest economy in the world. In 2006, California passed legislation (SB32) to reduce Greenhouse Gas Emissions by 2020 to the state's 1990 levels (431 MMTCO2e – million metric tons of Carbon dioxide equivalent). It achieved that in 2017, when the emissions were 424 MMTCO2e). California was serious about the **Kyoto Protocol goals** and was one of the few "countries" to achieve its commitments as per Kyoto. Inspired by the state, many of the cities in California, including the city of El Cerrito, also set targets and achieved them as per the Kyoto targets.

- ❑ Utility Scale Solar and Wind electric power generation increased from 3% in 19% in 2018. In the later stages this was spurred by legislation (SB350) passed by the previous Governor, Jerry Brown, in 2015 which had mandated 33% of electric energy come from renewable sources by 2020, and 50% by 2030 (**Renewable Portfolio Standard – RPS**). This is monitored and enforced by the California Energy Commission (CEC).

- ❑ California was one the first to establish a **Cap and Trade Program**, which is market based approach. In summary, it assesses the total carbon emission by the big emitters and issues allowances which later were auctioned. Over time the allowances are decreased so that the large emitters have to decrease their emissions or purchase allowances from those who have done more than their allowance. The program is a very complicated one that is described in detail in the accompanying website. To date, most emissions reductions have come from renewable energy increases and not from Cap and Trade. However, the California Air Resources Board (CARB) reported that as of 2018, the auctions from the sales of allowances to companies had gone to the Greenhouse Gas Reduction Fund (GGRF). From this the legislature had appropriated $6.1 billion, out of which $3 billion had been selected and $2 billion implemented in "Green" projects intended to reduce greenhouse gas emissions.

❏ **Goal of Carbon Neutrality by 2045**: In 2016, the previous Governor Jerry Brown signed legislation (SB100) that mandated that ALL (100%) electric energy in the state be carbon neutral by 2045 (meaning that all sources were admissible in this number as long as it did not emit carbon dioxide). This differed from previous legislation and requirements that a certain percentage be from only renewable energy (like solar and wind). However, Governor Brown went one bold step further. He signed an executive order mandating ALL energy (not just electric energy which is only about 10% of all energy consumed) be "carbon neutral" by 2045. The details of the law allow many options, because of which the energy mix can include nuclear, large hydro and natural gas with Carbon Capture and Storage (CCS).

❏ **Accompanying Increase in Renewable Energy**: For Electric Energy only, the bill (SB100) also increased the requirement that 50% electric energy be from renewables by 2026 (that does not include nuclear), and 60% renewables by 2030.

❏ Here are the achievements and goals in the **Transportation Sector**: California has always led the US in terms of established Corporate Average Fuel Economy Standards (CAFE) that require higher fuel efficiency for vehicles. California already has more electric cars than the other states. Governor Brown had also signed an executive order that established the **goal of having 5 million electric vehicles in**

California by 2030, and to establish 250,000 zero-emission vehicle chargers (that provide a slower charge), including 10,000 DC fast chargers by 2025 (which charge in a much shorter time, but need higher power). Initially, the California Energy Commission (CEC) is funding about **100 hydrogen refueling stations throughout the state** which are required to have at least 33% renewable hydrogen, with those supplying more than 40% renewable hydrogen eligible for a credit.

Efforts of the Government of California

The four agencies of the Government are the California Energy Commission (CEC), the California Air Resources Board (CARB), the California Public Utilities Commission (CPUC), and California Independent System Operator (CAISO). These organizations are engaged in different aspects of energy and Climate Change solutions activities. Efforts are being implemented that are aimed at building decarbonization – mainly electrification.

Challenges faced by California: The state will have a much easier time achieving the energy and emissions reductions goals in electric energy. But California faces big challenges in the energy and climate sectors by the way of decarbonization (mainly electrification) in the areas of transportation (with a large number of fossil fuel vehicles on the road that are increasing their vehicle miles traveled), in residential and commercial buildings, and in Industry.

So here is the Plan for California.

The current and proposed energy plan pie charts are shown below. The plan for California will mirror that proposed for the US above, as well as draw on the Global Plan, with the following added notes:

❏ **California needs a phased and time bound program to replace its natural gas power plants with solar plus battery storage units** – keeping only a few operational to deal with the variability of renewables until such time as other alternatives are developed.

❏ California is well poised to **develop solar electric highways** that vastly expand its electric charging stations throughout the state. Adopting the concept of solar-electric highways and roadways will make it much easier for California to blanket all land areas with solar-electric charging and green hydrogen refueling stations.

❑ **Vehicle Replacement:** California had 31 million vehicles on the road as of 2010. If 5 million electric vehicles are on the road by 2030 (California's current goal), assuming that they have replaced fossil fuel vehicles, then there still will be 26 million mostly fossil fuel vehicles on the road (assuming no growth in numbers). So from 2031 and 2050 the combined growth in battery electric vehicles and fuel cell vehicles (using hydrogen) and a "Cash for Clunker's" type program will need to be about 1.3 million vehicles a year. With this, there will be NO fossil fuel vehicles on the road by 2050. The Plan calls for all fossil fuel vehicle sales to end by 2035, so that the replacements for those can begin in 2045.

❑ With significant capabilities for clean energy research and development, the state should undertake the **RDD&D (Research, Development, Demonstration & Deployment) of the green production of storage fuels like hydrogen and ammonia**, and in their end use in electricity generation, transportation, shipping, and industry. The state is leading the US in establishing hydrogen refueling stations for cars, especially encouraging "green" hydrogen produced from renewable energy. The State needs to up its ambition considerably so that by 2050 it has about 9% of its energy coming from hydrogen and ammonia.

❑ The State can also pioneer in the US in terms of the **full scale electrification of homes, commercial buildings, industry, and agriculture** – transitioning what cannot be electrified with innovative technologies for storage fuels.

❑ With electrification, the electric energy demand will be 3 to 5 times what it is today. The State needs to build as much solar PV generation within cities or near cities, so as to reduce the need and expense of transmission lines. Still, with the **expansion of renewable energy based generation the transmission grid expansion** needs to be undertaken, and significant storage capacity developed locally (such as large battery systems) in order to deal with the variability of renewable energy.

❑ With the massive wildfires that have occurred in recent years, the State needs to undertake at a very high level, **Disaster Risk Reduction in regard to preparing for wildfires**, of the type described above by building fire breaks in existing forests, and designing new afforested areas with fire breaks so fires are easy to control. Massive programs need to be undertaken.

❑ **Carbon Sinks – Forests**: California should take up its share of the 80 million hectares that is the goal for the US in terms of reforestation and afforestation, with the areas designed to enable ease in control of wildfires, as described above. The reforestation of wildfires needs to be specially designed on these principles, with special attention paid to the locations of buildings and homes, and building fire defensible spaces around them.

❑ **Carbon Sinks – Coastal Ecosystems**: California is well poised to establish all types of coastal ecosystems along its entire Pacific coastline, coordinating with fishery experts to enhance the habitats for all kinds of fish and ocean life.

❑ **Low Carbon Transportation**: California has begun its investment in **high speed rail** along the coast. It should review the whole process and design and see how this can be expedited so as to establish this early. This will cut down vehicular traffic. California needs a statewide plan for low carbon transportation that will parallel that of the US – pedways, bikeways, mass transit, rail transit, solar-electric roadways, high speed rail and airports all integrated.

❑ **Just Transition**: The oil and natural gas industry is quite active in the state. California and the US and other fossil fuel dependent nations need programs and policies in place that help the companies, workers and communities involved in fossil fuel activities to transition to the new clean energy renewable economy. More on this follows.

❑ California needs to begin **enforcing its rules for its Cap and Trade Program**, so that the allowances of all polluting sources covered by the program are reduced to zero by 2045, and most of its auction proceeds are invested in implementing the above Plan. It is estimated that if the Cap and Trade program succeeds, it will reduce its greenhouse gas emissions by 15-20%.

❑   California needs to coordinate with national US policies in beginning the shut-down of its oil refineries and the possible conversion of these facilities to the making of storage fuels using renewable energy sources. The import of oil and the export of refined oil products need to be coordinated along with a Just Transition for all of its oil industry and natural gas industry workers.

We now present a snapshot of California's Energy Consumption during 2017.

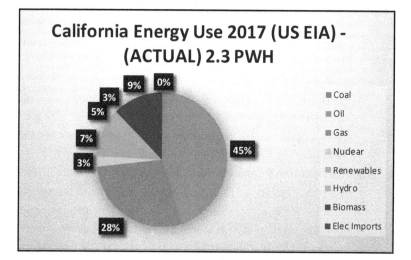

CALIFORNIA ACTUAL ENERGY USE IN 2017

This information is from the US Energy Information Agency – profile for California. Coal use is very small, essentially zero, but oil use is 45% and Natural Gas is 28%. Combined, dependence on fossil fuels is at 73%. Note that imported electricity is about 9% of total energy use. PWH = petawatt hours (10E15 Watt Hours, or 10E12 killowatt hours).

The Plan for California is essentially to achieve carbon neutrality by 2050 totally by fossil fuels. This can certainly be speeded up to be achieved by 2045, if the state wishes to meet its time bound goal by 2045. The reforestation and afforestation, and coastal ecosystems expansion are treated as bonuses because of their uncertainty, but they can be significant insurance that California more than meets its goals of reducing carbon and greenhouse gas emissions. California has a very good record of implementing energy efficiency activities, so the goal set is at 25%. Storage fuels are estimated at 9% of the increased energy. However, if energy efficiency does not achieve the necessary reductions, then storage fuels production and use can correspondingly expand. Here is the Plan for 2050.

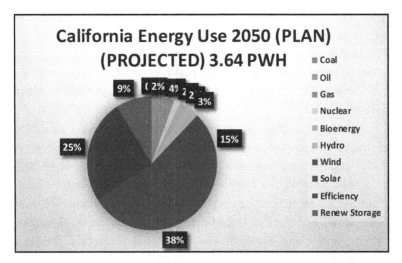

California Energy Use 2050 (PLAN) (PROJECTED) 3.64 PWH

CALIFORNIA ENERGY PLAN FOR 2050

Fossil fuels are down to about 5-6% (essentially gone) with the gas component larger. Solar PV has a big expanded role at 38%, with wind coming in next at 15%. If efficiency is excluded, California's actual energy use grows from about 2.3 PWH in 2017 to about 3.64 PWH by 2050.

Along with the European Union, California has always led the world in energy and Climate Change solutions. It is time for the state to up its ambitions in line with what is needed to achieve the 1.5 C goals and implement a Plan such as described above. There is much that the US and the world can learn from California as they begin to implement their national and Global Plans. This can provide the motivation and information that will lead to effective global treaties, effective actions by other nations, and an effective implementation of a US national plan.

We now turn to the US Green New Deal that has received a lot of public attention in the US.

The Proposed US Green New Deal (GND) –
Aspirations and Practical Implementation

The original New Deal was a whole package of measures that were pushed and implemented by US president Franklin Roosevelt from 1933 to 1936 to get the country out of a really big depression, at a time when most of the rest of the world was also in a depression. The New Deal was a number of programs, public works projects, financial reforms and regulations that helped lift the US out of its economic collapse and also provided protections against having the problems again.

The New Deal dealt with the excesses of the financial institutions and banks by establishing the Federal Deposit Insurance Corporation (FDIC) and the Securities and Exchange Commission (SEC), and by passing legislation that separated banking from speculative investments. At the same time it provided the people with a minimum level of income, employment, healthcare, retirement (Social Security), working conditions (hours of work) and labor protection. The New Deal also helped agriculture pull out of environmental degradations like the Dust Bowl (where agricultural soil was being blown away) by encouraging conservation. And It provided for a major reconstruction of the infrastructure of the country which helped manufacturing recover from the economic slump. The big problem then was the Depression and the New Deal helped solve this Depression, but also gave a new deal to the people and the environment.

The Green New Deal (GND) of the US is a good list of aspirations or desirable outcomes, and does lay out a bold plan for change that has been put forward in the US Congress by Congresswoman Alexandria Occasio-Cortez, who has sponsored it in cooperation with others and has been the principal champion of it in US politics and argued for it very eloquently. However, what the Green New Deal does need is a concrete plan of how, what and where, to solve Climate Change. As written, the two aspects – Climate Change solutions and better living conditions appear to be part of the GND package but items like wages and healthcare are mainly political aspects that are not directly related to Climate Change. The US Green New Deal is, however, the most ambitious political plan that has been proposed for the country to start to be part of the major global solution to Climate Change, while addressing the massive inequality and bad living conditions of much of the population.

The author and activist Naomi Klein provides a strong case for the Green New Deal. She emphasizes that it will be a massive job creator, lead to a fairer economy, increase pressure for action, be implemented even in times of recession, draw a lot of enthusiasm, help overcome opposition, and it's an idea whose time has come. She is an accomplished author who has come at Climate Change from many directions, from the environmental, political and spiritual ends. [41]

However, what it will really need is a lot of specific plans, programs, financing, regulations, new or revitalized organizations, and incentives, as well as comprehensive new industrial, transportation, urban development, energy transition, agricultural and ecosystem policies. This and other comprehensive actions are what the Book Plan lays out in the rest of this chapter.

The Green New Deal draws its inspiration from the US New Deal that the US used to recover from the depression in the 1930s, where the big problem now is Climate Change, and the solutions will give a new deal to the people and the environment. The Plan shows how to practically implement the US Green New Deal, but also to expand it to a Global Green New Deal. Some aspects, like unionization laws and programs are strictly public policy, but the Plan goes beyond what the US Green New Deal hopes to achieve.

How the Plan helps Effective Implementation of the Green New Deal

Here are the Green New Deal "Mobilization" Goals and Objectives (as shown within quotation marks), as stated in the Resolution passed by the House of Representatives, and how the Plan satisfies them – as a sub-note to each goal.

(A) *"Building Resiliency against Climate Change-related disasters"*

    a. The Plan proposes an advanced Disaster Risk Reduction (DRR) strategy for preparing for and dealing with hurricanes, typhoons, cyclones, coastal storms, massive floods, wildfires, and tornadoes, which is both high level and enables and empowers local communities to prepare and deal with these.

(B) *"Repairing and Upgrading Infrastructure"*

    a. The Plan presents infrastructure upgrades that do repair existing infrastructure, but emphasizes investments in new types of infrastructure that help mitigate Climate Change – renewable energy, electrification and ecosystem related.

(C) *"Meeting 100 percent of power demand in the US through clean, renewable and zero-emission sources"*

    a. The Plan not only shows how to do that for all fossil fuel power plants, but it also demonstrates how to overcome the variability aspect of renewable energy. But the plan shows how to achieve the maximum amount of electrification, and then how to meet the expanded demand through more renewable energy. A significant complement is the production of non-carbon storage fuels such as hydrogen and ammonia, that are produced only with renewable energy, and then used throughout to massively supplement electrification.

(D) *"Building and upgrading to energy efficient and distributed "smart" power grids"*

    a. The Plan shows how to achieve this, but the primary smartness up front that's needed is the "Smartness" of how to deal with the variability aspects of renewable energy (be able to shift energy dynamically around the grid), have local micro-grids that can function autonomously if the main grid supply fails or is disconnected, and local smartness that better manages supply and demand by turning things off and on as needed – to save energy and manage peak demand.

(E) *"Upgrading all existing buildings ... and new buildings to achieve maximum energy efficiency"*

    a. The Plan proposes the maximum achievable electrification of buildings and homes, the research into and use of energy efficient technologies, and the maximum level of local production of renewable energy in or around the buildings and homes.

(F) *"Spurring Massive Growth of Clean Manufacturing"*

    a. The Plan proposes the maximum level of the

electrification of all industrial processes. What cannot be electrified will be switched to new technologies using the renewable energy based production and use of non-carbon storage fuels. The Plan proposes the establishment of a major Industrial policy that is pro-employment, pro-environment and establishes net zero industries in all aspects of the new energy and eco-system plans.

(G) *"Working Collaboratively with farmers and ranchers to remove pollution and greenhouse gas (GHG) emissions"*

a. The Plan addresses the electrification aspect of agricultural machinery, and the use of ammonia as a fuel for agricultural uses (the farmers already use ammonia as a fertilizer and store it in tanks on the farm for this). Further, the Plan addresses the methane emissions from cows and livestock manure, which is another greenhouse gas that traps heat more than carbon dioxide.

(H) *"Overhauling transportation systems... to remove pollution and GHG emissions"*

a. The Plan proposes a novel concept "Solar Electric Highways" that will electrify all the highways and road-ways by establishing solar powered electric charging stations everywhere, and enable them to supply (and occasionally produce locally) non-carbon storage fuels like hydrogen. The Plan proposes the maximum level of electrification of transportation that is powered by renewable energy and the laying of high speed rail networks throughout the US and globally, to reduce the number of short haul flights that use jet fuel. Also, all of the green ways of transportation will be interconnected – walking and biking to mass transit, mass transit to regional and high speed rail and to air and road transportation – and added, the total encouragement of small electrified vehicles for local travel.

(I) *"Mitigating and managing the long-term adverse health, economic and adverse effects of pollution and Climate Change"*

a. The Plan addresses the whole aspect of adaptation to Climate Change related changes, and how the switch out of coal will be better for the health of local communities, and how local efforts can be supported and funded to help communities adapt to heat waves, floods, sea level rise and high winds. At the same time, the Plan proposes a major transformation of agriculture to a regenerative kind.

(J) *"Removing Greenhouse gases from the atmosphere"*

　　a. The Plan proposes a massive reforestation and afforestation of about 80 million hectares (1 billion hectares for the world) of boreal and temperate forests and the design of newly reforested areas to deal better with wildfires, encourage biodiversity, and also provide local benefits and incomes.

(K) *"Restoring and protecting threatened, endangered and fragile ecosystems"*

　　a. The Plan proposes a massive restoration and expansion of coastal ecosystems along the entire coastlines of Atlantic, Gulf of Mexico and Pacific coasts. Mangrove swamps, salt marshes and sea grasses, already do, but when expanded and established will store large amounts of carbon, will help restore ocean life and restore fisheries – all of which means much more beautiful coastlines and better incomes and benefits to coastal communities.

(L) *"Cleaning up hazardous waste and abandoned sites"*

　　a. These were US "Superfund" sites that industries and companies left behind when they polluted and dumped. These were called "superfund" sites as they were identified and a fund established by the government a few decades back to clean them up. Not all the sites have been cleaned up. The Plan does not address this issue, but what can be said here is that after the sites are cleaned up, they will be ideal for solar PV power plants as well as restored parks.

(M) *"Identifying other emissions and pollution sources and creating solutions to remove them"*

　　a. The answer to this will be the same as (L) above.

(N) *"Promote the International exchange of technology and help other nations achieve a Green New Deal"*

a. The Plan does all of that and more. It actually lays out a full strategy consisting of the aspects of global organization, taxes, financing, global agreement, technology development and sharing, transitioning out of fossil fuels, just transitions for oil producing nations, and assistance to the developing nations. **The Plan lays out a Global Green New Deal,** and a detailed plan for meeting a 1.5 degree Celsius goal by 2050. Detailed plans are also laid out for all the big emitters – USA, China, India, European Union and even a plan for California.

The Green New Deal (GND) of the US is more a list of aspirations or desirable outcomes to simultaneously solve Climate Change and improve people's lives. It does combine the need to solve Climate Change with a vast improvement in living conditions for all of the population. It is the national version of a global climate action plan and the United Nations Sustainable Development Goals that aim at improvements in the living conditions of people.

Part 4 of the Resolution written by the US Congress addresses issues that are important for the implementation of the GND. Many of the issues in this part are more addressed through effective public policy and programs, not having directly to do with Climate Change – these are the issues such as the support workers and their right to unionize, wages, healthcare, public ownership, workplace safety, trade negotiations, the protection of public lands, protection of the rights and interests of indigenous people, protections of businesses from monopoly capitalism, high quality health care, affordable and safe housing, and clean water, air, healthy and affordable food, and access to nature.

However, the proposed Plan does the following that addresses the goals of Part 4 in an effective way:

1. An industrial development policy and reindustrialization programs that are pro-employment and pro-environment.
2. Tax reform that favors the human factor and employment by implementing depreciation for human capital investments, and decreasing depreciation for machine and other capital investments not relating to renewable energy or electrification.

3. Direct economic development policies and programs that favor local production for local use, using forest and agricultural raw materials grown locally.

4. Direct business development and employment in all of the tasks of energy, Climate Change and ecosystem development laid out in the Plan.

5. Just Transition for all of the workers and companies (if the latter are favorable) which means that the workers will get financial and healthcare benefits for a few years, providing they sign up for the education and training planned for them, and then assistance with alternative employment (preferably in renewable energy jobs, but they can take other employment if they choose). The issues for companies will be taken up in talking about investment.

6. Application of the principles of energy democracy: In terms of income, control, jobs, and community owned or cooperative businesses, the Plan will produce the widest possible distribution of earning benefits, and meet the criteria of energy democracy – which means that the process should favor local community and worker owned cooperative type enterprises in their selections of vendors for goods and services, and in local utilities that produce renewable energy and supply it to the electric grid.

The Plans for the US, California and the Green New Deal will put the US in a good position to implement its part of the Global Plan, and to help other nations that need help. The lessons that are learned from California, as well as other nations that are leading, will help convince all of the nations of the world to agree to the Global Plan and model their own national Plans accordingly.

Chapter 7

National Energy, Climate and Ecosystems Plans for Other Major Emitter Nations

China, India and the European Union

Current Situation for China

China has already begun to suffer from the effects of Climate Change with temperature rises, massive floods, cyclones hitting the coast and the damage to agriculture. The rain was about 1.8% higher in 2017 than in previous years. The Tibetan Plateau has suffered from temperature increases that are about four times faster than elsewhere. In 2017, the annual average atmospheric concentration of gases measured at the Wanlinguan Station were 404.4 parts per million (ppm) for carbon dioxide, 190.7 parts per billion (ppb) for methane and 329.7 ppb for nitrous oxide. Chinese citizens have begun to recognize and understand the impact of Climate Change, understand the need for personal actions to reduce their carbon footprints, and are generally supportive of fiscal and taxation policies to solve the problem.

Rising sea level can be devastating for China as even a one meter rise in sea level will have a massive effect on the coastal cities of Shanghai, Tianjin and Guangzhou, and would displace an estimated 67 million people. The effect of drought and floods have been increasing in severity with damage to natural environment, infrastructure and agriculture, that worsen living conditions and poverty. In North China, with increasing temperatures and evaporation there is increased drought and water shortage. Although southern China gets more rainfall, the water flows away in floods, and generally water shortage issues are a concern for all of China. Then there are the bad effects on human health due to increases in infectious diseases such as diarrhea and cholera, the destruction of ecologically vulnerable areas and the increase in poverty of the populations living in these areas. Glaciers in the northwest part of China are melting and will be increasingly threatened by Climate Change.

The much higher levels of soot and smog have had a damaging effect on air quality in China with very bad effects for human health. The government has done much to try and reduce pollution of particulates (like smoke) and sulfur dioxide (that also causes acid rain), but the levels of ozone pollution have increased from cars, factories and power plants. However, after a slight decrease in the 2015-2017 period, coal use has expanded again. With China basing most of its progress on coal to produce electricity in power plants, the air quality in most regions of China has become very unhealthy. All of this, together with increasing temperatures, will worsen the air's effect on human health, and is leading to increased deaths from pollution. China has suffered severe impacts because of Climate Change by the way of melting glaciers, overflow of glacial lakes, decrease in the water of major rivers, rising sea levels (affecting the big coastal cities like Shanghai and Hong Kong), sinking of land in Shanghai, loss of biodiversity, and worsening natural disasters. [42]

China's Greenhouse Gas Emissions and Current and Projected Energy Use

China is the largest consumer and producer of coal in the world, and its share of coal in its energy consumption declined in 2010 from 80% to about 60% in 2017 (close to the percentage shown in the pie chart below). In this period, imports rose to make up for decrease in domestic production and new coal fired power plants were constructed to meet the increasing electricity demand. **As of 2018, about 260 GW (gigawatts) of coal power plants were under construction, and China was building coal power plants in other countries. China's coal production went from about 1,000 million metric tons (Mmt) in 1990, to about 1,500 Mmt in 2000 and then shot up to about 3,500 Mmt by about 2011. As of 2018, its domestic production was 3,550 Mmt, imports were 295 Mmt (mainly from Indonesia and Australia), and total coal consumption was 3,845 Million Metric Tons. In 2014,**

the installed capacity for coal based electric power production was 907 GW (Giga Watts) or about 77% of its total electric generation capacity. As coal power plants do not run at full capacity, the electrical energy produced may be less than that indicated by capacity.

Most of the coal used by industry is in the making of steel. Although coal is not allowed to be used in cities, rural areas use coal for domestic consumption (mainly cooking), which leads to very high levels of indoor air pollution and severe health problems among the rural population. The burning of coal emits arsenic, fluorine, aromatic polycyclic hydrocarbons and mercury. Severe arsenic poisoning, skeletal fluorosis (about 10 million people suffering from it), esophageal and lung cancers, and selenium poisoning, are some of the severe health problems that result. A World Bank study had revealed that air pollution, mainly from coal but also from car exhausts, leads to about 750,000 deaths every year. **Most importantly for Climate Change, because of coal, China has become the largest emitter of carbon dioxide, emitting about 25% of the whole world's emissions. This amount does not include carbon dioxide emissions from coal mine fires (often from abandoned mines) that are estimated to add about 360 million metric tons of carbon dioxide.**

China's oil consumption has been high also, and the consumption of natural gas has been growing. China has taken significant action in renewable energy, reaching about 4% of its total use by 2017. See below for the total energy consumption of China in 2017 as a pie chart. China has also engaged in a significant level of reforestation activity.

For emissions, from 3,300 MTCO2e (million metric tons of CO2, carbon dioxide, equivalent), its greenhouse gas emissions increased to about 5,100 MTCO2e by the year 2,000, to 10,900 MtCO2e by the year 2010, and on to a higher 12,800 MtCO2e by 2015 (Climate Tracker information). Its emissions were close to 15,000 MtCO2e by mid 2019. **So, while its emissions increased by about 50% from 1990 to 2000, during the that period 2000-2019, its emissions have TRIPLED or had gone up by about 300% and are essentially double the US emissions of 6,670 MtCO2e.**

Current Projections by an Energy Institute (ETRI) for 2050 are shown next after the 2017 pie chart. Based on the China National Petroleum Corporation's Energy and Technology Research Institute (CNPC-ETRI) report the 2017 total energy consumption was as shown on the following page. [43]

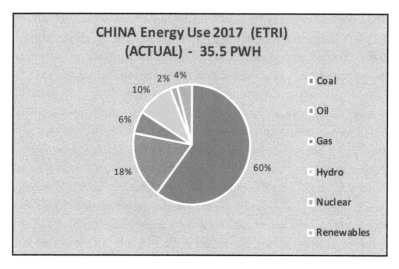

CHINA'S ENERGY CONSUMPTION IN 2017

China's Energy Consumption in 2017. As can be seen, this was met about 60% by coal, 18% by oil and 6% by natural gas, or about 84% by fossil fuels. Renewable energy, although small at 4% was growing rapidly. The total energy use of 35.5 PWH (Peta Watt Hours or 10E15 watt hours, or 3,050 Million Metric Tons of Oil Equivalent) was higher than that of the US, which was 28.8 PWH.

The projected energy consumption for 2050 is as follows:

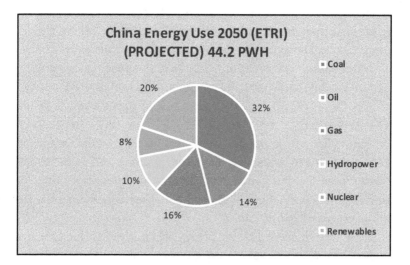

CHINA'S ENERGY CONSUMPTION PROJECTED FOR 2050

As can be seen, this is projected to be met about 32% by coal, 14% by oil and 16% by natural gas, or about 62% by fossil fuels.

Renewable energy (mainly solar and wind) grows to about 20%. The total energy use of 44.2 PWH (Peta Watt Hours or 10E15 watt hours), will grow from the 2017 energy use of 35.5 PWH, but the Carbon dioxide emissions would still very high at 7,700 Million metric tons of CO2, driven a lot by a high coal use. This is shown in the following pie chart.

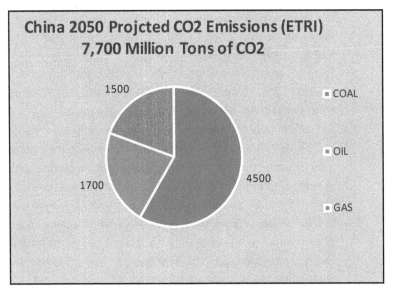

China 2050 Projcted CO2 Emissions (ETRI)
7,700 Million Tons of CO2

1500

1700

4500

- COAL
- OIL
- GAS

CHINA CO2 EMISSIONS PROJECTED FOR 2050

If this happens then the Global Climate Change goals
of 1.5C for the world will not be met!

We now present the Plan for China, that will be much better for China and for the world.

Energy, Climate and Ecosystem Plan for China

The Plan for China to achieve the above is as follows:

1. China as per its INDC, Intended National Determined Contributions for the Paris Agreement, said that its greenhouse gas emissions would peak by 2030, and committed to reducing its emission only after that. Instead, the Plan is calling for its emissions to start reducing immediately – as it has had since 1992 to increase its emissions for development.
2. Energy use of China will GROW from 35.5 PWH (petawatt Hours) in 2017 to 44.2 PWH by 2050, the same as projected by their ETRI. All of it will be renewable energy.
3. ALL of the coal fired and natural gas electric power plants will be REPLACED by a combination of renewable energy (mainly solar PV) and battery storage power plants, with evening night power provided initially by small natural gas plants and later by storage fuel power plants. It will benefit as it is the largest and lowest cost producer of solar panels.
4. ALL coal use in Industry will be **replaced** by electrification and storage fuels, and the added electricity generated by renewable energy (mainly solar PV). Eliminating coal will get rid of the polluted air that the Chinese people are suffering from. They do not need it when clean solar energy is available.
5. ALL oil use in transportation will be transitioned to electric cars and storage fuel vehicles by developing solar-electric highways, with the sale of fossil fuel cars stopping by 2030, and all fossil fuel cars (about 200 million currently) replaced by electric cars and storage fuel cars by 250.
6. China will need to engage in the technical and infrastructure programs to electrify its industry, transportation, and buildings, and produce the added electric power with use of renewable energy (mainly solar PV), and expand its electricity production 4-5 fold.
7. China will participate in an advanced RDD&D (Research, Development, Demonstration and Deployment) consortium for the development of Green methods that use renewable energy to produce and use "storage" fuels like ammonia

and hydrogen. Already it is doing much research, but it needs to proceed to practical application. It also needs to proceed to develop the means of storing, transporting and using storage fuels.

8. China has done well with High Speed Rail development along its eastern coast. It now needs to expand this in all directions going westwards, so as to replace much of the airline traffic to the interior, and reduce its air travel to the interior.

9. China has done a massive job in terms of reforestation. As part of the Global Plan to add 1 billion hectares (Chapter 6), China needs to bring the total to 80 additional million hectares (40 million hectares for temperate forests and 40 million hectares for tropical forests). However, it needs to pay more attention to biodiversity and the needs of and control by local communities that already live in these areas.

10. China needs a massive program for coastal ecosystems along its entire east coast (14,500 kilometers or about 9,010 miles from the Gulf of Bohai in the north to the Gulf of Tonkin in the south) along the lines of the global Blue Carbon Initiative and add mangrove swamps, salt marshes and sea grasses. China's coastal ecosystems are under attack, and since the 1950s, its coastline has lost 57% of the its coastal wetlands, 73% of its mangrove cover and 80% of its coral reefs. China needs to go beyond restoration to a massive re-introduction and replanting of its coastal ecosystems.

11. China needs to use all of the financing outlined in chapter 9 to fund its Climate Change transition. Aside from damage to Climate Change, it has been estimated that China needs to apply a tax of about 23% on the price of coal, to make up from losses to its economy (health, pollution, etc.) that are estimated to be as much as 7% of its GDP.

12. China then needs to cooperate with and collaborate with the rest of the world through the UNFCCC process and otherwise, so that the global Climate Change action plan can succeed. US and China should cooperate in this process to help the rest of the world, even as they aggressively implement their own plans.

The Plan proposes the following energy strategy for China.

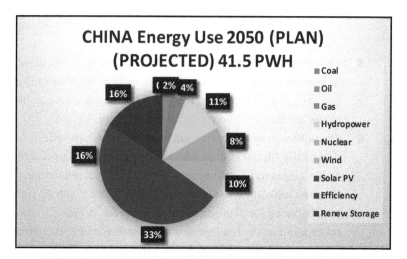

CHINA Energy Use 2050 (PLAN) (PROJECTED) 41.5 PWH

CHINA ENERGY USE PROJECTED FOR 2050 BY THE PLAN

Instead of 44.2 PWH, the Plan shows that 41.5 PWH could be achieved – still a big growth from 2017. Hydropower and nuclear are the same as projected by ETRI above. Fossil fuels go down to about 6% of the total, wind power going to a large part of China's wind availability, solar PV expanding to be about 33% of the total, efficiency at about 16%, and energy through renewable energy based storage fuels contributing about 16% also. This will meet all of China's energy needs and carbon dioxide emissions from fossil fuels will be down to very low levels.

As for the rest of the world, non-carbon storage fuels will be needed that can be produced with renewable energy. China has already done research on these fuels, and is engaging in research and development to develop the use of these fuels. As global RDD&D (Research, Development, Demonstration & Deployment) on storage fuels makes progress as per the Global Plan, then these fuels will become available, and China can use solar PV electric power to produce these fuels or import them as it imports oil and natural gas today. These fuels, like hydrogen and ammonia, will also replace gasoline (petrol) and diesel as automotive fuels.

Being the biggest nation of East Asia and one that has developed good financial and technical resources, China should cooperate with the other nations of east Asia, some of which have similar capabilities, to help the nations of the region meet their plans and help implement the Global Plan. China should modify its planning, get rid of coal and switch totally to renewable energy. That will be good for its health and economy. If it does not do that, and India does the same, the climate crisis will not be solved.

Current Situation for India

India has suffered and will be affected by Climate Change. At the same time, there are some significant actions that it is taking, but much more that it can do to help with the national, regional and global solutions to Climate Change.

First the impact of Climate Change.

The Impact of Climate Change on India

India is feeling the impact of Climate Change already through increasing temperatures, droughts, massive rains and floods, land-slides caused by heavy rains, melting glaciers, water shortages, cyclones, and coastal storms. The Indian Meteorological Department (IMD) says that these events are increasing in both frequency and severity. About 2,400 people in India have lost their lives during 2018-2019 due to extreme weather related events such as cyclones and floods.

Heatwaves: Data released by IMD indicate that from 1901-10 period to the 2009-2018 period, average temperatures in India rose by about 0.6 degrees Celsius (about 1.1 degrees Fahrenheit). However, there are other analyses and reports that indicate that average temperatures may rise by about 4 degrees Celsius by the end of the century. Heatwaves are becoming more common, and in Delhi the number of days that crossed 35 degrees Celsius in the period 2009-2018 increased to 1,613 days from 1009 days in the period 1959-68. Other major cities such as Mumbai, Bengaluru and Hyderabad have had similar heat waves. Although the cities see higher temperatures than the rural areas because of the heat island effect (a higher level of concrete in the cities), the rural areas suffer more from the heat waves as very few people there have air conditioning, and so they have a higher level of fatalities. As with heat waves in recent years, this was accompanied by drought and water shortages in many parts of the country. The city of Chennai, in southern India with a population of about 9 million, ran out of water in June 2019 as the monsoon was delayed and the reservoirs that previously supplied water ran dry. It had been recorded that for many years, in order to make Chennai into a "modern" hub with a high level of information technology, all wetlands had been paved over for new building developments making the situation worse.

What the heatwaves mean for the Himalayan region is harsher conditions in the hills and mountains. The Himalayan glaciers have begun to melt, and a number of glacial lakes have appeared as a result, together with the possibility of massive floods if these lakes suddenly release their water. Even more troublesome is the prospect for the supply of water in the northern Gangetic plane and for the Indus rivers going west through Punjab and Kashmir to Pakistan, that rely on snow melt to provide water for the rivers during the summer months. **When the glaciers are gone, there is the prospect of all of the rivers of northern India running dry in the summer months before the monsoon arrives.**

Catastrophic Rains, Floods and Landslides: As with other parts of the world, the increased global temperatures have led to increased evaporation in oceans, which come down in concentrated locations as very severe rains. India has been no exception. Next to the heat waves, the major effect on India of Climate Change has been the change of the Monsoon season, which usually lasts from June to September. As summer approaches, the winds from the southwest pick up moisture from the Indian Ocean, the Arabian Sea and The Bay of Bengal. They provide initial rains mainly in the western part of the peninsula, get contained by the Himalayan mountains and head northwest and provide rain over the Indo-Gangetic plain all the way to the north. Then as the winds shift, the monsoon retraces its path and provides rain along its path, and then after moving over the Bay of Bengal, provides a second period of rains over the peninsula.

However, Climate Change is disturbing this pattern in an unfavorable way. The changing weather patterns are often delaying the monsoon, worsening the heat wave and drought situations and then, because there is excess moisture, leading to very heavy rains and floods. In 2019, the rains were the heaviest on record and the retreat of the monsoon, which is normally by September end, got delayed to October 10. Although the average amount of rainfall is about the same, the rainfall is often heavier and more concentrated with more centimeters or inches of rain in shorter times, and often leads to catastrophic flooding events. The UN Office of Disaster Risk Reduction has said that in India, from 67 flood events in the 1996-2005 period, the flood events increased to 90 during the 2006-2015 period. A 2017 study showed that there was a three-fold increase in extreme rain events from 1950 to 2015.

Examples of extreme rain and flood related events are many. As early as 2005, the Indian state of Maharashtra was hit with heavy rains and floods. The city of Mumbai was hit with 944 mm (37.17 inches) of rain in a 24 hour period on July 26, 2005, and torrential rain continued during the next week. Inadequate drainage capabilities with little development of drainage projects, building developments that caused water retention and drainage issues, and the destruction of mangrove swamps for "development" only made things much worse. Five years later, during three hours of the early morning of August 6, 2010, in the area of Ladakh in northern India, the capital city of Leh and surrounding areas were hit with heavy rains that led to flash floods, debris flows and mudflows (landslides) in which at least a few hundred people died, including some foreign tourists. Some places received as much as 250 millimeters (mm – or 9.8 inches) of rain, and within one three hour period, rain fell at a rate as high as 150 mm per hour (5.9 inches/hour), with gushing water and mud as high as 10 feet (about 3 meters) in some places. Leh and some of the surrounding areas were totally devastated. Similar to Ladakh, the northern state of Uttarakhand was hit with heavy rains, flashfloods and landslides in 2013, that were described as a century scale event that led to largescale devastation. **I had vacationed in Leh earlier in the year, and had enjoyed the beauty mountainous ecosystems of Ladakh, and so was very saddened by the environmental destruction of Leh by a Climate Change related disaster. For those who wish to see the beautiful places of the world, we need to start doing it in zero or low carbon modes, if these places are not to be destroyed.**

Tropical Cyclones (what elsewhere may be called typhoons or hurricanes) have been worsening with Climate Change. The east coast of the peninsular part of India is more prone to cyclones from the Bay of Bengal, as compared with the west coast from the Arabian Sea. The Indian Government's National Cyclone Risk Mitigation

Project (NCRMP) reported that from 1891 to 2002, about 300 cyclones hit the east coast and about 50 cyclones hit the west coast. The east coast is also subject to storm surges of 3 to 12 meters (varying with location) and is also prone to tsunamis. In 2004, the ocean floor near Indonesia lifted by as much as 40 meters with a magnitude 9.1 quake leading to a tsunami that killed about 100,000 people in the city of Banda Aceh in Indonesia, and killing more on the shores of Thailand, India and Sri Lanka. The east coast of India, and the Bay of Bengal nations in general, need effective strategies and measures for emergency alerts to tsunamis, and effective disaster reduction strategies for cyclones, especially as these get worse with Climate Change.

In June 2008 India announced a National Action Plan on Climate Change (NAPCC) which took up eight national missions on water, sustaining the Himalayan ecosystem and developing knowledge on Climate Change, solar PV, energy efficiency, sustainable habitats, sustainable agriculture, and greening India (reforestation). Since most of the programs were with different ministries of the government and because they were not funded adequately, they remained with little to some effectiveness. The exception was the National Solar Mission, which was much better funded. The goal of the solar program was to establish 20 GW (giga watt or 20,000 MW – mega watt) of capacity by 2022, which was later increased to 100 GW. As of July 2018, the nation had an installed capacity of about 21.8 GW, so it had already met the goal of 20GW. However, in order to meet its goal of 100GW by 2022, India would have to add about 20GW each year. Roof top solar did not receive any special attention, funding or enablement, and so it remained very small (Down to Earth Article, 2018). [44]

India's Current and Projected Energy Use

India's energy consumption in 2018 grew very fast at an annual rate of 7.9%, and at 5.8% of total global consumption, India was the second largest energy consuming nation after China and the US.

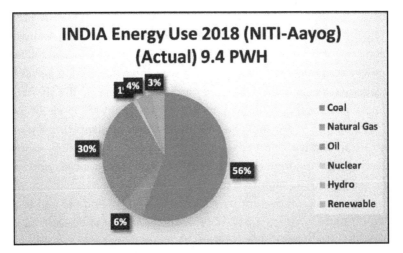

INDIA'S ENERGY CONSUMPTION IN 2018

India's energy consumption in 2018 was about 809 Mtoe (Million tons of oil equivalent) or 9.4 PWH (petawatt hours – or about 9,400 billion kilowatt hours) in electrical energy terms. As can be seen, India's energy needs were met 56% by coal, 6% by natural gas, and 30% by oil.

India is very heavily reliant on imports, and in 2018 imported about 46% of the energy it used. It imported about 31% of its coal, 53% of its small consumption of natural gas, and as much as 86% of its oil (petroleum). India also has a world class refining capacity, so that in 2015, even as it imported about 195 Mtoe of oil, it imported refined products like gasoline or petrol and diesel of about 23 million tons, and exported refined products of about 55 million tons. Its reliance on imports is only expected to grow, so that by 2030, its energy imports will be about 53% of its consumption. **In 2018, the nation generated 1.55 PWH (or about 1,550 billion KWH) of electric energy, out of which about 66% was with coal and a total of 80% was with use of all fossil fuels.** Although solar and wind together generated about 6.5% of its electricity, this is still small compared to what it does with coal and oil. [45]

The World Energy Outlook for 2018 by the International Energy Agency and the International Energy Outlook for 2019 by the US Energy Information Agency, as well as India's own information, are projecting that **India will have the fastest growing energy consumption of any nation in the world,** and given the size and higher growth rate of its economy, will be the second largest contributor (about 18%) to increasing global energy demand by 2035 (after China), and will consume more energy than the US by 2040. While wind and solar power are projected to grow in a big way, India is planning a significant increase in its nuclear power program, increasing the share of nuclear in electrical energy generation from about 4% to about 9% in the next 25 years. India has five nuclear power plants under construction and plans to add another 18 reactors by 2025, the second highest addition in the world. According to current policies, however, because of its high coal reserves, India is projected to continue to rely heavily on coal for its energy use, and continue to use coal significantly for electric power generation even up to 2050. India is aiming to do what China did from 2000-2019 – base its fast energy growth a lot on coal by using its domestic coal reserves. This will only add to a worsening of Climate Change as India's carbon dioxide emissions will grow. In 2017, India's GHG emissions were 2,380 MTCO2e (millions of metric tons of carbon dioxide equivalent), compared with China at 12,450 MtCO2e.

We now look at India's overall energy and electric consumption projections for 2050, as pieced together from the World Energy Outlook 2018 and the plan published by the Government of India. [26]

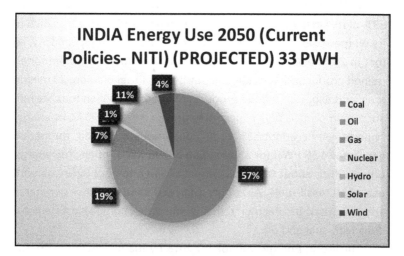

INDIA'S ENERGY CONSUMPTION PROJECTED FOR 2050

India's energy consumption is projected to rise rapidly if its economic growth rate stays comparable to today. The strategy for a very high reliance on coal becomes apparent (57%), with fossil fuels still dominating the energy consumption at about 83%. A big quantitative jump in renewables (solar and wind) is overshadowed percent wise by fossil fuels.

India's energy use is projected to more than triple from about 9.4 PWH in 2018 to about 33 PWH in 2050, becoming about equal to that of the US, and getting to be a close second to China (41-44 PWH). If this happens and since most of this is with coal, India's greenhouse gas emissions will grow to about China's level today, which are about 12,450 MtCO2e (million metric tons of carbon dioxide equivalent).

The Energy, Climate and Ecosystems Plan for India

The high level of India's planned use of coal and oil are clearly not favorable for Climate Change, and are not in India's interest, in both health and economic terms. The plans projected above clearly show the heavy reliance on fossil fuels by India, which plans to use its large coal reserves to power its economic growth, very similar to what China has done from 2000-2018, with some significant growth in nuclear energy and renewables. This strategy has clear disadvantages for India. Its reliance on imports of oil and natural gas are not good for its trade position. Its high expenditures on new nuclear reactors when even its thorium based technologies have not matured makes little sense. Its reliance on coal is not only meaning a very high level of pollution for all its citizens similar to China, but it means a massive increase in its greenhouse gas emissions, which only hurts India as it is one of the nations that is most vulnerable to Climate Change, as has been documented above.

So the Plan, as it has done for the world and for the US and China, proposes a massive replacement of all its coal fired power plants to renewable plus storage energies, an electrification of all sectors of its economy, the vast expansion of a durable, reliable and smart electrical distribution network, a big expansion of roof top solar by significant changes in its policies, a big expansion of small scale solar/bioenergy farms, a massive reforestation and afforestation effort, a massive enhancement of its land based wetlands combined with water harvesting, and the construction and rejuvenation of large scale coastal ecosystems, like its famous Sundarbans ecosystems to the east.

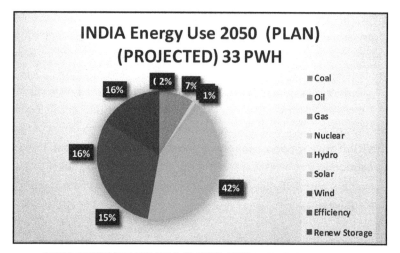

INDIA ENERGY USE PROJECTED FOR 2050 BY THE PLAN

The 2050 Energy Plan for India's shows a similar tripling of energy use (considering energy efficiency enhancements of about 16%). Fossil fuels are down to about 9%, and solar and wind have expanded to about 57% of the total. About 16% of the nation's energy needs are projected to be from non-carbon storage fuels produced from renewable energy (Renew Storage). With this, India will essentially be free of energy imports and its greenhouse gas emissions will be very low.

So here is the Plan description for India.

Energy, Climate and Ecosystem Plan for India

1. Energy use will grow from 9.4 PWH (petawatt Hours) in 2018 to 33 PWH by 2050. India has a very high solar energy resource, and with the low cost of solar electricity (demonstrated to be about US $1 per watt), solar energy will be India's mainstay.

2. ALL of the coal fired and natural gas electric power plants and captive or otherwise diesel generating sets will be **replaced** by a combination of renewable energy (mainly solar PV) and battery storage power plants, with evening night power provided initially by small natural gas plants and later by storage fuel power plants. It will benefit much from

improvements in health, cleanliness and beauty that the absence of coal brings.

3. ALL coal use in industry will be **replaced** by electricity based methods and the added electricity generated by Renewable energy (mainly solar PV), supplemented by use of storage fuels in applications that cannot be electrified.

4. With a high solar resource, solar-electric highways and roadways make a lot of sense, and will be implemented countrywide. Low carbon transportation modes need interlinking, from pedways and bikeways, linked to mass transit rail and bus lines, linked to high speed rail and all other modes.

5. India will need to engage in the technical and infrastructure programs to electrify its industry, transportation, and buildings, and produce the added electric power with use of renewable energy (mainly solar PV). India will need to expand its electric transmission lines 4 to 5 fold to meet the needs of full electrification of its economy.

6. India will participate in an advance RDD&D (Research, Development, Demonstration and Deployment) consortium for the development of green methods that use renewable energy electricity to produce and use storage fuels like ammonia and hydrogen, and develop the needed infrastructure for their use.

7. India needs to develop high speed rail throughout the country so as to replace much of the airline traffic, so that transportation within the country, both over long distances and within cities is "green" and zero carbon. This will massively reduce emissions from the burning of jet fuel for aviation. India should encourage and cooperate with South Asian, Middle Eastern and Southeast Asia countries in developing a high speed rail network that traverses this part of Asia, going all the way through Burma to Southeast Asia.

8. India has begun some reforestation. As part of the Global Plan to add 1 billion hectares (Chapter 6), India needs to bring the total to 30 additional million hectares in the non-mountainous regions. However, in the Himalayan region (hills and mountains) it needs to cooperate with Nepal and Bhutan to reforest and afforest the entire region, an added 20 million

hectares. This will do much to improve the micro-climate of the Himalayan region, and be combined with wildfire mitigation strategies during the hot dry summers.

9. India needs a massive program for coastal ecosystems along the lines of the global Blue Carbon initiative and add mangrove swamps, salt marshes and sea grasses. India's coastline length is about 7,500 kilometers (about 5,400 kilometers on the mainland, for the Bay of Bengal, Arabian Sea and Indian Ocean), and about 2,100 kilometers along its islands.

10. India then needs to cooperate with and collaborate with the rest of the world through the UNFCCC process and otherwise, so that the global Climate Change Action Plan can succeed. US, the European Union, China and India, as the biggest greenhouse gas emitters, should cooperate in this process to help the rest of the world, even as they aggressively implement their own plans.

Non-Carbon Storage Fuel Technologies for India

India, with its high level of solar insolation (which means that India receives a larger number of hours on the average of full sunlight), has solar panels that generate a significant amount of electricity. Instead of just 1,500 KWH (kilowatt hour or energy unit) generated on the average every year by 1 kilowatt (KW or 1,000 watts) worth of solar panels in temperate areas, solar panels of this size generate 2,000 KWH or more during the year. Also, considering that the cost of solar panels and total solar systems have been rapidly dropping, and will continue to drop, it makes a lot of sense for India to use some of its arid land areas to produce large amounts of "Green" hydrogen and ammonia, and store it and use it locally to produce electricity when the sun is not shining, or transport it to other power plants, or to the solar electric charging stations where it can be used as fuel for vehicles, to replace gasoline (petrol) and diesel and coal.

India already uses ammonia for agriculture in significant commercial quantities. As of January 2019, India's ammonia production capacity will grow from 15.6 million metric tons per annum (mtpa – million tons per year) in 2017 to 25.5 mtpa in 2022, about a 10.3% compounded annual growth rate (this compares with 175 mtpa of ammonia consumed globally). In 2017, about 93% of India's consumption was used for urea and ammonium phosphate fertilizers. Imports as a percentage of consumption is expected to decrease from 15.8% in 2017, to 8.1% in 2022. [46]

So, the Plan is proposing, as for the Global Plan and as for other nations, that India invest heavily in every way in the green production of non-carbon storage fuels, as a way of storing renewable energy, (mainly solar PV energy), and making these gaseous and liquid fuels available on a commercial scale in transport, in generating electricity and in powering industry. In storing renewable energy in the form of storage fuels, India and the world will totally overcome the issue of the variable nature of renewable energy generated electricity and make it available as and when and where needed. India needs to cooperate globally with all the nations that are active in this area, even in the RDD&D (Research, Development, Demonstration and Deployment).

Being the biggest nation in South Asia, it should also cooperate with all the other nations of South Asia in meeting their own and global Climate Change goals – as all the needs of the region will be similar.

Current Situation for the European Union

Europe was the center of the Industrial Revolution that has changed the world. Much of the Industrial Revolution of the past centuries was based on coal, from the start of the Watts Steam Engine to the steel factories that built the continent. In a sense, Europe has been thought of as the "developed" region of the world, which together with the other industrialized nations, represent what a "developed" area should look like and what the other nations of the world should aspire to. Culturally and architecturally, Europe has done well to preserve most of its cultural heritage, making it the most sought after tourist destination in the world. However, Climate Change is beginning to devastate Europe in a way that much of that "developed" nature may be unraveled.

The Impacts of Climate Change on the European Union (EU)

Europe is beginning to suffer from heat waves, floods, droughts, fires and sea level rise like never before. The heat waves and floods have been catastrophic. For the past decades, the impacts of Climate Change have been worsening for Europe. In July 2019, one of the worst heat waves ever hit Europe and caused widespread devastation. Several people died in the heat wave, France hit temperature records in many places, in Belgium and the Netherlands the temperatures exceeded 40 degrees Celsius (110 degrees Fahrenheit) for the first time in recorded history, and Greenland saw fires. Extreme temperatures have been increasing in Europe for the past 20-30 years. 2003 saw the hottest summer in 500 years till then, and resulted in an estimated 70,000 deaths. In 2000 and 2007, England and Wales saw heavy and record rains, in 2007 Greece saw a heat wave and wildfires, and in 2010 in Russia (although not part of the EU) saw a record heat wave that resulted in an estimated 55,000 deaths.

Europe has experienced heavy rains and floods like it has never experienced before. River floods used to occur sometimes, but recently, these have become heavy and catastrophic. In the last few centuries there was flooding, but now almost on a yearly basis there are heavy rains and floods in some part of Europe with severe disruptions, financial losses and its effect on tourism. The Netherlands has famous dikes to protect against the sea, but now with rising sea levels, all coastal regions will be affected and dike levels may have to be raised. Arctic ice has been receding, glaciers have been melting, water shortages have been looming (especially in the Mediterranean region that is seeing more severe heat waves and droughts), wildfires are being experienced and agriculture is being disrupted. A recent study of 571 cities concluded that floods, heat waves and droughts will be affecting all of them as Climate Change worsens.

Current EU Energy Situation and Use

The European Union (EU27) consists of 27 nation states. Its population is predicted to grow from about 505 million in 2017 to about 525 million. Its GDP (Gross Domestic Product or size of the economy) is projected to grow from about 13,000 billion Euros to about 22,000 billion Euros in 2050. If it can be considered a nation, the European Union has been leading the charge in renewable energy, with Germany being a leader in the implementing solar PV energy. Renewable energy production (including bio-fuels) contributed as much as 10% in 2017 to the total energy consumption. The European Union has the best and the most extensive networks of High Speed Rail in world, that extends from Germany and France to Spain. The EU has also led the charge in terms of energy efficiency, with efforts to make every aspect of its energy use more efficient, with the ultimate goal of reducing its energy consumption even as it grows economically.

As of 2017, even though the European Union had made much progress in renewable energy, it was still heavily dependent on fossil fuels.

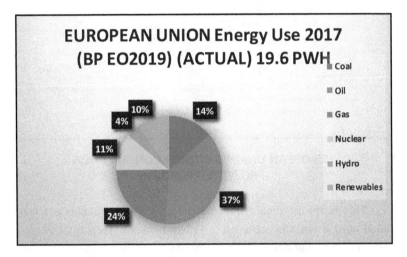

EUROPEAN UNION'S ENERGY CONSUMPTION IN 2017

As can be seen, the EU is still heavily dependent on fossil fuels for about 75% of its use, even though nuclear is a significant 11% and renewables (including bio-fuels) have reached more than 10%. The 19.6 PWH is in the unit of Peta Watt Hours, or about 10E15 watt hours, which is the equivalent of 1,689 Mtoe – million tons of oil equivalent. As of 2017, this level of energy consumption was double that of India, and about half of the US and China. [47]

There is a projection by a group that advocates the use BECCS (Bio-Energy Carbon Capture and Storage) – which means growing large amounts of Biomass (most probably on agricultural land), combusting it to generate electric energy and then capturing the carbon and storing it. It projects that if there are not aggressive moves towards reducing carbon emissions, in a Reference Scenario, fossil fuel use will remain high but renewables will grow to 14% of total. However, if aggressive polices are pursued to substitute fossil fuels with renewables (which they call Policy Success scenario), then the same group projects that fossil fuel consumption will decrease significantly. [48] [49]

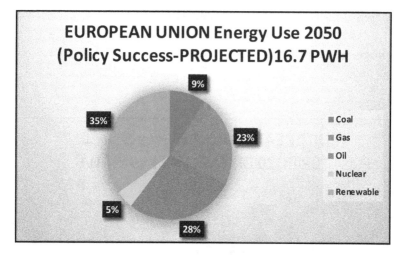

**EUROPEAN UNION'S ENERGY CONSUMPTION
PROJECTED FOR 2050**

This is the projection for 2050, if aggressive policies are pursued, and if what is achieved is Policy Success, then total energy consumption will decrease (from 19.6 to 16.7 PWH), with fossil fuels at about 60%. Renewable energy will be up to a much higher 35%. This will certainly not succeed in getting the European Union to be Carbon Neutral by 2050, which the EU is aiming to do.

The Energy, Climate and Ecosystems Plan for the European Union

Wind energy expands at twice the rate by using both onshore and offshore production. Solar energy expands at a much faster pace than others have projected. For the first time, it is assumed that Europe will use added renewable energy (wind, solar and tidal, etc.) to make and use renewable energy based non-carbon storage fuels like hydrogen and ammonia. The European nations have taken significant action in the area of actually undertaking research, development and demonstration of the production of these non-carbon fuels from green (renewable energy sources) – demonstration projects are already underway.

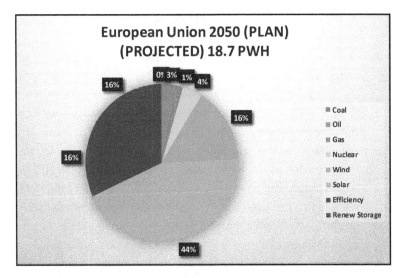

**EUROPEAN UNION'S ENERGY USE
PROJECTED FOR 2050 BY THE PLAN**

Total energy use FOR EU27 only declines slightly. Coal is gone totally, oil remains at 3% and gas at 1%. Nuclear at 4% is at about what others have projected. The big change is a big expansion in wind (16%), a massive expansion of solar (to 44%), a big increase in energy efficiency, and the coming of age of the use of non-carbon storage fuels produced through renewable energy.

Here is a description of the Energy, Climate and Ecosystem Plan for the EU

The Plan proposed here in this Book is much more aggressive in that it essentially gets fossil fuels down to near zero (with coal down to zero), and does all of the rest with renewable energy, or using energy storage methods that store renewable energy. Coal needs to be gone globally by 2050. **If Poland needs special help, then the EU should help it transition out of coal.** Here is the bullet point list.

1. Overall – Transitioning Out of Coal – Coal and natural gas power plants will be replaced by power plants that have solar PV + battery + natural gas backup. The gas plants will be replaced by "storage fuel" power plants as soon as these become available. Transitioning out of coal for industry – all

coal use will be replaced by electrification that is powered by renewable energy or uses storage fuels

2. Overall – Transitioning Out of Oil – Mainly the transition of oil based transportation on the roads and highways to reliance on electrical energy (mainly solar energy) and storage fuels.

3. Overall — Transitioning out of Natural Gas – Europe is overly dependent on natural gas and has to import most of it. This is a very unhealthy situation which is wholly unnecessary, as the EU can meet all of its power and heating needs with renewable energy, where it does not have to pay for the fuel. The entire Mediterranean region can use solar PV as well as concentrated solar power (CSP), which uses the heat of sunlight to generate electricity and can also store energy in molten salts for use at night.

4. Storage fuels RDD&D (Research, Development, Demonstration & Deployment) – Some European nations are leading the research (along with Japan and Australia, and some in the US) into the production of non-carbon storage fuels. This has to proceed beyond demonstration to large scale deployment. Main areas are: Green production, storage and distribution of fuels, use of fuels for power generation, and their use in vehicles.

5. Solar–electric highways, roadways and trainways – For road transportation, solar PV charging stations and storage fuel production and supply stations can be placed along highways and roads.

6. There will be full electrification of buildings, homes and industry to the maximum extent, with the rest of the needs being met with storage fuels. Electrical transmission capacity will need to be expanded accordingly.

7. Carbon Sinks – Reforest and afforest the European Union, add coastal ecosystems – Europe needs to add 40 million hectares – mainly temperate forests, all over Europe. This will begin to restore much of Europe's beauty and wildlife. However, as in other regions of the world, the forests need to be designed so that wildfires are easy to control. Europe needs to add coastal ecosystems along the coastlines for the Arctic, the British Isles, the Baltic Sea, the Atlantic Coast, and the Mediterranean sea. Mangrove swamps, salt marshes, sea grasses and coral reefs.

8. Energy Efficiency – new and existing – Buildings, homes, industry, transportation, and agriculture – The EU has been good

at this – all programs can be expanded and strengthened.

9. Adaptation to heat and floods – The EU needs to have a continental plan for preparing for heatwaves, not only by increasing green areas, but also by assisting all of its populations with cooling shelters and low carbon methods of cooling its homes and buildings. With the catastrophic floods in the recent past, Europe needs to put in place an advanced flood control, water harvesting, land wetlands restoration and coastal wetland building that will help it deal with both floods and coastal storms.

10. Aviation and High Speed Rail – Europe will transition to using aviation travel only for long haul or large distances, like flying into Europe from elsewhere. Europe already has major high speed rail networks in some of the main EU nations. All travel within Europe will transition to high speed rail, inter-city rail, mass transit and bikeways including human powered transportation with electric assist of all types. Europe is already much better in this than other parts of the world, with the exception of Japan and now China.

11. Shipping Transition – storage fuels – Scandinavian nations have started to experiment with use of hydrogen on ships. Other nations are looking into the use of ammonia on ships.

12. Global Leadership – With Europe being the first to announce that it will be climate neutral, with the exception of the state of California in the US, it is in an excellent position to convince the other nations of the world to aim for zero greenhouse gas emissions by 2050.

DIFFERENT TRANSITION STRATEGIES FOR DIFFERENT NATIONS – ALL CONVERGING OR COOPERATING TO BE PART OF THE TOTAL PLAN

The Intergovernmental Panel on Climate Change (IPCC) in its 2018 report on "Strengthening and Implementing the Global Response," has said that although some nations and regions have begun to do some of the activities and have achieved a little, the "geographic and economic scales at which the required rates of change in the energy, land, urban, infrastructure and industrial systems would need to take place are larger and have no documented historic precedent".

Of the nations that signed the Paris Agreement, the Climate Action Tracker has evaluated the responses of 32 nations that make up about 80% of the global emissions of Greenhouse Gases. As of October 2018, only seven of these nations had made commitments or made efforts to begin to achieve the commitments they voluntarily made at Paris. Morocco and The Gambia led the pack and were the only nations committed to and proceeding to take of the actions needed to keep the world average temperature rise below 1.5 degrees Celsius. The other five nations that have proceeded to act on commitments to keep temperature below 2 degrees Celsius were Bhutan, Costa Rica, Ethiopia, India and Philippines. Morocco has committed to large scale renewable energy projects (42% of its energy needs from renewable by 2020), increased natural gas imports and reduced its fossil fuel subsidies. Gambia is engaging in a massive reforestation project. India is proceeding to generate 40% of its energy from non-fossil fuel sources and is promoting electric vehicles.

Each of the different sets of nations need to have different strategies to get from where they are now to achieve the Plan proposed this book. Broadly speaking, these are the richer income industrial nations, medium income industrial nations, less industrialized, oil producing nations, lesser income nations, and island/small nations.

What the Plan Proposes for the Other Categories of Nations

Industrial and Semi-Industrial Nations

1. All of the Annex I nations (categorized as such in the Kyoto Protocol) need to adopt a plan as outlined in this book and phase out all fossil fuels by 2050 – this includes coal and oil, but also, in the later stage, natural gas. They aggressively need to adopt renewable energy for ALL of their energy needs, and adopt solar PV if they do not have wind potential or access to geothermal or hydro power.

2. Having more resources, they need to aggressively fund all of the tasks needed for RDD&D (Research, Development, Demonstration & Deployment), especially of the means of

producing storage fuels by use of green methods or through use of renewable energy, and getting them to be used on a large commercial scale, up to about 25% of total global energy needs. Japan, Australia, China and to some extent some European nations have begun research in storage fuels that have been described above. More nations need to participate in this and cooperate so that the world can use these fuels to replace fossil fuels entirely. They need to take the lead in setting up the infrastructure for production, storage, transport and supply.

3. They need to enhance and smarten all of their electric grids so that these can meet all of the energy needs of their economies – the interconnection of electric grids between nations must be taken up so that nations can sell surplus electrical energy to neighboring nations.

4. These nations need to end the use of oil and natural gas in their transport sector, and move to electric renewable energy and storage fuels produced by green methods. All of their roadway fleet of vehicles need to transition out of fossil fuels and be replaced – half by 2030 and all by 2050.

5. These nations need to lead the rest in developing the technology and the automatic funding mechanisms that will fund their own transitions and those of the "developing" nations.

OPEC and Other Oil Producing Nations

1. These nations immediately need to use the income from oil to internally transition to renewable energy – many of these nations are in areas where there is ample solar energy – so they should use solar PV in a massive way.

2. In the other direction, they must participate in the production of renewable energy based storage fuels.

3. And finally, they must end the export of oil and reorganize their economies so that they do not rely on this export income any more. Possibly, the world should give them priority in switching to the green production and export of storage fuels.

4. This strategy is true of OPEC nations, but is also true of larger nations like the US and Russia that are major oil producers, for the oil producing and using parts of their economies.

5. Oil producing nations like Saudi Arabia, Iraq and Iran should

use their arid regions to produce solar energy and use that in turn to become exporters of storage fuels, instead of oil or petroleum.

Larger "Developing" Countries

1. These include China, India and Brazil.
2. These nations, especially China and India, need to end the use and/or expansion of the use of coal for electric power production and move to invest instead in a major expansion of renewable energy, detailed plans for China and India are described earlier in this chapter.
3. These nations have had more than 25 years to expand their fossil fuel use to help the poor in their nations escape poverty. Except for the short term expansion in the use of natural gas, these nations need to aggressively transition out of fossil fuels. Solar energy is now lower cost than the other options, and so this makes sense.
4. As China and India have larger populations, they should pay special attention to the needs of their population for energy democracy and to make sure that all of their populations benefit from the energy transition.

Smaller "Developing" Countries

1. These are the vast majority of nations. They should be assisted in making the energy transition out of fossil fuels, maximizing use of renewable energy based electricity and the supply of storage fuels to replace the fossil fuels.
2. As with China, India and Brazil, these nations should pay special attention to the needs of their population for energy democracy and to make sure that all of their populations benefit from the energy transition.
3. At the signing of the Kyoto Protocol and again at the signing of the Paris Agreement, these nations were promised help with technology transfer, financing and institutional advice, which was never delivered. Now the time has come for some automatic funding mechanisms that will be described in a later chapter to fund their actions in a timely manner.

Coal Producing and Exporting Nations

1. These nations have to begin to close down their coal production, transport and export activities and move to transition their electric power production out of coal, first by beginning with the use of renewable energy (mainly solar PV), and then through the use of storage fuels produced by renewable energy.

2. Indonesia, Australia, Russia, Colombia, South Africa and the United States need to begin planning to shut down their mining operations in a phased manner, so that they can stop the export of coal by 2040. This will give time to all the coal importing nations to begin ramping down their coal operations immediately, and start replacing all of their coal use with renewable energy and storage fuels.

Natural Gas Producing and Exporting Nations

1. These nations should continue the production, storage, transport and export of natural gas until such time as it is replaced by renewable energy and eventually by the use of renewable energy based storage fuels

The primary challenge the world faces is to transition out of coal as it is the most polluting and it emits the most heat trapping gases for each unit of heat energy than any other fossil fuel. The construction of new coal fired electric power plants needs to stop immediately and be replaced by solar PV plus battery power plants. Stopping the use of coal will bring many health benefits as well.

Chapter 8

Organizing Globally –
An Implementation Plan that
will be Adequate, Effective
and Timely

To begin with, let us not have any misunderstanding here. This plan, or something like it that the world agrees to, will need a level of cooperation that the world has never seen, a level of leadership that the world has never seen, a level of effective and empowered global organization the world has never had, a level of innovative financing for a global effort that the world has never seen, a level of economic justice the world has never seen, an effectiveness in overcoming the opposition to solutions that the world has never seen, a level of technological, business, social and economic innovation the world has never seen, and a decisive level of organization and timely implementation the world has never seen. Only a good plan, with ALL of that will succeed in keeping the temperature rise to below 1.5 degrees Celsius (2.7 degrees Fahrenheit). It will take something like this even if the world decides to do better.

First, I recommend we start with this Plan and use the above plan and the plans for the major emitting nations in the succeeding chapters, to determine what the respective roles for each nation should be. Since 1992, all developing nations have had the chance to use fossil fuels to further their development. Since ALL fossil fuels now have to go to zero by 2050, there is no question of fair carbon emissions per capita any more. What is true is that the developing nations need help, and that they are helped to make the transition along with the whole world.

The main thing is to agree to a plan and then work the plan in a rapid manner. The aspects that have to be decided are how the global part is to be funded or invested in (see financing section in the next chapter), which nation is going to do what by when, what is the nature of the global organization that will be expanded or created, how much of their internal funding will be provided, the fair and effective manner in which the external global funding will be distributed, and what will the manner in which the global organization they put in place will organize, coordinate and regulate the whole process.

Once this process has been completed, the world will need to draft, sign and ratify a new agreement or protocol that will make it official. However, as compared with the original treaty signed in 1992, or the Kyoto Protocol signed in 1997, or the Paris Agreement, this time the financing aspects will be automatic (no question of nations committing and doing nothing). Also, it will not be either voluntary or mandatory, but the action plans will be jointly worked on by the empowered new or expanded global organization and each nation or group of nations. The Global Plan and the individual plans will be monitored, assisted or coordinated from a "war room" on a continuous basis to solve problems, resolve issues, and direct resources for the plan. This will especially be needed for the processes of Research, Development, Demonstration and Deployment of new technologies or expanded versions of new technologies.

There is a desperate need for national and global leaders to step forward and say that enough is enough, and that now the world needs to *act*. They must begin to think in terms of a Global Plan for the world, such as described in this book, and agree on the rough outlines of a Plan through relatively rapid discussions and high level agreements, at a much faster rate than the UNFCCC process and the annual meetings of the Conference of Parties. There need to be strategy and discussion session in between at high levels and then a discussion on how they will sell it to the world, so that all the nations can agree to it through their democratic processes. **All national leaders need to realize that the time for climate denial is over, and the time for action on effective solutions to Climate Change is now.** In the past, the United States has provided leadership that helped bring about the Paris Agreement. The US needs to not only stop obstructing and non-cooperating, but must show leadership and begin to embrace multi-lateral approaches through the United Nations, or allied gatherings of the world's nations. It must begin to sell to its population internally that they need to cooperate with the UN and the rest of the nations of the world, to make it happen.

The world must move decisively to counter the misinformation by climate deniers and the opposition by fossil fuel producing nations, companies, and political and activist organizations that are spreading misinformation. There needs to develop a substantial understanding that the world must sort through this confusion fast and act. There is effectively now NO uncertainty that we humans are causing global warming and need to act effectively to solve the problem fast.

Defining the New Global Organization Needed

At the present time, the global organization that is central to running the whole process is the UNFCCC (United Nations Framework Convention on Climate Change), with its Secretariat located in Bonn, Germany. As per the UNFCCC website, there are a number of governing, process management, subsidiary, and constituted bodies (organizations) that work with them. Currently, the Conference of Parties (COP) is the supreme body, in which all the nations who sign up are represented, that decides what is agreed on, governs the whole process and holds annual meetings at different locations around the world. The Parties to the Kyoto Protocol and the Parties to the Paris Agreement serve as subsidiary bodies of the UNFCCC, and all are assisted by a Bureau and the Secretariat in Bonn in carrying out the tasks they have decided on. All of these are of course linked with the United Nations and as agreed to by its main enabler, the UN General Assembly. Besides various groups and committees there is of course the IPCC (Intergovernmental Panel on Climate Change) that plays a crucial role in informing the world and the United Nations, and can provide the information and guidance on paths of action.

To organize and implement the plan outlined above in terms of energy planning, emissions reductions, mitigation, rejuvenation of carbon sinks, adaptation and disaster management, will require a much stronger organization that is adequately funded to be able to do all the needed actions in timely manner. The type of organization and strategy should have the combined capabilities of timely effectiveness in implementation and be organized to be as democratic and consensus oriented as possible, while implementing things in such a way as to make the transition just, and apply the principles of energy democracy. The disadvantaged groups, communities and nations should not only be helped to minimize the damage of Climate Change, but also be a major recipient of the benefits and empowerment of the whole process. Such processes are already described in the Sustainable Development Goals defined by the United Nations, but now need to become part of the strategy for Climate Change solutions.

The plan proposed in this book is intended to include ALL of the major aspects that need attention globally, in order to make sure that all important aspects of what is needed are acknowledged and there are no piecemeal approaches that enable success in one area, while ignoring what is needed in another important area. **As stated above, the plan presented in this book is only expected to provide the starting point, and will be modified by the various organizations, governments, and the global organization that coordinates or implements it as one goes along.** So this chapter describes the nature of new or strengthened global organization, planning, finances, strategies and resources that will be needed to organize, negotiate, finance, research, enable and implement a plan that is globally agreed to, in a timely and effective manner.

Here is the framework for a new or strengthened organization.

1. The New Global Organization should be under an empowered UNFCCC organization and a more effective Conference of Parties (COP), which is the democratic assemblage of nations for this purpose. This should be part of a new global agreement and Protocol.

Proposed Organization Chart of New Global Organization Implementing the Global Plan

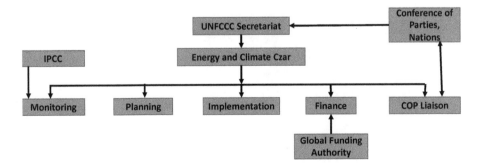

2. The New Organization should have an effective leader and have all the different departments to make it a truly effective organization – see recommended Organizational chart.

3. The Conference of Parties (COP) should act like a legislature is terms of appropriating funds that become available, but the New Organization should have some discretionary funds that it can apply for small and urgent tasks, based on priorities established by the COP.

4. There needs to be a Global Funding Authority formed or an organization that establishes and collects the taxes that all the nations submit after they have met their own needs as per Plan. There needs to be an automatic funding mechanism for helping the developing nations. All approvals and funding should be by stages, so that the early tasks are effectively implemented, and only when there is clear evidence that the implementation is proceeding with integrity, should the following tasks be funded – again in stages.

5. The processes should be such that several committees should be formed of different groups of nations that are empowered to make decisions and take actions during all of the year, based on guidelines established by the global organization and the Conference of Parties. In short, the guidelines and monitoring should be set up front, and a regular and effective auditing function added, but the implementation processes should move ahead with speed, in order to meet the timelines to achieve everything on schedule by 2050.

It is now time for the nations of the world to resolve and move towards a cleaner and more beautiful world, in a way that world has never seen.

Chapter 9

The Investments We Need and Ways of Financing Them

The World Energy Outlook 2018 Report looks at its three scenarios in terms of investments. For the 2010-2017 period, average annual investments in energy were about $2.1 trillion per year. If the current polices were to continue (business as usual), the energy investments are **already projected to be about $2.1 trillion per year from the years 2018-2025 and about $2.8 trillion per year for the 2026-2040 period,** with about half of that going to fossil fuels. If we assume that $2.8 trillion per year is also needed for the 2041-2050 period, **then the total investments planned anyway calculate to about $80.5 trillion for the 2021-2050 period.** Their Sustainable Development Scenario (SDS), which means more renewables, electrification and energy efficiency, calls for only slight increases in energy investment so that it would be about $2.3 trillion per year for the 2018-2025 period and about $3.2 trillion per year for the 2026-2040 period (**calculating to about $91.5 trillion for the 2021-2050 period**), with some annual investment in coal fired power plants continuing! [3]

By comparison, **International Renewable Energy Agency (IRENA) is projecting that for its Reference Case (Business as Usual scenario), the energy investments are** *already* **expected to be about $93 trillion for the 2015-2050 period or about an average of $2.6 trillion per year.** About 42% of this would go to fossil fuels, 29% for energy efficiency, 9% for power grids and flexibility, and about 9.6% for renewables. Compared to that, for their ReMap Case (where they project a big increase in renewable energy and energy efficiency) they are projecting that energy investments of about **$120 trillion will be needed for the 2015-2050 period or about an average of $3.3 trillion per year or about an extra $700 billion per year over what the world would spend anyway.** [4]

For the WWS plan proposed by the Solutions Project, the total power to be added of about 50 Tera Watts (or TW – 50 million Mega Watts or MW) would need a total investment of about $125 trillion (about $2.5 million/MW), compared with a Business as Usual (mainly fossil fuel investment) needed of about $2.7 million per MW, or about $3.5 trillion investment per year. [5]

In contrast, the Global Plan proposed in this book actually is more aggressive than other plans and would get the world to Zero carbon emissions from fossil fuels by 2050. Because it plans to do this mainly by an expanded solar plan it needs about an estimated $4.4 trillion a year globally, or about $132 trillion total over the next 30 years. This assumes a level of decrease in solar energy and battery costs based on published projections. If cost fell more then the amounts needed will be lower. The next table compares what the different plan investments needed. Costs have been estimated for expansion of renewable energy (mainly solar PV), electrification of all sectors, expanding the transmission grid, all of the work needed to develop and deploy storage fuels, and some amounts to handle fossil fuels and then retire them.

The World GDP in 2019 was about $88 Trillion, and the expected economic growth is projected to increase it to about $202 Trillion by the year 2050, if current trends continue. Let us understand this – what the world ALREADY plans for Energy Investments (Business as Usual), mainly in fossil fuels are $2.5 – 3.1 Trillion per year (about 3-3.5% of the 2019 GDP). The Plan calls for an investment of about $4.4 trillion per year or only about 5% of 2019 GDP (about 2.2% of 2050 GDP) – that's only about $1.3 trillion more than what the world was planning to do anyway.

Plan or Item	BAU* ($t)	Better Plan** 30 Years ($t)	Better Plan** Per Year ($t)	Percent of 2019 GDP (%)	Percent of 2050 GDP (%)
WEO 2018	80.5	91.5	3.1	3.5	1.5
IRENA	93	120	4.0	4.55	2.0
WWS Solutions		125	4.2	4.7	2.1
BOOK PLAN		132	4.4	5.0	2.2
World GDP - 2019			88		
World GDP – 2050			202		

TABLE – COMPARISONS OF THE INVESTMENT ESTIMATES OF THE DIFFERENT PLANS $TRILLIONS (2021-2050)

*BAU – Business as Usual – What the world was planning to invest anyway – Energy Investments that are already projected
**Better Plan – For WEO2018, this is the SDS case, for IRENA this is the ReMAP case, and then there is the Plan proposed in this Book.

Since the world is already planning to spend $80.5 trillion dollars over the next 30 years (or about an average of $2.68 trillion per year) in energy investments, what the Plan is proposing is an estimated $132 trillion (or about $4.4 trillion per year). This means that if the anticipated investments can be diverted to the new activities, we only need an additional $51.5 trillion (or about $1.72 trillion per year). So, in order to have effective implementation, we need this added amount to be effectively raised in an automatic and guaranteed fashion as possible, so that the Plan or anything like it gets implemented in a timely fashion and all of the tasks are completed by 2050. For this we propose the following financing plan.

FINANCING THE BOOK GLOBAL PLAN

The strategy that is proposed for the whole plan is to discourage activities that need to stop and encourage activities that we need to transition to. The global and US financing are presented together. It is proposed that the Plan be funded from the following sources:

1. Taxes or fees on activities that need to be discouraged.
2. Public Investment (Government budgets of federal, state and local levels).
3. Private Investment.

So far, the approach of getting the nations to invest the money in Climate Change solutions, nationally or globally (source number 2 above) has failed miserably. At Paris, the richer industrial nations pledged $100 billion to help other nations, but only a fraction of that actually got contributed. In 2016, only $56 billion had been received against that commitment. Trusting the national governments to contribute the money out of their national government budgets each year will not work and will be too dependent on the political moods in the nations, each particular year – guaranteed to fail miserably. **If we have to solve the Climate Change problem, and implement a Plan such as in this book, then the funding mechanism has to be global and it has to be automatic** – i.e. a higher reliance on taxes and fees. Once taxes provide a certain amount of automatic funding, then national governments can supplement this by investing in crucial tasks nationally and globally. Once business circles begin to see that this is the economy of the future, private investments can come in to accomplish the detailed technology and product development tasks, and supporting all of the products and services that will be needed by the transformed economy.

The Basic approach that is proposed here is as follows: "Tax the fossil fuel activity and invest the money in developing renewable alternatives as per Plan". The exception is the financial transactions tax. The basic strategy will be to use the taxes to develop the new activities and demonstrate these. Then, these activities will be used to provide the public with options, with incentives given to adopt them, as the taxes and fees on the undesirable activities are gradually increased, and at the same time increase the incentives to encourage everyone to adopt the new options. In this fashion, the public can be guided and assisted in making the transition, and as often as possible, empowered and enabled to take charge and self-propel the process. Before we begin that, we need to address the issue of fossil fuel subsidies.

Phase Out Subsidies for Fossil Fuels

Global subsidies for fossil fuels were recently estimated by the International Monetary Fund (IMF) at about US Dollar $5.2 trillion in 2017, or about 6.5% of the size of the global economy (US Dollar $80 trillion, as measured by Gross Domestic Product – GDP). The biggest subsidizers of fossil fuels are China ($1,400 billion), United States ($649 billion), Russia ($551 B), European Union ($289 B) and India ($209 B). The working paper estimated that if these subsidies were not there, then in 2015 the global carbon dioxide emissions would have been 28 percent lower, fossil fuel air pollution deaths 46% lower, tax revenues higher by 3.8% of global GDP, and the net economic benefits (environmental costs less economic costs) would have been 1.7% of global GDP. So, clearly, we have to begin to get rid of direct and indirect subsidies of fossil fuels. That in itself will help the whole process. We next address the funding methods.

So, here are the taxes or fees that are proposed and the activities they will be invested in.

Carbon Tax

Around the world, various nations have imposed some carbon taxes and some nations have tried to do so, with various levels of success. Denmark and Sweden have been successful in using it to reduce their carbon emissions. The higher price for fossil fuels that discourages the use of these fuels, combined with using the funds for renewable energy or carbon emissions reductions activities, can be the best way forward. This would also provide finance at the levels that will be needed, but without having to rely on the richer nations having to contribute these amounts out of their national budgets.

If coal, oil (petroleum) and natural gas have to phased out by 2050, the best way is to tax them and to use the funds to finance the tasks of the plans that are in addition to what the nations can do themselves. In the World Economic Outlook report for 2018 (WEO 2018), published by the International Energy Agency (IEA), that was discussed in Chapter 3 above, for 2017, consumption of coal was 3,750 Mtoe (millions of metric tons of oil equivalent), oil was 4,435 Mtoe, and natural gas was 3,107 Mtoe. If one taxes each of the fuels based on the metric tons of greenhouse gas emissions per common heat energy unit of each fuel, the tax on coal will be the highest, oil will be next and natural gas the least.

For quite some time, there has been talk in political circles in the US of the need for a Carbon Tax, and there is even pending legislation or a law (US Congress House Resolution HR 763) that is proposed to be enacted. In the first year it is proposed to have a carbon fee rate of $15, going up to $25 in the second year, multiplied by a carbon emissions content for each fuel (stated in metric tons). Using this second year rate, and using the fossil fuel consumption levels for 2017 in the previous paragraph, this would lead to a global carbon tax of about $600 billion every year. In the US Congress, the pending legislation says that after administrative and other expenses have been deducted, the rest of the money from the "Carbon Dividend Trust Fund" shall be rebated to all eligible individuals, where an eligible individual is any citizen or lawful resident of the country. [50]

Some form of carbon tax has been proposed and used globally in about 27 nations, some of whom have already implemented carbon taxes, and the US recently proposed legislatively but has not voted or adopted a carbon tax. The US idea is to tax each fuel based on its carbon dioxide emissions per unit of heat or energy, and then immediately turn around and refund this amount totally to the residents of the US (except for some small administrative expenses). The approach proposed here is to provide a tax refund to those with taxable incomes below a certain level, but use only 25% of the taxes collected, and use the other 75% to invest in either the US or Global Plan or both.

Financial Transactions Tax

A financial transactions tax is a levy that is not like an income tax, but only applies a fee each time a financial transaction occurs. There are many kinds of financial transactions taxes, some domestic and some multinational. In 2011, about 40 nations had some form of a financial transactions tax, raising an estimated US $38 billion. So the plan proposes a global Financial Transactions Tax. Since this will be global, there is no question of anyone escaping taxes by moving transactions around the world.

It was estimated in December 2018 by the US Congressional Budget Office (CBO) that a 0.1% transactions tax would give revenue of $776.7 billion in the period 2019-2028 (ten years), or an average of about $77 billion a year. So, the Book Plan is proposing a 0.2% US Financial Transactions Tax that will raise a revenue of about $154 billion a year or about $4,620 billion over the 30 year period (2021-2050). Similarly, for the whole world, all of the stock exchanges will have similar financial transactions tax on stocks type transactions, that will raise an estimated $18.48 trillion over 30 years (2021-2050). Again, as for the carbon tax, it is proposed that 25% of the proceeds be refunded or used to reduce the burden of those earning less than a certain amount that is tied to the poverty level.

Aviation Transport Tax

Currently, aviation emissions are clearly out of control, and the use of jet fuel is a very carbon intensive process. The immense global and US tourism activity only adds to this, as rich and the upper middle classes think nothing of going all over the world on vacations to places that are still beautiful, but are getting devastated by global warming. Currently proposed efficiency increases and use of biofuels are not adequate in addressing the issue.

For 2017, the US Department of Transportation (USDOT) reported that for all domestic and international the total number of passengers carried were 849.3 million (741.6 million domestic and 107.7 million international). Only a $10 fee per flight will yield a revenue of $8,493 million or about $8.5 billion per year, or about $255 billion over the 30 year period (2031-2050). Almost all of this needs to go to implement a US National High Speed Rail Plan, as well as other low and zero carbon transportation modes (Mass Transit, biking, pedestrian, etc.). Globally, ICAO (International Civil Aviation Organization) reported that in 2017, the number of passengers were 4,300 million, and so at a $10 fee per passenger, this works out to $43 billion a year or about $1.29 trillion over 30 years.

Meat Tax

The consumption of meat, by the way mainly of beef, pork and chicken, is devastating the forests of the world and directly adding to carbon and methane emissions. Hence, a global meat tax proposed is aimed at reducing this devastation, and using the funds for the Global Reforestation and Afforestation Plan of adding 1 billion hectares from 2021-2050. US meat consumption is about four (4) times the global average, and so, if the effect of US meat consumption on deforestation is to be reduced, there needs to be a US meat tax, and globally there needs to be a global meat tax.

In 2018, US consumers ate about 98 billion pounds of beef (or $44.46 million metric tons). At current average prices, the value of this meat was $274 billion. A 5% tax on this will yield a revenue of about $13.7 billion per year or about $411 billion over the 30 years (2031-2050). So, the Book Plan proposes a US national tax of 5% on all meat consumption that will yield these amounts, all of which will be applied towards reforesting and afforesting the US to the extent of adding 80 million hectares, and towards adding coastal ecosystems along the entire US coast – all of which will absorb enormous amounts of carbon. In 2013, the US meat consumption was 50 million metric tons, as compared with a global meat consumption of 320 million tons (or about 6.4 times the US consumption). Hence, the proceeds from a global meat tax are estimated to be $2.63 trillion.

Fossil Fuels Vehicles Tax

The US currently has about 250 million vehicles on the roads, which are nearly all fossil fuel vehicles (running on gasoline, petrol or diesel). It appears that currently the sales of new vehicles is about 17 million per year and old vehicles that are retired for age are about 11 million vehicles, so that about 6 million vehicles are being added every year. The Plan proposes taxing fossil fuel vehicles every year for 30 years (2021-2050), considering the increases every year and increase in the fossil fuel tax from a start of $10 per vehicle to a linearly increasing tax of $300 per vehicle by the year 2050. As the fossil fuel vehicles are gradually increasing, and the tax per vehicle is gradually increasing, with the proceeds starting at about $2.5 billion per year, and rising to a peak of about $28 billion per year by the year 2038, before decreasing to zero by the year 2050. It is proposed to stop the sales of all fossil fuel vehicles by 2041, so that those sold that year can be retired in 2051.

Globally, there were 1,320 million vehicles on the road in 2020. Doing a similar calculation for the world, with declining number of fossil fuel vehicles and increasing tax, gives a total tax proceeds of about $2.33 trillion, with all fossil fuel vehicles gone by 2050.

SUMMARIES OF TAX ESTIMATES

Shown in the following table is a summary of the global tax proceeds from the five types of taxes, and the 25% refund of carbon and financial transaction taxes, providing an estimated $57.33 trillion a year or, on the average, about $1.91 trillion a year. This exceeds the added estimated amount needed of $51.5 trillion or about an average of $1.72 trillion per year.

Table – Total Tax Proceeds as per Plan for the World

CATEGORY	30 YEARS	25% DIVIDEND	30 YEARS NET
	$ TRILLION	RESIDENT REFUND	$ TRILLION
CARBON	49.49	12.37	37.12
FINANCIAL	18.48	4.62	13.86
AVIATION	1.29		1.29
MEAT	2.63		2.63
VEHICLES	2.33		2.33
TOTAL	74.22	16.99	57.33

The numbers for the US are as follows.

Table – Total Tax Proceeds as per Plan for the US

CATEGORY	30 YEARS	25% DIVIDEND	30 YEARS NET
	$ TRILLION	RESIDENT REFUND	$ TRILLION
CARBON	7.52	1.88	5.64
FINANCIAL	4.62	1.16	3.46
AVIATION	0.25		0.25
MEAT	0.41		0.41
VEHICLES	0.56		0.56
TOTAL	13.36	3.04	10.32

It is proposed that National governments impose and collect these taxes in a globally coordinated fashion. The less well-off nations use all of their tax proceeds internally to accomplish their domestic goals. The better off nations collect the proceeds and use a big portion of the funds for their domestic tasks, but then contribute some percentage of their funds to a Global Organization, such as the one sketched in the previous chapters, which then helps implement global tasks, and some of the less well-off nations that need help to implement the Global Plan. The processes of taxation, appropriation of funds and spending need strict controls in order to make sure that the goals and activities of the Plan are achieved in a timely manner, so that the whole transition occurs by 2050.

Investing the Proceeds to Implement the Plan

With this Plan, it is proposed that about 25% be used in such a way as to benefit and empower the parts of the population that are at the bottom of the economic ladder globally, and to reduce the burden from the carbon tax, in the manner described in the last section of the chapter on the Global Green New Deal and in support of the global sustainable development goals that were described in that section. The rest of the money will be spent to fund all the parts of the plan described in chapters above with the following order of priority:

1. **Coal:** Replace all coal fired power plants with renewable energy (usually solar PV) plus battery power plants, ultimately backed up with storage fuels. The next in priority for coal will be to electrify all processes that need it and produce that electricity using similar renewable energy power plants.

2. **Oil:** Replace all gasoline (petrol) and diesel fuel applications, especially for vehicles, by electrifying all of the transportation and basing that transportation on renewable energy, battery vehicles and storage fuel vehicles – investing in the Solar-Electric highways.

3. **Natural Gas:** Replace all natural gas power plants with renewable energy (usually solar) plus battery power plants, ultimately backed up by storage fuels. The next in priority will be to electrify everything that uses natural gas (home and building) with energy efficient processes, and produce that added electricity with renewable energy.

4. **Transition Nations, Companies and Workers Dependent on Fossil Fuels:** Help all nations currently dependent on fossil fuels to transition to renewable energy for their energy needs. Help all companies and workers dependent on fossil fuels for their income to transition to other energy or income activities.

5. **Transition All On Road and Off Road Vehicles to Zero Emissions:** Provide global assistance for the development of infrastructure for Solar-Electric Roads for electric, battery and storage fuel vehicles. Replace all fossil fuel vehicles with zero carbon emissions vehicles. Solarize and electrify all pathways and supply them with clean renewable energy or storage fuels.

6. **Energy Democracy:** Help all of the people, organizations and communities at the lower rungs of the economic ladder to begin to participate in all of the above activities so as to benefit from incomes, businesses, activities and consumption.

7. **Just Transition:** Fund all of the transition activities of workers that are involved in fossil fuel production or end use activities through income, education, training, healthcare and job relocation benefits.

8. **Storage Fuels:** Do the massive global program to replace all mobile fuel applications and back up and peaking electric power with storage fuels (hydrogen, ammonia, methyl cyclo-hexane, etc.). Some nations are aggressively pursuing this research, which as soon as it is demonstrated as being successful and economic, it will need massive funding for Research, Development, Demonstration and Deployment (RDD&D) – the last means making these universally available so as to replace all mobile fuels for use in vehicles, planes, ships, etc.

9. **Carbon Sink Rejuvenation:** Help all areas of the world to reforest and afforest to the level of One billion hectares, and all the coast lines of the world to develop ecosystems (from a few hundred yards or meters, to as much as 32 kilometers (20 miles) wide.

10. **Adaptation:** Help all of the world adapt to heat, drought, and floods, and help global agriculture transform to adapt to Climate Change.

11. **Disaster Management:** fund the global Disaster Risk Reduction actions for all major climate related disasters – coastal storms, tornadoes, wildfires and landslides.

Funding Solar-Electric Highways and Roads and Other Transportation

As of July 2014, the global on road vehicle population reached about 1.2 billion, which if current trends continue will reach 2.5 billion by 2050. As of that date, the US had about 250 million vehicles and China about 100 million vehicles. In 2013 the global new vehicle sales were 84 million, which is projected to grow to 127 million per year by 2035. Just 2.5% of those vehicles are expected to be battery electric, plug-in hybrid or fuel cell vehicles (last one using storage fuels). Many nations have begun to talk about stopping the sales of new fossil fuel (gasoline or petrol and diesel) cars and transitioning to all battery electric cars. In 2017, the total number of new vehicles sold were about 97 million, of which about 73 million were cars, and about 24 million were larger commercial vehicles (light duty and heavy duty trucks, and buses).

Off road or non-road vehicles have become a key contributor to pollution, besides their carbon emissions. In the US, these vehicles emit about 75% of the particulate matter (PM2.5) and 25% of nitrogen oxides (NOx). Globally, this is mainly because pollution emissions control methods in these machines lag far behind on road vehicles. Because of this and because the market and sales of these off road vehicles are fast expanding, they have become a major source of pollution worldwide. Globally, they are also a significant contributor to carbon and greenhouse gas emissions. In addition to mining, construction and agricultural machines, the other vehicles that need attention are railway locomotives.

Then, let us not forget all of the other internal combustion and turbine engines (and engines of other kinds) that burn fossil fuels. Engines for standby power generation also add much to local pollution and are also contributors to greenhouse gas emissions. Besides all of the engines used in the civilian sector, there are all of the vehicles and engines that are used by the militaries of the world, which is a sector that has received even less attention than off road vehicles for pollution controls. **All of these vehicles need also to be converted to zero carbon emissions vehicles and engines.** For off road, railway and military vehicles and engines that are very mobile and need to be used all over the distributed countrysides, the best option is their conversion to storage fuels, and for greater efficiency, these will need to be battery hybrid vehicles and engines.

The Plan proposes a total conversion of transportation (on road and off road) by 2050, with a combination of conversion to all electric vehicles and those using zero carbon storage fuels (hydrogen, ammonia, etc.). The highways and roads will be converted to solar electric roadways where solar panels along the roads provide pure electric power (to vehicles using catenaries like electric buses do in cities today), electric charging for battery vehicles, and the supply of storage fuels that are produced locally along the roadways using solar power, or transported to these stations from locations that produce storage fuels and transport the fuels using storage fuel vehicles. The gas or petrol stations around the world will be replaced by ones that supply storage fuels and provide charging hookups. The solar panels, and in some cases wind turbines, powering the roadways and these new or modified stations will be located all along these roadways. At least one lane in multi-lane highways will need to be converted to use by all-electric vehicles, although other vehicles could run in these lanes as well. The plan calls for the research, development, demonstration and deployment (RDD&D) process **to have demonstration sites in all nations with significant road miles or kilometers converted to Solar-Electric Highways by 2030,** and then the total conversion of the infrastructure globally from 2031 to 2050.

On the vehicle side, the plan calls for the following steps in transitioning from fossil fuel cars, commercial vehicles and all off road vehicles to zero emissions vehicles by 2050:

1. For companies and nations to immediately begin the RDD&D needed to develop the vehicles – all-electric, battery electric, and storage fuel powered (on road and off road) – to be completed by 2030. Implement a global program to convert ALL vehicle factories (globally) to the production of these kinds of vehicles. This will require a massive re-tooling effort, with some of the investment coming from in-company and some from private sources. Governments can provide incentives to companies as needed.

2. The sale of all new fossil fuel vehicles (on road and off road) to cease by 2030, from 2031 onwards, transition to

only the sales of all-electric, battery electric and storage fuel vehicles. If the current rateof new vehicle sales has to be maintained that means the TOTAL conversion of ALL factories to the new vehicles by 2030, and for these to have the capability to produce 100 million on road vehicles per year (assuming that is what the market needs).

3. The new or re-tooled factories are to ramp up production so as to prepare for the other parallel task needed – that of changing out all fossil fuel vehicles (on road and off road). **Assuming that there are 2 billion total on road vehicles by 2030, this would mean that we would need to change out 100 million vehicles per year for twenty (20) years, from 2031-2050.** This will require incentives and financing to provide owners the motivation to switch to zero emissions vehicles. Because of the magnitude of the tasks, it will help if the total population of on road and off road vehicles are stabilized at 2030 levels, and the next 20 years spent in changing out the fossil fuel vehicles with zero emissions vehicles.

4. **Fossil Fuel Vehicle Tax to Finance the Transition:** Starting 2021, all fossil fuel vehicles (on road and off road) will be taxed in terms of an annual added fee (to be added to whatever is currently in place for normal vehicle and license plate registration). The tax proceeds are shown in the table above. Part of these funds will be used to finance the RDD&D to develop the ideas and the methods for the infrastructure and the new vehicle designs for the transition. All of this will be supplemented by financing and investments from private sources, which will grow as the plan grows in speed. The plan calls for a rapid increase in this fee or tax starting 2031, to start providing vehicle owners the incentive to switch out of fossil fuel cars (gasoline or petrol, diesel and even natural gas) to zero emissions vehicles, with bigger incentives given for the purchases of the latter. This tax is proposed to rise to a level high enough by 2050 to make it uneconomical to own or operate a fossil fuel vehicle after 2050.

5. After 2050, globally, fossil fuel cars and off road vehicles will be totally phased out and the sale of fossil fuels at gas, petrol, diesel or natural gas stations will be very low. **After 2050, all vehicles (on road and off road) will be zero emis-**

sions vehicles.

6. For local travel and in small cities, the growth and the use of small electric "vehicles" will be developed and encouraged, such as manual and battery electric bikes, trikes and quad (four wheel) bikes, for local personal and light duty travel (for local shopping trips) together with added solar PV powered charging infrastructure for all of these smaller "vehicles". For this, there will need to be total conversion of cities and small towns to introduce bike and pedestrian paths for pedestrians and for human powered and light battery electric transportation of all kinds and small electric vehicles (bikes, trikes and quad bikes).

7. For larger distances in cities and metropolitan areas, there will be the considerable expansion of mass transit (buses and light rail trains) that can be combined with the use of the smaller light manual and battery electric "vehicles" described in item 6 above. Besides private and public finance, the new fossil fuel vehicle taxes will be used to support this development, especially in nations that have less availability of public and private finance.

Funding Aviation and Tourism Conversion to Zero Carbon Modes

It must become totally clear to all "tourists" that they cannot be engaging in behavior that's bad for Climate Change. Many tourists are going to enjoy the beauty of nature and beautiful sceneries. All tourists and potential tourists have to understand that if they are emitting large amounts of carbon and other greenhouse gases, that they are destroying what they are enjoying! To get from their homes to their tourist destinations, they have to insist on the lowest carbon mode. It makes good sense for global society that if they want tourism to continue, they have to make low carbon modes conveniently available. Again, tour and cruise operators have to ensure that their vehicles and ships run only on zero emissions vehicles – as with all shipping, all cruise ships will need to be converted to use carbon free storage fuels and sails, or whatever technology gets them to zero emissions.

Aviation is the other big elephant in the room that needs to be addressed seriously, as described in Chapter 2. It is estimated that as of 2017, there were 39,000 planes in the whole world (including military aircraft, but not light or small planes). Another source claims there are about 24,000 planes. Of these, there are an average of about 16,000 planes in the air globally at any given time, although this number varies over the year. The International Civil Aviation Organization (ICAO) of the UN says that the number of planes double every 15 years, and Boeing has said that the number of planes to be added (new) will be about 40,000 planes by 2037. In 2018, airline flights emitted 895,000 million tons of carbon dioxide and they carried about 4.4 billion passengers, and this is expected to double by 2030.

The burning of jet fuels, besides emitting carbon dioxide, emits nitrogen oxides, water vapor, soot and sulfate particles. It has been claimed that biofuels made from algae, plants like jatropha and waste byproducts can be used in planes, and that this may be a good way of recycling carbon and help reduce aviation's carbon footprint. But the use of these fuels is still in its infancy.

The Book Plan for aviation has been presented in Chapter 3. Here we address the question of how we are to finance the transition of aviation to a zero carbon mode. The Book Plan for financing this is follows:

1. **Aviation Tax:** A Tax will be placed on Aviation for each passenger for each flight. A starting tax of just $10 per passenger will raise about $44 billion now, and this number will double by 2030. The aviation tax should gradually be raised every year until it meets the financing needs of the tasks outlined in Chapter 3 and further described below.

2. **Storage Fuel Engines:** After being supplemented by the financing by the plane manufacturers, at least 50% of these funds must go towards developing aircraft engines that use storage fuels, and the best candidate may be ammonia.

3. **Funding for Research:** The RDD&D for these technologies (say for turbines that burn zero carbon storage fuels) should be ready by 2030. Thereafter, all new planes sold must use these types of engines,

4. **Retiring and Converting Planes:** From 2031-2050, the next part of the funding will go to retiring all planes using jet fuel or converting them to the use of bio-fuels that are from plants grown on non-agricultural land.

5. **Storage Fuel Production for Planes:** Next, solar PV power plants located near airports will need to be funded so that

they may produce most of the storage fuels, although these can be transported to the airports from other locations.

6. **Substitute With High Speed Rail:** Short haul flights need to be replaced as much as possible with high speed rail travel, especially where there is heavy traffic. As described in Chapter 3, the next part of the funding will need to go to building a high speed rail network throughout the world, so that there are few flights over continuous land areas, and most flights are over oceans or where distances are greater than 1,600 kilometers (or 1,000 miles).

7. **Funding Conversions for Tourism:** On landing after crossing an ocean, the rest of the transport over land must be by the zero carbon mode. For this and for tourism on cruise lines, all transport will be funded for conversion to the zero carbon mode – either through electrification, electric or battery vehicles and vehicles or cruise ships using storage fuels.

Stopping Deforestation Being Caused by Firewood, Wood Pulp, Beef, Soybean and Palm Oil

1. As described in Chapter 4 the major part of the deforestation is caused by forests being cut and converted to other land uses for commercial purposes. The Union of Concerned Scientists has highlighted **the four commodities that are the biggest drivers of deforestation: beef, soybean, wood products and palm oil.** The UN has pushed a Billion Trees Program that has encouraged trees to be planted. Recently (in 2019), Ethiopia planted 350 million trees in one day, which broke the previous record held by India that had planted 50 million trees in one day. That is very commendable, but in order to have a sustained growth in forest cover, and achieve a net addition of 1 billion hectares of forests (tropical, temperate and boreal forests), it is necessary to systematically address the commercial or direct use products that are the reason for current deforestation (besides the massive increase in forest fires).

2. **Firewood:** For nations whose populations depend on firewood, which are mainly in Africa, there needs to be a double pronged approach. They need to be assisted in planting massive plantations of firewood trees, but combined with

agroforestry, so that the rate of afforestation is much larger than the rate of deforestation. The planting and harvesting of trees will create many livelihood opportunities. The other side of this solution is to support the production and distribution of efficient cookstoves that use much less wood, an effort the UN is already much engaged in, and the use of solar ovens. The long term solution is to enable these nations to move to electric cooking that is powered by solar PV electricity.

3. **Paper and Wood Pulp**: Here, South Korea has clearly emerged as the leader, as it currently recycles 85% of its paper and has engaged in massive reforestation for many decades. So, the solution for the world is to engage in a systematic program so that all nations of the world meet South Korea's level of recycling. Paper can be recycled 5-6 times before the fibers become too small to be used for paper. Also, paper production from the cutting of the tree to the making of paper, is a very chemically and energy intensive process. Also, paper used for napkins, paper towels and such purposes needs to be recycled too. **The plan proposal is to tax the process of making wood pulp from wood the first time this occurs, and use the funds to support recycling.**

4. **Lumber**: While lumber for home construction is a significant contributor to deforestation, the wood used does not end up being burned or add to carbon, although the whole process of cutting, transport and processing does add to greenhouse gas emissions. However, this deforestation does withdraw the cut trees from the process of absorbing carbon and is often bad for the species that live in these areas. The whole rules for lumber need to be changed, so that clear-cutting is banned and anyone who cuts a tree for lumber has to plant more trees than that, and the tree plantations have to be managed so as to be favorable for absorbing carbon, supporting wildlife and be planned so as to minimize wildfires.

5. **Tax Beef and Use the Funds to Reforest Cattle Ranches**: The world needs to have global tax on beef, and on the export of beef, and use these funds to reconvert deforested areas

back from cattle ranches to tree plantations in suitable and sustainable ways. These reconverted areas may need some extractive activity, whether it be for wood pulp, lumber or firewood, but the rate of reforestation and afforestation of other areas need to exceed the rate of cutting down trees. The plan recommends that about 20% of the funds be spent on educating global consumers to reduce the intake of beef, because of the ill effects it has on the planet's health and on personal health (heart disease, cancer, diabetes, stroke, etc.).

6. The historic book *Beyond Beef* by Jeremy Rifkin states that, "There are currently 1.28 billion cattle populating the earth. They take up nearly 24% of the land mass of the planet and consume enough grain to feed hundreds of millions of people. Their combined weight exceeds that of the human population." Since 1992, when the book was published, the disastrous effects of beef consumption and raising cattle have on deforestation (especially in the tropics and the Amazon forest in South America), has become very well known. The book proposes taxing beef consumption and using the funds for both reforestation and direct education. [51]

7. **Tax Pork and Use the Funds to Divert Soybean Away from Hog Farms:** Hog or pig farms in developed nations are amongst the most polluting of operations and consume most of the soybean grown in those nations. Most of the soybean grown in the world goes to feed pigs, poultry and cattle. The plan proposes taxing pork and chicken production too, and using the funds to reforest lands deforested to grow soybean. Soybean needs to be diverted to the making of vegetable protein for human consumption, as it can help considerably with the food supply. Again, the plan proposes using 20% of the funds for education to reduce the consumption of pork and chickens, both for planetary health and personal health, and divert populations towards the consumption of soy proteins.

8. **Create Alternative Livelihoods to Palm Oil Based on Reforestation:** Palm oil is used in processed foods, personal care products, biofuels and vegetable oil. Converting forested areas to palm oil plantations has a double whammy as there is not only deforestation, but much of the land converted

is often also peatlands, that contain much carbon in the soil. As the peatlands are drained, much of that carbon is released. While some nations and companies have begun to discourage this by saying they will not purchase products that lead to deforestation by palm oil, this is not enough. **The plan proposes taxing palm oil consumption and exports and using the funds to reforest deforested areas, reverting the peatlands to wetlands, and use of the products from the reforested areas on a sustainable extractive basis.**

9. Clearly, the massive appetite for meat, paper products, firewood, lumber and palm oil are driving deforestation. Those who are involved in these commercial operations often wish to imitate the high consumption patterns and fashions of the richer nations. Besides promoting more holistic lifestyles, taxing these activities to fund reforestation and establishing new coastal ecosystems, is the best way to divert these activities to reducing their carbon emissions and increasing their carbon absorption.

Promoting Sustainable Development Goals – The Global Green New Deal

From the 1960s to the end of the century, as it was understood that a big part of the global population was either being left behind or suffering from increased poverty, there was a declared "War on Poverty." By the end of the last century it was realized that this "war" was not really working and things were getting worse for most of the world's population even as the richer part was doing very well.

So, as a follow up to the United Nations Conference of Environment and Development (popularly known as the Earth Summit) in 1992 in Rio de Janeiro, Brazil, the world agreed to what were called the Millennium Development Goals (MDGs) in the year 2000. These were eight goals meant to balance the tasks of global finance and environment with an attempt to improve the lives of common people around the world, especially the disadvantaged.

In order to improve on this process, the Sustainable Development Goals (SDGs) were introduced and agreed to by the United Nations General Assembly in 2015, as part of its "2030 Agenda."

These SDGs were: [52]

1. No Poverty
2. Zero Hunger
3. Good Health and Well-being
4. Quality Education
5. Gender Equality
6. Clean Water and Sanitation
7. Affordable and Clean Energy
8. Decent Work and Economic Growth
9. Industry, Innovation, and Infrastructure
10. Reducing Inequality
11. Sustainable Cities and Communities
12. Responsible Consumption and Production
13. Climate Action
14. Life Below Water
15. Life On Land
16. Peace, Justice, and Strong Institutions
17. Partnerships for the Goals.

Of these, Goals 6, 7, 11, 13, 14 and 15 have to do directly with Climate Change. The others may be described as a "Global Green New Deal". As compared to the US Green New Deal, which is directly linked to Climate Change, the Sustainable Development Goals have a much weaker connection. However, the situation that the world faces today is that if Climate Change is not reversed, all of the SDGs can be expected to begin showing a worsening trend.

Most nations scored very low (did very badly) on Goal 13 (Climate Action), Goal 14 (Life Below Water) and Goal 15 (Life on Land). Progress on Climate Change solutions was very poor, and protecting life on land and sea (health and biodiversity) was also going badly. So the net conclusion is that nations are doing very poorly in proceeding towards solutions for Climate Change, and biodiversity (species and life on land and sea) were continuing to suffer. Meanwhile, as of June 2019, more than half the nations of the world were not on track to eradicate poverty (SDG 1).

Even the International Energy Agency (IEA) includes in a very prominent way in its World Energy Outlook 2018 (WEO2018) a

Sustainable Development Goal (SDG) scenario that would ramp down the use of fossil fuels and ramp up the increase in renewable energy, with these rates of ramping up or down being much faster than what current policies or even new policies being considered, would do. This was described in Chapter 3 above, before presenting the Book Plan.

Book Plan for the Global Green New Deal

The book calls for a strategy that implements the Plan as described in the preceding chapters, but does it in such a way as to vastly improve the lives of all of the world's population while proceeding to solve Climate Change! The few following sections in this chapter describe what the Plan approach is for implementation.

Chapter 12 describes in detail how the principles of energy democracy were to be applied and how the whole climate transition needs to be a just transition. The principles of an extractive economy that is worsening Climate Change needs to be replaced by a regenerative economy. Since renewable energy resources like solar, wind, storage and geothermal energy, and energy conservation, are distributed, this represents an excellent opportunity for there to be more distributive and democratic control and operation of all of these energy systems. For this, the parts that need to be funded are community based decentralized development of energy generation and conservation, at the local level through distributive initiatives. This requires communities to participate in the planning, building and benefitting of an alternative decentralized renewable energy model.

Besides that, all other initiatives in this book, from transitioning out of fossil fuels, to building new renewable energy systems, to reforestation, afforestation, and agricultural adaptation, should invest in and empower community based and democratically controlled initiatives and organizations. It makes sense to convert all utilities to nonprofit organizations whose sole aim and charter is to transmit electrical energy and distribute storage fuels, and empower them to work cooperatively with the community. Even disaster management, which needs to be primarily the focus and role of national governments and global organizations, needs a strong component of community participation in training and providing input in planning and organizing ways for dealing with Climate Change disasters.

All financing, whether from public or private sources, or from the various taxes listed above, should finance and empower such alternative economic, industrialization, energy distribution, agricultural and forest development models.

Chapter 10

Overcoming the Obstacles – Climate Deniers and Fossil Fuel Financial and Political Interests

But before we can begin to implement any plan for solving or minimizing the damages of global warming, or get agreement on goals and schedules, we have many obstacles to overcome. The first is the anti-science people who refuse to accept what most of the world's scientists are saying. People like these have used every trick in the trade to try and dispute or discredit scientific evidence on many major health, scientific and environmental issues. When major economic and financial actors have seen that solving or tackling such issues would decrease their profits, they have lined up in opposition, and used any means possible to delay national or global actions, sometimes for decades, including coming up with sophisticated financial and economic arguments of what is or is not possible.

Then there is the big elephant, which is the immense inertia of our fossil fuel civilization that relies on coal, oil and natural gas. With global civilization basing everything on fossil fuels, it has become difficult to get off this "steam train", as almost everything so far has been moving in the direction of relying more and more on fossil fuels, or continuing to rely on fossil fuels in a big way. The companies, countries, economies and activities that benefit from all of this have a stake and a vested interest in this continuing, as a result of which they have fought changes in every possible way.

Some More Science – Planet Earth's History
and How It Gave Us Past Global Cooling

According to the Big Bang Theory (the most widely accepted among scientific astronomers), the universe began as an incredibly dense and hot speck about 13.61 billion years ago (age calculated by scientific observations of the rate at which the universe is expanding). It is postulated (an explanation offered based on scientific evidence) that our solar system was born when a shock wave from a supernova (explosion of a dying star that becomes unable to sustain its ignition, first collapses and then explodes – such events happen all the time elsewhere) a hot pre-solar nebula (cloud of gas and dust), and caused it to condense into the proto-planetary disk (essentially a round flat surface) of our solar system about 4.6 billion years ago. Most of the planets, except for Pluto, are on the one flat plane of the proto-planetary disk.

The flat rotating disk consisted of a star (our sun) and a rotating disk of particles, dust and gases which came together to form our planets. The moon is explained as having been formed when a giant meteorite hit the molten ball of Earth and broke away a chunk that became the round moon. Scientific dating methods, that date a rock based on when it first solidified, date Moon rocks that were recovered during the US mission to the moon at close to 4.6 billion years. Since planet Earth remained a hot molten ball, rocks that formed when the crust first started to solidify, dated a few hundred million years later. We are part of the Milky Way Galaxy, which is one of billions of galaxies in the universe, and our sun is one of about 100 billion stars that rotates in the flat spiral of the galaxy about once every 200 million years. Among scientific astronomers and other scientists, there is a whole lot of agreement that the scientific evidence points to the above as being true.

There are other books that detail the science based history of our planet Earth from a molten ball 4.6 billion years ago and today. The author's book, *Rethinking Progress – Towards a Creative Transformation of Global Society"* details in an entire chapter the biography of our planet. What is relevant for Climate Change is that planet Earth went through many cooling stages, the first of which was by the evaporation and condensation (rain) cycles of water in the atmosphere that ended up forming our oceans. Then as life developed, and as fossils of dead animals and matter sunk below and formed the petroleum or oil deposits over hundreds of millions of years, they took carbon dioxide out of the atmosphere which helped to continue the cooling of the Earth's atmosphere, as there was less heat trapped by the greenhouse effect. Then came the dense carboniferous forests, which under temperature and pressure formed the coal seams that again took carbon dioxide out of the atmosphere and further cooled the Earth's atmosphere. The remaining carbon dioxide in the air gave us enough warming so that life like ours and as we know it today, could flourish. Then the Earth's atmosphere cooled enough that we got the ice ages, the formation and melting of which have been correlated by some scientists with the changes in the axis of spin of the earth, which currently rotates at about an angle of 21.5 degrees relative to the plane of Earth's orbit around the sun. The angle of this axis as the Earth rotates around the sun gives us our beautiful seasons. [53]

The planet Mars is much smaller than Earth, and as a result it cannot hold onto much of an atmosphere. That, and the fact that it is further away from the sun than planet Earth, makes it much colder. The planet Venus is about the same size as the Earth, so its gravity can hold on to its atmosphere. But because it is closer to the sun, its surface is hotter, so all of the water boiled off and was not able to form any oceans. Then because its atmosphere is made up of mainly carbon dioxide, the atmosphere of Venus is very hot, about 460 degrees Celsius (about 860 degrees Fahrenheit)! Early US and Russian probes to Venus did not last long because of the higher temperatures. **This is what happens when you have a runaway greenhouse effect! This is what can happen to us unless we change course!**

So here we take up the science disbelievers (the Climate Deniers), the science manipulators, the problem of inertia, and the political and financial opposition, that have so far been quite effective in blocking progress towards solutions for Climate Change. Except in climate denier circles, there is total consensus in global scientific circles that human-caused Climate Change by the burning of fossil fuels is making matters worse. **The IPCC (United Nations based, Intergovernmental Panel on Climate Change) is by far the most credible authority on the Science of Climate Change, and any uncertainty that may have been there in 1990, is now totally gone – one can say that there is about 99.9 % certainty that we humans are contributing to global warming and Climate Change – the scientific statement that there may be 0.1% uncertainty has now become meaningless.**

Here are some of the methods, arguments and false claims made by climate deniers and their financial and political supporters.

The first chapter of the book described the science of Climate Change or global warming. There was evidence provided as to why the science based reports of the Intergovernmental Panel on Climate Change (IPCC) were the main basis for clearly describing the manner in which the Earth's climate was changing, and absolute evidence that almost all of it was due to human activity in general, and the burning of fossil fuels in particular. So why is it that some influential parts of the political and financial circles continue to reject and discredit this science? To understand this we look at what they have done before when global society has been faced with similar health and environmental threats. How have groups that opposed solutions to health or environmental threats acted in the past, and what is the strategy that they have adopted? One of the main tactics has been to use the Tobacco Institute Approach! Here is how they have used it!

The Tobacco Institute Approach

The Tobacco Institute was formed in 1958 as a trade association by cigarette manufacturers and initially supplemented the work of the Tobacco Industry Research Committee (TIRC), which later became the Council for Tobacco Research. While TIRC attacked scientific studies that showed the bad effects of tobacco on human health, the Council tried to show tobacco in a good light. Besides putting out good news about tobacco, the Council attacked scientific studies by sowing doubt, but not providing scientific rebuttals. The Tobacco Institute tried every way of trying to head off any regulation of tobacco, and at one time had as many as 70 lobbyists in the US capital Washington, DC.

The Tobacco Institute published lengthy White Papers that attempted to rebut scientific reports critical of tobacco, including a rebuttal in 1979 of the Surgeon General's report on "Smoking and Health". Later, in 1986, they attacked the Surgeon General's report on second hand smoke with a press release and a longer rebuttal paper, claiming that he had distorted the evidence and was suppressing contrary viewpoints. They also criticized the 1993 US Environmental Protection Agency's 1993 report that had declared tobacco smoke to be a class A human carcinogen. In one case, while secretly hiding their involvement, they indirectly paid Stanley Frank $500 to write an article favorable to tobacco for the January 1968 issue of the *True* magazine, and then paid $500,000 to Rosser Reeves to publicize it and then distribute a million copies of it.

When their anti-scientific behavior, and their misdeeds and misinformation activities finally caught up with them, they entered a Master Settlement Agreement in November 1998 with the Attorney Generals of 46 US states, that settled all Medicaid lawsuits for compensating the states for tobacco related healthcare costs. In the Agreement, they agreed to stop their tobacco marketing efforts, dissolve the Tobacco Institute and related organizations and for the four major original participating manufacturers or companies participating in Tobacco Institute to pay $206 billion over the first 25 years of the Agreement. [54]

Whatever may have been the results of the settlement with the US Tobacco industry, the important point that is being made here is that there was a **Tobacco Institute Approach** that attempted to do the following things:

1. Discredit all scientific and medical reports and findings that disputed the bad health effects of tobacco smoke.

2. Fight with all the money and influence they had to head off legislation and regulations that would educate the public on the bad effects of tobacco smoke, and on the sale and advertising of cigarettes.

3. Bring out contrary scientific reports of their own, which had not been peer reviewed, as all scientific journal articles are, that attempted to create an alternative (false) scientific narrative to confuse and fool the public and influence politicians.

4. Pay others to create scientific reports, that had no scientific basis whatsoever, by secret payments to people and to others to publish and publicize the false information.

Today, everyone knows scientifically and health wise that to-bacco smoke is a carcinogen, and that so is second hand tobacco smoke. Yet the Tobacco Institute thwarted efforts from 1958-1998 (40 years) to stop the bad effects on the health of the US public (and on the health of the global public). The same approach is being used in other areas.

Using the Tobacco Institute Approach
to the Destruction of the Ozone Layer

The other major case where the Tobacco Institute Approach was used to delay solutions to a major global environmental threat was in efforts to protect the Ozone Layer. The Earth's Ozone layer is a higher layer of the atmosphere called the stratosphere, which pro-tects us from excessive Ultra-Violet light that is harmful for humans and most other life forms on land. Ozone consists of three atoms of oxygen, whereas what we call oxygen is really a molecule that consists of two atoms of oxygen (the oxygen in the air we breathe).

In the late 1920s, a US scientist Thomas Midgley came up with a new class of chemicals made up of chlorine, fluorine and carbon, named as chlorofluorocarbons (CFCs) that replaced other chemicals as refrigerants and in air conditioners. Then two chemists (Sher-wood Rowland and Mario Molina) at the University of California at Irvine published their theory on atmospheric chemistry in 1974 that showed that CFCs could be destroying large amounts of the ozone layer. [55] Since 1974 the American Chemical Manufacturers Associ-ation (ACMA), currently known as the American Chemistry Coun-cil, used the Tobacco Institute Approach to try and discredit by all means possible the theory that CFCs were destroying the ozone lay-er. Besides ground based measurements by a British Scientist, Joe Farman, in Antarctica, it took two NASA (US National Aeronautics and Space Administration) air flight expeditions into Antarctica to confirm the chemical scientific information that the theory was right based on the chemical content inside and outside the Ozone Hole that had been discovered around Antarctica.

There was now enough scientific evidence that the theory that CFCs were destroying the Ozone Layer was correct, and it was only then that the US financial and political opposition was finally over-come. However, it was because of the US Chemical Industry's use of the Tobacco Institute Approach that action on effective solutions was delayed from 1974 to 1987, when the Montreal Protocol (action protocol to protect the ozone layer as a follow up to the Ozone LayerTreaty) was signed. By then there was evidence that the problem was worse than anticipated, and so in 1990 in London the nations of the world decided to totally phase out these chemicals by the year 2000. Even with all this, the Ozone Layer will continue to be destroyed till about 2050, and only then is the layer expected to begin to recover.

Applying the Tobacco Institute Approach to Climate Change

A more powerful version of the Tobacco Institute Approach has been used to discredit the science of Climate Change, to create bad science, to mislead the public, to spend large sums of money to influence the politics, and to use enormous financial power to seize political control. On the topic of Climate Change it is important for people to really understand what is going on, because the world cannot afford this confusion anymore.

Although there are many related fields that study how the planetary climate system behaves, the two main fields are those of Atmospheric Chemistry and Atmospheric Physics. Good science is what uses this knowledge as published through peer reviewed papers and articles in scientific journals. **Bad science is that which has not been put through the same wringer** of peer reviews, that is not confirmed by experts in the field, or relies on information that has not been scientifically checked, and is **almost always published by people who have little or no understanding of Atmospheric Chemistry or Atmospheric Physics, and little or no ability to analyze the climate system of planet Earth.** Such people have come up with many false claims and arguments – we take up a few of these and refute them.

Countering the False Claims and Arguments

Claim #1: Carbon dioxide (CO_2) is not causing global warming and Anyway Is Good For You: An increase in carbon dioxide gas in some greenhouses is good for plant growth.

Countering Claim #1: Some higher levels of carbon dioxide may be beneficial inside a physical greenhouse for plant growth. However, scientists the world over (except Climate Deniers) agree that the rising temperatures, the effects of droughts and floods, and the natural disasters made worse by Climate Change, **are very bad for agriculture.** Carbon dioxide (CO_2) concentrations in the atmosphere were very high about 500 million years ago, and temperatures were very high. Over hundreds of millions of years, CO_2 was removed from the atmosphere and buried as the fossils of animals, hence giving the deposits of fossil oil, and burying the carboniferous forests, leading to fossil coal seams. In the Eocene period of the Earth's history (lasting from about 55.8 to 33.9 million years ago), the oceans and forests developed the capacity to absorb the greenhouse gases. This process caused a cooling of the Earth to a point that the temperature of the atmosphere became favorable for us (the human species) and for life as we know it.

To point to the devastation that high CO_2 levels can cause, we look to past scientific data based on fossil dating scientific techniques. About 250 million years ago, we had the Permian-Triassic mass extinction of species that occurred after CO_2 levels rose dramatically, most probably due to volcanic activity, that wiped out 90% of the known species. Besides increased temperatures, ocean acidity rose significantly, much as we see today. The claim that corn yields in northern climates like Alberta, Canada will be increased, fails to mention that agriculture will become worse to the south in the US, and in most places of the world, where higher temperatures, heat waves, irrigation water shortages, catastrophic floods, and adverse plant and insect competitors will hurt crop yields.

Claim #2: Solar Flares are the Cause of Global Warming – Not Green House Gases: It is claimed that solar flares from the sun cause the warming that has been observed, so that changes and activity in the Sun are claimed to be the cause of heating.

Countering Claim #2: Scientific observations (again by scientists in peer reviewed journals), do not detect any significant change in solar activity. From measurements it has been observed that while the lower atmosphere is heating up (due to global warming), the stratosphere (or the upper atmosphere) has been cooling. Based on scientific understanding, if heating was being caused by solar flares, then it is known that the upper atmosphere would see hot spots, which have not been observed.

Claim #3: We are actually seeing Global Cooling: Little dips in the historical record of temperatures, and areas that suddenly experience colder than normal weather for short times are used to make the claim that the Earth's atmosphere is cooling and not heating.

Countering Claim #3: Since we had descended into the lower temperatures of the Ice Ages, after the lifting of the last ice age about 10,000 years ago, geologically speaking the Earth is in a period called the Holocene Interglacial period. If human actions had not intervened we would have headed into another ice age about 10,000 years from now. Thanks to global warming, besides not having an ice age, we will get into a period of much warmer temperatures.

There is no scientific basis for the claim that at the present time the Earth's lower atmosphere is cooling, as clearly shown by the global surface temperature measurements. If one takes the ratio of temperature highs and lows as a measure of temperature rise, in the 1950s the ratio was about 1 (meaning that temperatures were stable). Although there was a small dip in this ratio in the 1960s and 1970s (down to about 0.75), the ratio rose to about 2 by the year 2000 (meaning there were twice as many recorded highs as there were recorded lows), and the ratio was 5 in 2012. Thereafter, we continue to set temperature records with each subsequent year.

Claim #4: Scientists Don't Agree on Climate Change: Over the past decades, the deniers have continued to claim that there is no agreement among scientists as to the causes of and solutions for global warming. They have at times tried to advance scientific sounding type articles and then point to those as proof. They then say that more time is needed to study and research the problem, and hence there needs to be a delay in actions for solutions.

Countering Claim # 4: About 20,000 scientific papers, articles and reports were reviewed by the IPCC for their Fifth Assessment Report. A survey conducted for the 1991-2011 period showed that of the 4,103 papers reviewed, 3,894 agreed with Climate Change science and only 83 disagreed – or **99 out of 100 scientists were of the consensus that significant global warming was occurring and that it was man-made. Only Climate Denier type scientists, that are in a very small minority, disagree with the overwhelming scientific consensus.** We now look at some false arguments.

Other False Arguments by Deniers That Argue
Against Solutions to Climate Change

A look at Climate Deniers shows that almost all of them do NOT have a scientific background, and are either not capable of understanding Atmospheric Chemistry and Physics, or do not want to understand or accept what the genuine science is telling us. They appear to be mainly ideologues who want by hook or by crook to discredit the widely accepted science of Climate Change or the solutions that have emerged. So, when they are not using the Tobacco Institute Approach to try and fool the public, they are making outlandish statements that often have little basis. Here's what some of them sound like.

False Argument #1: "If US cuts green-house gas emissions, the rest of the world will not."

This argument is false because it was US leadership under President Barack Obama and commitments that his administration made to reduce Greenhouse Gas emissions, that convinced almost all of the nations of the world to get serious. This led to the Paris Agreement of December 2015, where as many as 192 nations participated, most of whom made specific voluntary commitments for the first time (even most of the less well-off nations). The US, having historically done most of the past emissions and still the second largest emitter (after China), needed to show leadership and cooperate with the rest of the world. It will take US leadership for the Plan presented in this book to be accepted and implemented. **One thing is true, as this book is emphasizing, that the time has come for ALL nations, including China, India, Russia and other nations to come to the table and start their energy transition to renewable energy, and reduce their fossil fuel emissions to zero by 2050.**

False Argument #2: "Claims of green house gas emissions by rich nations are not reliable."

The claim is that industrial nations have simply outsourced their greenhouse gas emissions to Asia by moving those activities, and so, local emissions may be cut, but these may go up in other nations. Some of this may be true, but what is not true is that claims of green-house gas emissions cuts are not reliable. The International Energy Agency publishes energy use by all nations, and the IPCC has been coming with increasingly accurate ways of confirming claims by nations of their current emissions and reductions of emissions achieved. The richer nations do need to take a wider responsibility for the products they import and the greenhouse gas emissions caused in their production and shipping.

False Argument #3: "Global warming is a socialist conspiracy."

Regardless of which political persuasion you are, such false arguments are used to cause the capitalist sections of the world economy to oppose solutions. One of the ways that climate deniers try to put down all efforts for solution to Climate Change is to call it "socialist" and warn about Stalin type takeover of the economy by the government trying to do things like forcefully redistribute wealth. Nothing could be further from the truth. All solutions that have been proposed for global warming, whether in the US or globally, are proposed to work within the capitalist economy that dominates the world. Whether it is renewable energy (solar, wind and hydro), or energy efficiency, or mass transit or biofuels, these are all interventions in the existing economy that aim at providing economic incentives, investments and programs that are not aiming at an overthrow of the capitalist system – just aiming at changing some of the rules of the game so that the US and the world can begin to de-carbonize the economy. While just transition and energy democracy are championed, ideological arguments are beyond the scope of this book. Many do believe that capitalism is responsible for Climate Change types of problems, but that argument is not dealt with in this book.

False Argument #4: "Solutions to Climate Change will wreck the US and global economy."

There is absolutely no evidence that the solutions for Climate Change that have been implemented already or ones that are being proposed, will wreck the economy! Let's look at some examples of solutions that have already been implemented, to see what effect they have had on the economies of the US and the world. First, in the US, for many decades now, the US has used steady increasing Corporate Average Fuel Economy (CAFÉ) standards to improve the fuel efficiency (increasing miles per gallon or kilometer) and reduce carbon emissions per mile traveled. This has done much to reduce carbon dioxide and nitrous oxide emissions per mile of car driven, but the automobile economy has thrived in the US. Similar efforts in other countries have had similar effects. **There is NO evidence that CAFÉ has hurt the US Auto industry.**

Solar Energy of all types and sizes has grown everywhere and has become part of the new US and global Solar Energy economy. Solar for electric production is cheaper and cleaner today, and is benefiting the overall economies while reducing carbon emissions in the big way. The same is true of wind energy as on land and off-shore wind farms have grown globally and the costs have come way down. **This has created a thriving wind industry and wind power generation activity.** The story has been very similar with solar energy, mass transit, biofuels and hydroelectric power. Plus, the solutions create many new businesses and jobs in clean energy and all related areas. **There is NO EVIDENCE that solutions will wreck ANY economy.** On the contrary, solutions to global warming reduce costs, make economies more competitive, help reduce the increasing natural weather disasters that are starting to devastate economies, and provide cleaner air and water for all. As described in the next section below, Sweden reduced its green-house gas emissions by 20.9 % from 1990 to 2009. In a similar time frame, Sweden's economy actually grew by 44% from 1990 to 2006, showing that emissions reductions, environmental restorations and strong economic growth were possible at the same time.

In fact, everything in this book points to the fact that financially and economically, things will be a lot better with Renewable Energy, storage technologies and the restoration of carbon sink ecosystems (forests and coastal). Energy costs will decrease (the fuel is free), there will be much less pollution, and the Earth will be a much more beautiful and desirable place to live. **So, actually, the opposite is true. If the problem of global warming is not solved in a timely fashion, the economy and environment of the USA, the world and the planet, will be wrecked.** The combination of severe weather, air pollution, global spread of tropical diseases and viruses, water pollution, water and food supply problems, environmental and species degradation and extreme heat, will take a toll of everything.

False Argument #5: "There is too much uncertainty and more research and time are needed:" One of the arguments that climate deniers have put forth often are that there is still much uncertainty, and there is much that needs to be studied and investigated before any actions are taken. When the IPCC says that the high level of certainty exists that Climate Change is occurring and that it is human caused, climate deniers seize on the flip side of it – namely there is still "some" uncertainty. There was a high level of certainty that we have a real global problem when the Kyoto Protocol was signed, and the level of certainty was enough for global society and the US to begin to act to reduce the severity of the problem. It has become clear without a doubt to almost all of the world's climate scientists that human activity, especially the burning of fossil fuels, is the cause of Climate Change. It is the anti-science claims of the climate deniers and their scientists that are flawed.

The "scientific arguments" put forward by "experts" such as Dr. Patrick McMichaels (then professor in the Department of Environmental Sciences at the University of Virginia) in November 1995, to the US House Science Committee, attempted to show that the findings of the IPCC were flawed. The book, *The Heat is On* (1997) by Ross Gelbspan, has a very detailed analysis of McMichaels testimony, including rebuttals by others and the IPCC, that showed his scientific references to non-peer reviewed information and publications, and interpretations of Global Circulation Models (GCMs – that are scientific models of the climate system), showed that his conclusions were severely flawed. He made false statements about Climate Change calculations, claims that the raw data was not provided to scientists on his side of skepticism (when even IPCC relied on peer-reviewed scientific reports and not raw data), and false statements that claimed that the IPCC conclusions were in error, and that newer analysis by scientists on his side of the fence would yield more correct results. When we see that he went on to be the Director of Science at the Cato Institute, which receives about 40% of its funding from the oil industry, and continued his tirade against the established and generally accepted climate science, it's easy to understand how and why his testimony was scientifically flawed and biased. [56]

More False Arguments and Misinformation in
Planet of the Humans Documentary

Now to add to all this comes another piece of Climate Denier misinformation in terms of a documentary by Michael Moore. With a lot of outdated information the movie tries to bunk renewable energy like solar and wind energy, without even talking about the immense damage being done by fossil fuels and their dig, burn and dump cycles, in terms of pollution, destruction of nature and Climate Change, and the trampling on the rights of local and indigenous peoples. The movie uses outdated information about solar PV energy about low efficiency, pollution created in mining and use of fossil fuels – the solar PV industry has moved far past its early days with vast increases in the efficiency, cost and reliability, and the minimization of damage to environment in processing, and high level of recycling of products.

At the time of the writing of this book, solar panel efficiencies (how much solar energy is converted into electrical energy) are much higher than the 8% quoted and have vastly increased, with most panel manufacturers providing "production" guarantees (that the panels will produce at a level equal to at least 80% of their initial capacity), for 25 years – with the panels actually lasting much beyond that. As pointed out in Chapter 2, there are more than 62 utility scale solar PV power stations worldwide of a size greater than 200 MW (megawatt), which is usually the size of a nuclear reactor generating electricity. The same has happened with wind energy, with big increases in efficiency, cost and reliability. Wind Farms are always sited at locations where there is a high wind potential (always measured with instruments for at least a year at the height of the wind turbines), and, although they are changes in wind speeds, they usually are producing energy day and night at relatively constant levels – this has been observed to be true in the Midwest of the US.

The movie gives a lot of misinformation about batteries in terms of their size and reliability. Actually, batteries for all applications such as cars, and utility scale systems (that work along with the electric grid) have increased vastly in terms of cost, efficiency, reliability and in the recycling of materials. They also are increasingly able to take away the disadvantage of the variability of renewable energy (like there is no solar energy when the sun is not shining), by storing that energy during the day in battery packages sized properly for the application. The movie makes a big deal of being off the grid and misses the biggest point – renewable energy is on the grid in order to replace fossil fuel electric power generation – so it needs to be connected to the grid – also, so that when it is producing more energy than needed by the user, the energy flows back into the grid for use by others.

Stand-alone off grid solar PV plus battery systems are only needed in far off places and farms or locations where they are not close to any grid – then they must be sized properly, with larger battery systems. Lastly it makes a big deal by criticizing the burning of wood from trees (biomass), whereas most Climate Change solutions folks have moved away from it. Clean energy is solar, wind, geothermal and battery energy and *not* ethanol plants, natural gas, biomass or biofuels. In fact, most Climate Change folks discourage the use of any technology that burns anything and emits greenhouse gases – without the arguments of the recycling of carbon (that carbon dioxide is absorbed in wood, plants or animals and then later emitted back, hence supposedly making it carbon neutral). Also, incinerators of waste have not been encouraged by any genuine environmentalist. Another point the movie gets totally wrong is the wringing of hands about overpopulation – the big problems of planetary natural destruction and pollution are being caused by the fossil fuel and destructive consumption habits of fewer rich people, and the manner in which they *force* the rest of the population to have *no choice* except to be dependent on fossil fuels.

Lastly, the film attempts to discredit Climate Change activists such as Bill McKibben, Al Gore and those of the Sierra Club by using their old outdated statements and by connecting them with companies that may or may not be doing what they are supposed to be doing, are a lot of smear tactics. As described in the next section, the fossil fuel industry and the Koch brothers have been in the forefront of fighting to keep fossil fuels, in funding climate deniers and in issuing false arguments and information. The cost of renewable energies have fallen to a point where coal fired power plants are not only more expensive to install (about $1,000 per kilowatt for a solar PV System, versus about $3,500 for a coal fired power plant, according to the US Energy Information Agency) and operate (fuel cost for coal versus zero fuel cost for solar), but are more than a thousand times worse than solar energy in the damage they do during mining, transport, burning and solid waste disposal. The Sierra Club has very courageously fought with its Beyond Coal Campaign, and for clean energy and related jobs throughout the US, and in the tradition of Rachel Carson and John Muir have fought big battles to reduce the poisoning of the environment and the destruction of nature. Bill McKibben and Al Gore have very eloquently and selflessly, in their writings informed about and fought for Climate Change solutions for many decades, and are continuing to do so.

Funding the Denial Machine

As it happened for tobacco and for the chemicals that were destroying the Ozone Layer, the funding for fighting against solutions to Global Warming is coming from those companies whose profits would be reduced if these solutions were implemented.

Major Funders: The first and foremost in funding and supporting these efforts is the fossil fuel industry (oil, coal and natural gas) that has benefitted by enormous profits for more than a century and sees the threat of its profits being reduced. All the of the major US oil companies have lined up to fund these efforts, including ExxonMobil, Chevron, Conoco Phillips and Occidental Petroleum. Coal companies funding such efforts are like Alpha Natural Resources. There are many groups and companies that are active in financing climate denial groups worldwide such as Anschutz, Bradley, Coors, DeVos, Dunn, Howard, Pope, Scaife, Searle and Seid.

Global Oil's Anti-Climate Lobbying Actions: Although it appeared that the oil majors were not spending much directly on lobbying, a research analysis by InfluenceMap revealed that the five major oil companies (ExxonMobil, Royal Dutch Shell, Chevron, BP and Total), invested over a $1 billion in the three years after December 2015, when the Paris Agreement was signed, on lobbying and branding efforts that worked against the purposes of the agreement in solving the problem of Climate Change. Instead their efforts were aimed at making sure that the social, legal and political measures stayed in place that would help them to continue expanding their fossil fuel operations. Nearly $200 million of these funds per year have been used to control, delay, or block climate solutions related measures. In spite of their positive statements in regard to Climate Change, and with sales of $1 Trillion and profits of about $55 billion in 2018, they have planned a combined capital investment of $115 billion in 2019, most of it for expanded oil and natural gas exploration and production, but only 3% of that will go to low carbon investments. This is **Greenwashing** at its best (see below).

While all of the majors continue to push the importance of the need for increased oil and gas production, supposedly to meet growing energy demand, Chevron, BP and ExxonMobil have led direct efforts to oppose a whole range of policy initiatives and actions that aim at climate solutions. The aim has been to build public support while ensuring that climate policy initiatives are defeated. In a social media strategy, led by ExxonMobil, the majors effectively used a $2 million social media campaign to promote increased oil and gas production, while successfully fighting a number of climate solutions related ballot measures in various states in the November 2018 US mid-term elections. At the same time, this strategy is complimented by about $195 million per year investment by the five companies through their jointly funded Oil and Gas Climate Initiative, which admits the need for climate regulation, while emphasizing voluntary action and low carbon investments. Meanwhile, ExxonMobil's plan to reach 10,000 barrels of biofuels production a day by 2025, would amount to about 0.3% of its current refinery capacity!

InfluenceMap assessed the full corporate carbon policy footprint of these oil companies that accounts for their direct operational and supply chain greenhouse gas emissions and emissions resulting from direct product use, and adding that the actions of these companies oppose actions that lead to solutions for Climate Change. Their corporate lobbying has consisted of influencing the political stories and public's understanding of Climate Change. These narratives by the oil companies have advanced many of the false scientific statements and the false arguments referred to above by their Chief Executive Officers (including Rex Tillerson, who became Trump's Secretary of State), fighting climate solutions, regulations, the US Environmental Protection Agency, and political battles at the same time. Spending on their branding activities has meant pushing their oil related products that lead to global warming, by putting them in a good light, which again has been about $195 million annually.

The oil producing nations are not standing idly by. Like the other climate deniers, they engage in their own version of greenwashing. While voicing strong support for the Paris Agreement,

OPEC (Organization of Petroleum Exporting Countries) has come out strongly criticizing the push for switching to renewable energy by IPCC. Like the US oil industry it claims that oil is needed to alleviate poverty in much of the world, although the world economic system has been busy creating poverty for many years.

In the US it has been the Koch brothers that have funded the denial machine. Between 1997 (the year of the Kyoto Protocol) and 2017, the Koch family foundations financed 92 groups up to about $127 million to attack Climate Change science and solutions. Among other actions, the Koch brothers' efforts excelled at using the Tobacco Institute Approach to fight California's efforts. Their funding for the Pacific Research Institute (PRI) enabled the latter to recycle a criticized "Spanish Study" that was an attack on the renewable energy industry, that aimed at discrediting California's efforts to create more clean energy jobs. The oil industry fights all of these solutions tooth and nail while claiming to be proceeding in a "Green" direction in regard to Climate Change.

Greenwashing

This is the process by which a company talks as if it is totally in agreement with all the things that are being said about the need to start solving Climate Change, then doing a little bit in terms of lower carbon activities, highlighting these small activities in a big way to make it seem that they are totally on board, and then doing the exact opposite in terms of their main actions, and on the side fighting all of the financial, media, and political battles to defeat actions aimed at climate solutions. So, these businesses portray themselves as being environmentally responsible, engaging in "green advertising" based on half-truths and lies and then actually behaving in a contrary way! All of the actions of the big oil majors have been strong in the area of greenwashing.

The Politics of Climate Change

Very reluctantly, and after great goading by the United Nations Environment Program (UNEP) and people such as Maurice Strong, the world signed the global warming treaty in 1992 (UN Framework Convention on Climate Change). The treaty was just a statement of principles and did not commit any nation to do anything. It took a lot of leadership and goading by many people, including Bill Clinton and Al Gore, to bring the nations together to actually commit to actions, which resulted in the Kyoto Protocol in 1997 (five years later). The Kyoto Protocol committed the industrial nations, as described above, to reducing their green-house gas emissions to 1990 levels by about 2008-2012.

Although during Al Gore's time as vice-president, and Bill Clinton as President, the US did sign the Kyoto Protocol in 1997, the US never ratified it because the Republican Party controlled Congress and Senate refused to sign it. Anyway, the Protocol actually went into force much later on February 16, 2005, when the required 55 nations had ratified it. With the coming of the Republican administration of George Bush in 2000, the US showed strong signs of withdrawing from the Kyoto Protocol. In the absence of national or federal level leadership, many communities around the US, and states such as California pushed ahead with their own compliance. California passed a law (AB32), which committed it to reduce its green-house gas (GHG) emissions to 1990 levels (about 400 million metric tons of CO2 equivalent) by the year 2020. California's GHG emissions actually peaked in between, and it was successful in reducing them to below 1990 levels in 2018 itself. California's economy is booming and it is having the largest addition of businesses and jobs in the whole nation. In fact, so many jobs are being created in California, that the housing stock has not been able to keep up with it.

By 2009, based on emissions from fuel combustion only, Germany and Sweden met their Kyoto targets. Sweden reduced its greenhouse gas emissions by 20.9% from 1990 to 2009. In a similar time frame, Sweden's economy actually grew by 44% from 1990 to 2006, showing that emissions reductions, environmental restorations and strong economic growth were possible at the same time. Sweden reduced its emissions from housing and services by about 50%, mainly due to the use of heat pumps and burning pellets, and reduced its emissions from transportation by switching to clean energy buses, and introducing road toll taxes to reduce traffic and pollution. The nations of the Eastern Europe and the former Soviet Union also met their Kyoto targets, but mainly because of the collapse of their economies after the collapse of the Soviet Union.

In a way, the denial machine became more active in the US in 2001, when the former US president George W. Bush and vice-president Dick Cheney changed the US climate policy, rejected the move to limit greenhouse gas emissions, essentially withdrew from the Kyoto Protocol, and began to cooperate with organizations that supported misinformation on global warming. They adopted very weak policies in regard to emissions, with their goal being to avoid emissions regulations on the fossil fuel industry, and steer the political conversations in that direction. They encouraged an alliance between the fossil fuel industry and contrarian scientists in order to promote the denial machine. What started in the past in the tobacco industry and in fighting the ozone layer by chemicals destruction theory got energized into doing the same for Climate Change – the Tobacco Institute Approach.

In the 2016 US presidential election they supported Republican candidates other than Trump. However, with Trump as US president, they have gotten what they dreamed of. First, they have a US president who is a climate denier and has called global warming a "Hoax". Trump has not only rejected all the reports of the IPCC, but has also rejected the fourth US national Climate Assessment published by 13 of his own US government agencies. The disinformation machine, the scare tactics, the Tobacco Institute Approach, and political actions have been in full gear, all helping the Denial Machine get stronger. For America and for the world, this may be called, "The Great Leap Backwards".

Meanwhile China continues to base its development on coal and says it will only peak its greenhouse gas emissions by 2030. With the US reversing its position on Climate Change, China has been able to delay any significant actions. China has continued to use coal to fuel its progress, even as it talks about its solar energy and other renewable energy activities.

We now come to a major aspect of our entire civilization, that constitutes a barrier to solutions.

The Inertia of a Fossil Fuel Civilization

Chopping wood for personal cooking and heat occurred early in human civilization. Then came the use of wood as a fuel at the start of the industrial revolution to provide fuel and power for stoves, furnaces and small machines. To make the wood fuel more portable, it was converted to charcoal by partial burning, which was used in early industry for quite some time. Employing wood and charcoal for personal and industrial use led to the large scale deforestation of major land areas. Much of North America was deforested during this time. Most of the rest of the world has historically suffered deforestation when wood was used as fuel.

Historically, as coal began to be used, factories, buildings, homes, ships and steam railway engines were fueled with coal. So the cities, transportation and industries were designed to burn coal. Then with the coming of electricity, coal began to be used for generating electricity, which is mostly what it is used for today. Then, as oil or petroleum based fuels began to replace coal and wood at many locations, the entire civilization was redesigned and organized for the use of these fuels (mainly gasoline or petrol, diesel and jet fuel). Since automobiles or cars and trucks were the principal mode of transport using oil, all cities and new urban areas in the industrial nations (like the US, Canada, Europe, Australia, and Japan) began to be designed for cars and fossil fuel vehicles, developed and built to be spread with houses, buildings and parking lots taking up large areas. Most houses were even designed with garages to house the cars. This mode of urban development, that has been called urban sprawl, made sure that the oil fueled cars and trucks were favored, as the highways, city roads, houses, buildings and factories were designed only for them.

The latest stage is the growth of natural gas as it emits the lowest greenhouse gases among the fossil fuels, and is the cleanest burning locally (although its production causes significant emissions of methane, a strong greenhouse gas). Also, the use of "Fracking" or hydraulic fracturing of rock formations to release the trapped gas, has been a major cause of the pollution of ground water and the setting off of mild earthquakes. So the US (including California), China and the European Union have been increasing their use of natural gas. In fact, the US boasts that it has become an exporter of natural gas, and a low cost producer.

Then came the big jump on surface transport as the US led the world and developed and built large networks of limited access "Highways" that enabled fossil fuel cars and trucks to zoom along without being delayed by signal lights, stop signs or crossings. The rest of the world wanted to be like the "developed" USA, so they copied it, and all of the international loans to many of the developing countries were to encourage and finance the building of these kinds of highways, and the mega factories to build cars for them. Big limited access highways became a symbol of being "developed" and most nations and regions of the world adopted them, making the fossil fuel cars and trucks and their highways the biggest source of greenhouse gas emissions globally. As noted above, oil based agricultural machines replaced animal and alcohol fueled vehicles. When alcohol made from crops was becoming a significant fuel for agricultural machines and cars, US oil companies used the excuse of alcohol prohibition to shut down the alcohol production from crops by farmers or other alcohol energy producers.

The situation today is that the oil companies and the oil producing nations have made sure that all aspects of energy use are totally dependent on fossil fuels and the greenhouse gases they emit. Almost everyone drives gasoline or petrol fueled vehicles for personal transport, and almost everyone uses diesel fueled vehicles to transport goods and services. Even items ordered from the internet or on-line are actually delivered to houses or businesses by fossil fueled trucks. All other aspects of civilization – agriculture, homes, buildings, shipping and air travel are fueled by fossil fuels. We live in a fossil fuel civilization where very little today gets done or moves without the burning of fossil fuels and their greenhouse gas emissions. But this fossil fuel use is hurting economically.

There is much damage that is being done by Climate Change to society and to business. The most recent US National Climate Assessment noted that US businesses suffered losses from extreme weather events and natural disasters of about $91 billion in 2018, and that the losses could climb to $500 billion per year. The Sierra Club Magazine also described how Climate Change was starting to hurt business in a big way. **[56] The United Nations reports that between 1998 and 2017, the affected countries reported direct losses of about $2.2 trillion out of total losses of about $2.9 trillion from all sources.** That's more than twice what was lost in the previous twenty years, and about 77% of total losses from any cause. This compares with the losses of only $895 billion from 1978 to 1997.

The commercial and political interests have long fought wars for the control and domination of oil producing areas, all the way from the colonial era to today. They are expected to continue their fight in the political, financial and military arenas for quite some time – not only for control of these areas but also the continued use of these fuels. But the world has to begin the transition away from fossil fuels that are driving the Climate Crisis and it needs to wean the commercial, political and military interests away from the destruction of fossil fuels into a new energy and world economy that is fair to all and begins to solve Climate Change in a timely manner. That is what the Book Plan is aiming at.

Chapter 11

Global Plan for Reducing Other Greenhouse Gas Emissions

This chapter describes the current situation with the other Greenhouse Gas Emissions that are leading to Climate Change (almost all of which are man-made), and besides the Plan described in the above chapters for reducing carbon dioxide (CO2) emissions, also describes the Plan for the non-CO2 gases, such as methane, nitrous oxides, and fluorinated gases, all of which add to Climate Change like CO2. The UN Intergovernmental Panel on Climate Change (IPCC) published a report in October 2018 that clearly laid out the fact that in order to keep the global average temperature rise to at or below 1.5 degrees Celsius, the following reductions in emissions are needed by 2055 (Except for CO2, the other percent changes are approximate and were picked from graphs in the Report):

❏ Carbon dioxide (CO2) emissions needed to be reduced to zero by 2055
❏ For Other non-CO2 gases:
❏ Methane (CH4) gas emissions needed to be reduced by at least 50%, and
❏ Nitrous Oxide (N2O) emissions reduced by about 25%
❏ In the report targets are not mentioned for fluorinated gas emissions.
❏ Black carbon emissions reduced by about 50%, and will be addressed in the future

These targets were adopted by the Plan as goals for emissions reductions for the year 2050, as defined in Chater 1.

APPROACH TAKEN IN THIS BOOK:

❑ **All carbon dioxide emissions reductions are achieved main-ly through transition away from fossil fuels to zero carbon renewable energy. The rest through stopping deforestation and afforestation.**

❑ **Carbon Absorption through reforestation, afforestation and coastal ecosystems, as per Plan in Chapter 3, are consid-ered as a bonus, that will be subject to the level of wildfires and storms, with credit for only 5% of the emissions reduc-tions.**

❑ **BECCS is not considered a significant candidate** as it will need large scale diversion of croplands from food crops in agriculture and will need massive inputs of fossil fuels (or at least energy by itself) as needed by the current "green revolution" agriculture.

❑ **While Carbon Dioxide Removal (CDR), and Carbon Capture and Sequestration (CCS) may come to represent significant strategies quantitatively, as of now these appear to be very expensive, will themselves consume much energy, and very little exists by the way of demonstration projects.**

Current Situation with Greenhouse Gas Emissions

In spite of all the publicity it has received, global greenhouse gas emissions (as reported by the Global Carbon Project) grew in **2019, with the carbon dioxide (CO2) emissions growing by 0.6% over 2018 to 36.8 billion Metric Tons,** and have grown for the last three consecutive years. Add the estimated 6 billion metric tons emitted from forest wildfires in the US and the Amazon, and the actual car-bon dioxide emissions were about 43 billion metric tons.

Here are the Greenhouse Gas (GHG) Emissions for the top sev-en GHG emitters globally for 2017. These emissions include other greenhouse gases, and also include livestock and transport figures. These are reported by the World Resources Institute (WRI) as report-ed in Wikipedia.

WORLD GREENHOUSE GAS EMISSIONS FOR 2017

Nation	GHG Emissions, MtCO2e	GHG Emissions, Percent Approx. (%)	GHG Emissions Per Capita, TCO2e	Cumulative GHG Emissions, Percent (%)
World	45,260	100	6	
China	12,450	28	8	12.5
US	6,670	15	19	25
EU28	4,220	9	8	22
India	2,380	5	2	3
Russia	2,200	5	15.5	6
Japan	1,350	3.0	10	4
Brazil	1,018	2	5.5	-
Others	14,972	33		

Total emissions reported in MtCO2e – or Millions of Metric Tons of Carbon Dioxide Equivalent. These do not include emissions from land use change and forestry, nor from imported goods. The emissions numbers of all other non-CO2 gases have been converted to carbon dioxide equivalents using their 100 year Global Warming Potential (GWP). Meaning the actual emissions data for a gas (say methane or CH4) has been converted by multiplying its emissions by its GWP number. For the 100 year number, methane has a GWP of 28, and nitrous oxide has a GWP number of 265. EU28 is the European Union of 28 nations, lumped together as a nation. So, for example if carbon dioxide was the only gas, then 45,260 Million Metric tons of it would trap the same amount of heat as the combination of gases that calculate out to 45,260 MtCO2e. [58]

Here is the same data for total GHG emissions shown visually as a pie chart.

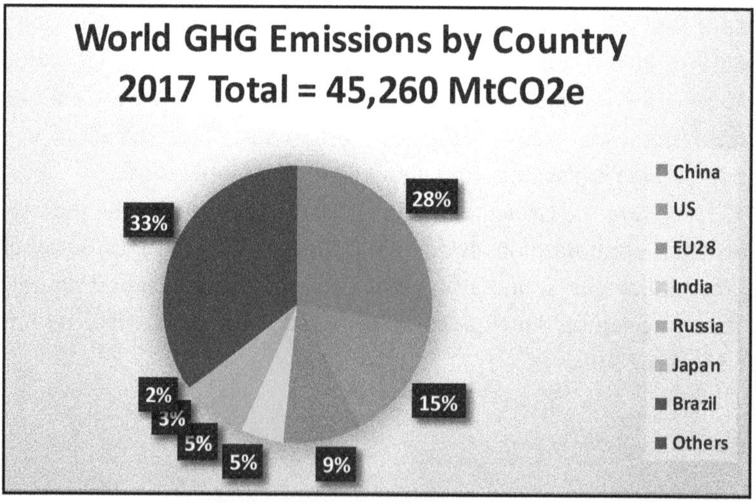

World GHG Emissions by Country
2017 Total = 45,260 MtCO2e

China
US
EU28
India
Russia
Japan
Brazil
Others

28%
33%
2%
3%
5%
5%
9%
15%

Figure 10.1 – GHG Emissions of different nations as a percentage of total (45,260 MtCO2)

As can be seen from the above table and pie chart, the top seven (7) emitter nations emitted about 67% of all emissions or about 2/3rds of the total. Also, China's emissions have grown to be about double that of the US, whereas, as of the year 2000, China's GHG emissions were about half that of the US. Also, **China's per capita (per person) emissions at about 8 Metric Tons CO2 equivalent are now about at par with those of other developed nations (although still half of those of the US) – while India is still at 1/4th that of China.** *On this basis, China needs to start to reduce its emissions immediately, and not by 2030.* Also the table indicates that the US and the European Union (of 28 nations) combined have historically emitted nearly 47% of all emissions from preindustrial times. Here are descriptions of the three main contributing Greenhouse Gases.

Carbon Dioxide (CO2): Consists of one atom of carbon and two atoms of oxygen. This is primarily emitted by the burning of fossil fuels and has been the subject of most of this book. However, it is also emitted by deforestation, land clearing for agriculture and soil degradation. It can also be absorbed in a significant way by reforestation, improved fertility soils and expanded coastal ecosystems, as has been described in an earlier chapter.

Methane (CH4): Consists of one atom of carbon and four atoms of hydrogen. This is emitted by agricultural activities, waste facilities, energy use (leakage at oil and gas facilities), and burning of biomass.

Nitrous Oxide (N2O): Consists of two atoms of nitrogen and one atom of oxygen (although there are other nitrogen oxides), and is primarily emitted by fertilizer use, and the combustion of fossil fuels (while a fossil fuel is being burned).

Fluorinated Gases (F-Gases): The most notorious ones were CFCs (Chlorofluorocarbons) that were used in air conditioners and refrigerators, but which also destroyed the Ozone Layer, high in the atmosphere, that protected us from ultra-violet light, an excess of which was bad for life and resulted in skin cancer for all humans. Today there is a big list of these gases that were intended to substitute for CFCs, in order to have less destructive effect on the Ozone Layer, but they ended up having a big effect per unit of gas on global warming. These now need to be substituted by gases that cause less global warming.

We now look at what the emissions of each of these gases are in terms of how they affect global warming.

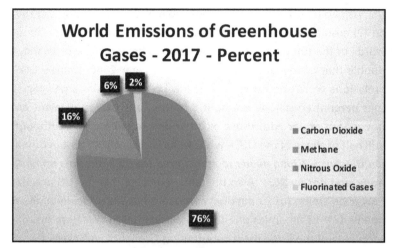

WORLD EMISSIONS OF GREENHOUSE GASES – 2017
What this pie chart shows is that carbon dioxide contributes to about 76% of the global warming, methane about 16%, nitrous oxide by about 6%, and fluorinated gases by about 2%.

The emissions of methane, nitrous oxide and fluorinated gases is calculated using their Global Warming Potential (GWP). The following table provides the Global Warming Potentials (GWP) of each of these main gases, which is the amount each of these gases trap relative to carbon dioxide over time.

GLOBAL WARMING POTENTIAL OF MAIN GREENHOUSE GASES.

Gas Name	Chemical Formula	Lifetime (Years)	GWP (20 – Year)	GWP (100- Year)	GWP (500- Year)
Carbon Dioxide	CO2	30-95	1	1	1
Methane	CH4	12	84	28	7.6
Nitrous Oxide	N2O	121	264	265	153
F-Gases	Different	10-50,000	5,000-20,000	2,000 – 24,000	500-24,000

This tells you that the molecules of a gas trap heat that many times more than carbon dioxide.

What the above table means is that a ton of methane gas traps 84 times more heat than a ton of carbon dioxide over a 20 year period, while a ton of nitrous oxide traps about 264 times more heat in the same period. The GWPs of the F-Gases are much more and these gases stay around for longer periods of time, and are entirely man-made and do not occur in nature. Depending on which GWP time period is used, the actual emissions of methane and nitrous oxide are multiplied by the selected GWP number to calculate the emissions contributions as Carbon Dioxide Equivalent (CO2e), as shown in the pie chart above in which carbon dioxide is shown as 76% of the emissions. These emissions are then added to the carbon dioxide emissions in order to calculate the total greenhouse gas emissions.

It's the increases in the concentrations of these gases in the atmosphere, caused mainly by the burning of fossil fuels, that are at the heart of Climate Change. These are the gases that increasingly trap the heat of sunlight all the time, thus causing the Earth's lower atmosphere to heat up, which causes the oceans to heat up.

The increases in the atmospheric concentration of these gases from pre-industrial times, that existed before the year 1750, are listed in the following table.

INCREASES IN THE CONCENTRATION OF GASES SINCE 1750.

Gas Name	Chemical Formula	Unit of Measure	Concentrations in Atmosphere	
			Pre-1750	Recent
Carbon Dioxide	CO2	ppm	280	410
Methane	CH4	ppb	770	1,800
Nitrous Oxide	N2O	ppb	270	325

Ppm = parts per million. So 410 ppm of CO2 in atmosphere means that there are 410 molecules of CO2, out of a total of a million total molecules (a molecule is the smallest unit of the gas, and consists of one atom of carbon and two atoms of oxygen combined attached to each other). Ppb means parts per billion. So a methane or CH4 concentration of 1,800 ppb means that out of a total count of one billion molecules, 1,800 of them are CH4 molecules.

The Pre-1750 levels of these gases were actually good for life on Earth, as some heat was trapped keeping the global average temperature in a range that is good for us humans and life as we know it, because otherwise the temperatures would be very cold. However, the reverse of that has happened, and as we have pumped massive amounts of these gases (mainly CO2) by burning fossil fuels, these have given us an excessive level of heating that is not good for us humans and life as we know it, and it is adding greatly to the current extinction of species. The past chapters of this book addressed how we reduce carbon dioxide mainly through a massive energy transition strategy. We now present plans for reducing the other greenhouse gases

Plan for Reducing Methane Emissions

The five major sources of methane emissions are:
1. Leakage from the production of oil and natural gas (methane is part of natural gas) – the largest contributor.
2. Enteric fermentation in the guts of cattle, pigs, sheep and goats.
3. Emissions from large lagoons where manure from animals is stored.
4. Emissions from landfills, where the organic wastes produce methane when they are biodegrading.
5. Leakage of methane from coal mines.

Globally, the Plan for reducing methane emissions is as follows:
1. In the short term, requiring all methane emissions from oil and natural gas extraction and production to be burnt, captured and burnt off (emitting some CO_2).
2. In the long term (by 2050), eliminating the use of fossil fuels, so that there is no extraction and processing of oil, gas and coal – hence no emission of methane from this biggest source.
3. Reducing the population of animals (cattle, pigs, sheep and goats), which are major contributors of deforestation as well, as described in an earlier chapter. The meat tax will help with this process.
4. Having closer control of manure in lagoons, by enclosing them and porting the methane so that it is burnt off (emitting some CO_2).
5. Eliminating the green and organic wastes (mainly kitchen wastes) from landfills, so that all future garbage does not generate methane emissions, and all the methane emis-

sions from organic wastes that are already there are collected and burnt. All of the kitchen and green waste will be directed to composting and industrial scale composting facilities will be set up for this.

6. The only remaining source of methane will be enteric fermentation from the guts of animals, and all other sources will have been eliminated or used to generate energy by burning it, with some emissions of CO_2 resulting. Some of this can be reduced by changing the feed of these animals.

7. By these means, methane emissions will be reduced by more than 50% by 2050 (which will exceed the goal)

Plan for Reducing Nitrous Oxide Emissions

The major sources of Nitrous Oxide Emissions are:

1. The biggest source of emissions is from agriculture through the use of nitrogen fertilizers, from manure and from the burning of agricultural residues (70-80% of emissions).

2. Nitrous oxide is also emitted when fossil fuels are burned, mainly through automobile exhaust emissions.

3. Emissions of the gas occur in industry when chemicals involving nitrogen are being produced or handled.

4. The fourth major source of the gas is from wastewater treatment during nitrification or denitrification of mainly fertilizer runoff present in wastewater.

Globally, the Plan for Reducing Nitrous Oxide Emissions is as follows:

1. Since car exhausts emit a significant output of nitrous oxide, improving the emissions reductions by better technology in catalytic converters will reduce emissions.

2. However, replacing all fossil fuel vehicles by battery electric or non-carbon fuel vehicles will eliminate ALL emissions from cars by 2050 – so that is what the Plan is.

3. Plan calls for the reduction in the use of nitrogen fertilizers by switching to organic fertilizers produced on the farm, and alternating crops to use nitrogen fixing crops that capture nitrogen from the air, store it in the soil, and use it for plants. The manure management practices will be changed

to reduce N2O emissions.

4.   Plan calls for implementing technology upgrades in the production of adipic acid that releases N2O. Adipic acid is also known as hexane dioic acid, 2.5 billion kilograms (or about 5.5 billion pounds) of which are produced globally annually – **this is a white crystalline powder that is used in the production of nylon**.

Plan for Reducing All Fluorinated Gas (F-Gases) Emissions

Plan calls for:

1.   Reducing all leaks of these chemicals from refrigerant systems.

2.   Substituting all of these chemicals with ones that neither destroy the ozone layer (in the high stratosphere of the atmosphere), nor cause global warming.

3.   As was done for CFCs earlier, these gases need to be emptied from units (refrigerators and air conditioners) where they are and then neutralized and disposed of. These units need a program to replace them with units having the substitute chemicals. This can be handled as part of the treaty to protect the ozone layer.

So, by the year 2050, The carbon dioxide (CO2) emissions will be reduced to zero by eliminating fossil fuels and ending deforestation, the methane (CH4) emissions will be reduced by 50%, and the nitrous oxide emissions will be reduced by 25%, and the goals will have been met.

Chapter 12

The Jobs and Economy Aspects of the Plan – Including Just Transition and Energy Democracy

The transformation for Climate Change is both a challenge and an opportunity. It is a challenge in terms of making sure we achieve the greenhouse gas emissions globally in a timely manner and an opportunity to make sure that the benefits of the transformation are widespread. To the maximum extent possible the plan of this book and strategies to implement it must be designed to help small cities, regions and companies so that the local people benefit from and increasingly control the activities, institutions and finances.

For solar energy, the fuel is free and it falls everywhere, so aside from some equipment and installation costs, and some fee for being connected to the grid, "consumers" and "customers", namely ordinary folks, should not have to pay much for the energy (definitely less than what they pay today). Transmission costs can be high if all of the renewable energy power plants are big and centralized and need very large new transmission lines, as the transmission costs will be high. That is why the renewable energy sources should be located as close to the end users as possible and the transmission lines added should be smaller.

This chapter addresses:

1. The Jobs and Economy aspects of the Plan,
2. The Just Transition aspect (the transition for those involved in fossil fuels – both production and use), and
3. The Energy Democracy aspects (greater local democratic control of new businesses).

Jobs and Economy Aspects of the Plan

We first look at what others have said about employment and job additions.

Jobs Projections by IRENA: The International Renewable Energy Association (IRENA) estimated **that in 2016, about 40 million people were employed in the global energy sector, of which about 30 million were employed in fossil fuels and about 10 million in renewable energy.** In their best case for a transition (their REmap case), they projected that by 2030 fossil fuel employment would go down to about 24 million and the combination of renewable energy, increased efficiency and grid enhancement would employ about 61 million people, for a total of 85 million (or about 45 million more people employed in 2030, compared to 2016). Again, for their RE map case, by 2050, the total employment would have shrunk down to about 76 million, with only 21 million employed in fossil fuels, and about 55 million employed in combined renewable energy, energy efficiency and grid enhancement (Climate Change solutions areas). **So, they are saying that by 2030 about 51 million more people will be employed in these Climate Change solutions areas and that by 2050, about 45 million more people will be employed. So, IRENA is projecting big jobs growth benefits of the transition away from fossil fuels.** [4]

We think that IRENA is still projecting too high a level of continued fossil fuel employment even with moving aggressively towards the Climate Change solutions areas – about 21 million people. **In this Book Plan, by 2050, almost** *all* **the fossil fuel employment should have shifted to the renewable energy, emissions reductions and ecosystem rejuvenation areas, and only a residual of a few millions should remain employed in fossil fuel clean up and remaining activities. So here is what the Book Plan proposes.**

All of the areas of the Plan will need a large number of new businesses and, as IRENA estimates, a big increase in employment. Employment will increase in the following activities.

ENERGY

1. Renewable Energy of all kinds, but especially solar PV – from production, transport, construction, installation, and then maintenance and management.

2. Storage technologies of all kinds, but to begin with battery technologies of all sizes and types – a big expansion.

3. Other storage technologies will also need work, depending on what is locally feasible – water pumped storage, molten slats produced by concentrated solar plants.

4. The green production of storage fuels, their storage, transportation, and then their end-use in making electricity, and in industry, buildings, ships and vehicles.

ELECTRIFICATION

1. Production of all of the electrical hardware for transmission – cables, substation hardware (switching, transforming, etc.), towers, and other hardware.

2. Installation of transmission lines and interconnection points between a spur line (where electricity is being produced) and main line (which carries it to the end user).

3. Electrification technologies and hardware for buildings, homes, industry, and agriculture, and their installation by contractors.

TRANSPORTATION

1. The production, sales and delivery of a very large number of battery electric vehicles.

2. Solar-Electric Highways – the global production, installation and operation of solar-electric charging stations.

3. The production, sales and delivery of a very large number of fuel cell vehicles that use storage fuels.

4. The production and installation of solar PV and other renewable energy based production units on-site that produce, store and supply green storage fuels.

5. The construction of major pedways and bikeways in cities and surrounding areas.

6. The construction and operation of expanded mass transit bus, light rail, rail lines.

7. The construction and maintenance of a global high speed rail network, directly linked with and connected with airports, mass transit lines and bikeways and pedways.

INDUSTRIALIZATION

1. Every aspect of the energy transformation will need big increases in production of all of the hardware and technologies for every aspect of the areas above.

2. One area of new industrialization is for the making of new equipment that will enable small businesses to engage in local production for local use, that will help in the upliftment of depressed communities. Most of these local industries will process forest and agricultural products from some of the newly afforested and transformed agricultural areas, except from the areas that need to encourage biodiversity.

3. All industrialization needs to be dependent on new clean renewable energy, and be pro-employment and pro-environment. Production processes will be such as to maximize employment and be skill intensive rather than automated, with tax reforms favoring greater employment.

REFORESTATION AND AFFORESTATION

1. The One billion hectares of reforestation and afforestation will require massive employment in all activities from tree nurseries to planting and taking care of these areas.

2. The newly afforested or reforested areas will require manpower so as to design and implement the features that require an ability to control and minimize wildfires.

3. The new areas that need a revival of biodiversity will need local communities to tend these areas and earn employment through eco-tourism and only extractive harvesting that leave the forest intact.

4. Those areas that are allowed to be tree plantation areas can harvest trees on a selective basis as long as they plant more than they harvest, no clear cutting is allowed, and tree diversity is such that biodiversity of plant and animal life is still encouraged.

COASTAL ECOSYSTEMS

1. All of the coastal ecosystems will need the proper design and construction of shoreline and offshore civil engineering structures so as to create the special aspects that will enable the planting of the trees and plants needed by the coastal ecosystems.

2. For mangrove swamps will need the planting of mangrove trees, and for sea grasses, it will need the underwater planting of sea grasses (like eel grass).

3. These activities will create much employment as they will be on a larger scale than ever before.

4. Since these ecosystems will lead to a revival of ocean life and fish varieties, the fisheries will be renewed, and this will create a resurgence and much increase in employment for the fishermen and the fishing industry.

Some of these areas are qualitatively described here.

For **Sustainable Transportation** the city is suitably planned to maximize the use of walking, biking and public transportation. **The city will be designed so as minimize the distances needing to be traveled, and hence reducing the distances that cars need to travel, and discourage the use of car transportation – both to relieve congestion and to reduce the carbon emissions from vehicles.** The design of the city will be such as to maximize the areas in which the people could walk and bike and take public transportation, and minimize the use of transportation needing fossil fuel combustion – hence minimizing noise, pollution and carbon emissions from vehicular travel. The transportation plan for the habitat must offer quiet, clean, healthy and safe low carbon choices – also ones that are suitable for the elderly and the disabled. Transforming our cities to this mode, and creating new developments will create many jobs. **This is the type of infrastructure that we need to invest in – not more and more infrastructure spending on roads and bridges supporting cars and trucks!**

Sustainable or Regenerative Agriculture can create more jobs, income and employment in the farm sector. This type of agriculture has been described in Chapter 6. Regenerative agriculture means farming that uses less tillage, more natural fertilizer, none or very little pesticides and herbicides, conserves water, and uses a lot of different types of mostly traditional varieties of seeds and crops. This type of agriculture is more skill intensive, requires more attention to land management, and at the organic end, produces farm output that fetches a far better price. Best of all, it is capable of providing more jobs and better livelihoods and incomes for more people. In the US, a study of 13 counties in the state of Missouri showed that converting to sustainable agriculture would provide support for more than 165 farm households per county, and more than 300 additional farm and non-farm households in total. Plus, it would support local production for local use as described below, as more people could earn their income processing the agricultural output.

Sustainable Forestry is another area that can create many jobs. This needs to be combined with the Plan strategy to reforest and Afforest the Earth as described in Chapter 3. The definition of sustainable foresty adopted by the international Food and Agricultural Organization (FAO) is: "The stewardship and use of forests and forest lands in a way, and at a rate, that maintains their biodiversity, productivity, regeneration capacity, vitality and their potential to fulfill, now and in the future, relevant ecological, economic and social functions, at local, national, and global levels, and that does not cause damage to other ecosystems." In this approach, resources are harvested from forests (including timber), in a manner that the forest itself is standing and performing much of its ecological function and serving as an important carbon sink. Sustainable forestry is not plantation style forestry that uses clear cutting through mechanized operations, reduces labor content and leaves a devastated countryside and the clear cutting of old growth forests. On the other hand, sustainable forest management can create many jobs through afforestation, reforestation, management of existing forests, revival of urban green spaces, improvements of watersheds, protection of forests from fire (or an ecosystem approach) and the growth of forest tourism. Such investments would further revive rural areas and raise their living standards. It must be added here that other land ecosystems such as savannahs, grasslands and chaparals must also be restored and afforestation should not occur at the expense of these other 'ecosystems.'

Employment in fishing has been declining globally for some time now. Employment could be revived if sustainable fishing practices were adopted, as in many cases they are. **Sustainable Fishery Management** means that the fish catch must not exceed the regenerative capacity of the fishery, so that there is enough fish left that enable them to reproduce in sufficient numbers. This will be combined with the Plan for the expansion of coastal ecosystems as described in Chapter 3. The marine ecosystems' health will improve over time, so that the species that depend on it can reproduce and have a habitat that enables them to survive and thrive. All of the coastal ecosystems globally need to be revived as they have degraded by too much human development – marine coastal ecosystems such as mangrove swamps need to be revived and expanded, so that storm surges are lessened and species get habitats to survive in. This may mean in some places giving less importance to beaches and more to the coastal ecosystems. This would make the coastal areas more able to absorb the effects of hurricanes, cyclones and coastal storms.

The next is **Sustainable Industry**, which uses mainly renewable raw materials, helps develop alternatives or replacements faster than depleting mined raw materials, has a low carbon footprint, is more skill intensive rather than capital or energy intensive, does not create toxic wastes or effectively treats them, recycles the rest of its wastes, and only sustainably uses resources from carbon sinks (forests, agriculture or fisheries) – so that these do not deplete too fast so as to collapse the ecosystems on which these depend. This needs to go hand in hand with the Plan for the electrification of industry and making it more reliant on locally and on-site produced renewable energy (mostly solar PV). Also, truly sustainable industry is that which encourages and enables the people involved (management and workers) to be empowered to continuously improve their knowledge and skills, greater representation of employees in management, and have full encouragement for their creative and productive skills, conserve capital and energy, and reorient production methods so as to make them interesting, safe and healthy. This takes us to the next important activity – that of creating a new and transformed industry for all of the activities for the Energy, Climate and Ecosystem Transformation.

The next big opportunity is that of transforming our cities, towns, villages and homesteads or establishing new ones that are **Sustainable Habitats** or eco-cities. **As per Wikipedia an Eco-city or Sustainable City is one that follows the principles of environmental sustainability (so that the environment or nature around them has been able to sustain itself), functions as a zero-carbon city (net zero carbon emissions), produces all of its energy from renewable sources, functions like an ecosystem in terms of recycling its wastes, and lives in harmony with many types of life.** So, the type of infrastructural development should be such that there are areas set aside for these activities co-located near to each other – the production of renewable energy, the growth and sale of agricultural produce, the treatment and recycling of waste (compost, water treatment, etc.) and the treatment and recycling of water. This is the type of infra-structural development that we really need – not spending more and more on supporting the fossil fuel powered transportation. **Urban sprawl that relies on the automotive mode of transportation mainly should be discouraged, and all new developments should be built on the basis of eco or sustainable city criteria, and be designed so as to be friendly for walking, biking and mass transit.**

The following sketch for a newly designed eco-city defines many of the features that need to be there for the small and large cities of tomorrow. First, there needs to be a combination of a nearby solar PV plus battery power plant powering the city, with a small produc-tion unit producing storage fuels from solar energy, that then gener-ates electricity at night. The city should be tied to the larger grid, so it can exchange energy (back and forth) as needed. The city power system can be designed as a micro-grid, so that if there is a power failure on the big grid, the local community micro-grid can operate independently for some time and some important loads for all time. The residential areas will mainly have pedways, bikeways (or human powered transportation), electric powered vehicles (mainly bikes, trike and quad bikes), and practice the principles of urban forestry. There will be a car park just outside the city with solar powered elec-tric charging stations, where most vehicles will be parked, that peo-ple use to travel to elsewhere, on the solar electric highways, that are linked also by electric bus transit, and electric rail transit and freight lines. The residential areas will have wetlands close by that get water from the residential area by water drainage through the wet season, with some of the water being harvested and cycled for city use.

The city will have an industrial scale composting facility that composts urban (mainly kitchen), agricultural and forest green wastes, for use by the nearby farms. Adjacent to the city will be new-ly designed and implemented agroforestry areas, as well as bigger afforested areas that are designed on the principles of both biodiver-sity encouragement and wildfire control. In the city there will also be factories that process the products from the forest and agricultural areas, that are harvested on a sustainable basis, so that the resi-dents of the city can have adequate livelihoods from the sale of the

SEGMENTED FOREST
BIODIVERSITY & WILDLIFE DESIGN

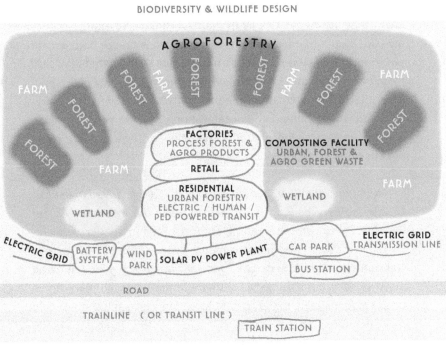

Concept of a small eco-city that can be used for new or redesigned cities.

finished products , as well as the benefit of consuming some of their own food and agricultural products, with the retail areas selling both these products as well as the food grown on the local farms. The residents will be able to walk or bike over easily to the nearby wetlands and forest to enjoy the beauty of nature without the pollution of fossil fuels.

JUST TRANSITION FOR FOSSIL FUEL WORKERS

A *just transition* means a deal for the workers involved in the fossil fuel industry – not only in the extraction, transport, refining and distribution of the fossil fuel, but also, all of the end users in terms of engines, generators, furnaces, heaters, burners and fossil fuel cars. The world needs programs and policies in place that help the workers and communities involved in fossil fuel activities to transition to the new clean energy renewable economy. This help can also be extended to fossil fuel companies if they are willing to invest their resources wholly in the new renewable energy economy (and stop the process of opposing the transition or engaging in greenwashing – appearing to do much while doing very little). *Just transition* means that fossil fuel workers need a specific package of measures to help them make the transition in terms of financial support, education, training and/or relocation – say five years of salary, benefits and retraining and other benefits so these workers come out ahead after the transition.

All of the 30 million people globally that are involved in the fossil fuel industry have to be helped to make the transition. As per the 2017 US Government report, about 1.1 million people were employed in the fossil fuel industry in the US, and about 800,000 people were employed in low carbon, and renewable activities (although they included the natural gas industry in the latter number). It will be the responsibility of the current fossil fuel companies to not only make the transition themselves, but also help the workers make the transition – they should invest most of their earnings going forward in this activity. But the nation states must also invest some portion of the global taxes in helping the workers transition, and also provide incentives to the whole industry to transition. Global society and the nation states must also practice the principles of energy democracy as outlined below, so that all of the rest of the population of the world also benefits from the whole process. In this way, all of the benefits of the implementation of the Plan and the transition will be fairly shared by all, always for the future.

Also included in a just transition must be support for oil exporting and heavily using countries (like OPEC). The global program should provide them with financial and institutional help – although a good part of this should come from their own oil "carbon" taxes.

The real challenge will be as to how to make this transition globally, so that all those who are part of the world fossil fuel economy are helped to make the transition over the 2021-2050 period. Anytime a coal powered plant is replaced by a solar PV plus battery plant, all of the workers involved in mining, transporting, storing and using the coal will need to be part of the package – possibly gaining a significant part of the employment and business as part of the new activity.

ENERGY DEMOCRACY FOR ALL GLOBAL CITIZENS

The book's Energy Democracy Plan will enable the economic and financial strength and well-being of large numbers of common people to get a significant part of the action and benefits, both in terms of lower energy costs, more business ownership and employment through changes in economic development strategy. Local people will be able to enjoy and have a greater level of democratic control of the whole transition process, and many land areas (such as reforested and revived coastal areas) benefit through greater local business and livelihood development, as well as the direct local use of the food, fuel, energy and fiber from these activities, even as they grow and manage these natural resources, as well as local renewable energy development.

The Energy Democracy movement that is developing seeks a fundamental shift from the destructive extractive economy to one that is regenerative and provides social, economic and environmental justice, while empowering local communities in the ownership and control of distributed energy resources. Since solar energy is available everywhere, it makes it possible for it to be locally produced and locally owned. The communities and workers will be helped through local democratic control and economic development to develop alternatives like local production for local use, forestry and ocean activities, renewable energy activities and a pro-employment re-industrialization strategy.

The concept is to transform the energy system away from fossil fuels into an energy economy that is based on local, decentralized renewable generation, equity, and community leadership. Special "green" zones can be created where local communities and especially lower income communities are provided technical and financial assistance to establish renewable energy power generation (especially solar PV) that is locally owned and operated, and which would be connected to the grid. Worker and consumer owned cooperatives or some combination of the two can provide employment, lower cost electricity, work place democracy, and local wealth building. [59]

A significant percentage of the tax proceeds that were described in the earlier chapter can be directed towards developing locally owned and operated renewable energy power generation, or local roof top solar activities, so that energy democracy flourishes.

A significant percentage of that will be used to provide added incentives to low income communities, and the all-round technical, legal and financial assistance provided so that these communities develop the expertise to operate these themselves.

Chapter 13

What the Transformed World Will Look Like After the Plan

The way things are going, the picture out there is worsening day by day, year by year. Thirty years or so ago, there might have been uncertainty, but now all of the uncertainty has gone, because the damage of Climate Change is being felt everywhere, and is getting worse. One does not have to be a scientist to see it or be alarmed by it. There may be some climate deniers in the world who continue to dispute the science and the obvious evidence of worsening conditions, but the majority of the people of the world now are very concerned about the fact that things are getting worse. Many are very depressed, others are angry at their leaders for doing nothing and continuing to increase the use of fossil fuels, and feel that their situation and that of their children and grandchildren will be getting worse, if not catastrophic. Over the years, there have been many climate protests to try and get the rich and the powerful to begin to solve Climate Change in a meaningful way, but they have not listened.

Then recently a young girl named Greta Thunberg, a protester against this continuing damage and relative lack of action, caught the imagination of people that are concerned about Climate Change. She has started acting as the conscience of the world. Greta represents the future generations that will have to live and suffer in the worsening conditions caused by Climate Change. It started out as a protest sign of a school girl as "School Strike for the Climate" in front of the Swedish Parliament, and has mushroomed into a global movement especially among school students, but growing into adherents of all ages. It is pressure like this which will build up to bring change. The aim of this book is to provide ammunition to people like

Greta Thunberg and the climate movement so that there is no place for the rich and the powerful to hide. [60]

Still there are strong climate deniers as well as political leaders, some dictatorial in nature, that want to go backwards from whatever little progress had been made at Climate Change solutions, and go backwards and use more fossil fuels in their nations and globally for political and financial gain, and ignore worsening conditions. Their scientific, financial, economic and political arguments, which have been refuted in an earlier chapter, are beginning to look weaker and weaker. One thing is sure, with business as usual or even with small efforts at reducing the damage or adapting to it, the global situation for all of human civilization will get much worse, first in terms of living conditions and damage to the beauty of the earth, and then descend into a downward spiral of conflict, war and further degradation.

However, if a plan such as described in this book is accepted and effectively implemented, the worst consequences of Climate Change will have been avoided and we will transform to a much more beautiful planet with good living conditions for all. Rather than the worsening damage caused by the extraction, burning, transporting and dumping of fossil fuels that occurs all over (dig, burn and dump), we will have clean energy delivered to us via the sun and the wind, more than enough for our expanding needs, with more of it directed towards local wealth building and empowerment. The air and water will be much cleaner, and there will be less pollution everywhere, our land and ocean areas will be clean and rejuvenated again. **That is why this book has emphasized Energy Plans first so that there is more than enough for everyone, and with lower costs of energy everywhere, because the "fuel" is free.**

Not only will there be much less pollution and the damage caused by fossil fuels be a thing of the past, but the beauty and productivity of our Earth will be enhanced everywhere. We will have reforested and afforested all of the land areas of the world and rejuvenated other land based ecosystems in a way that not only absorbs carbon, but also provides a combination of beauty and biodiversity (forests, plants and wildlife) on one side with a better livelihood for many through sustainable extraction of food, fuel and fiber combined with better incomes. On the other hand, as we look to the oceans, all of our coastlines will have been rejuvenated through coastal ecosystems like mangrove swamps, salt marshes, sea grasses and coral reefs, in such a way that they not only absorb massive amounts of carbon, but also lead to revival of ocean species (who then will have better habitats in the coastal ecosystems), a revival of fisheries, and in many cases an ability to absorb some of the worst impacts of coastal storms.

The adaptation and transformation of agriculture globally will lead to soils that are healthier and more fertile. As they transform to a more organic agriculture, the organic content of the soil will increase so that it can absorb more carbon. Currently, there is much damage caused by chemical fertilizers (nitrogen fertilizers emit nitrous oxide), herbicides and pesticides (that poison land areas and ground water), excessive water use that causes water logging, soil salination and long term water shortages, use of mono-cultural crops that are more prone to large scale disease, and the air and water erosion caused by excessive tillage with diesel powered agricultural machines. This will be replaced by a regenerative agriculture that uses more composted fertilizer, decreases the use of poisonous chemicals or eliminates them, uses the least tillage needed (decreasing wind and water erosion), uses much less water (conserving a precious resource so ecosystems close by can revive), and uses a much greater variety of crop seed diversity so that the farmers can earn more and the agricultural areas are much less prone to disease that will wipe out entire crops.

With the average global temperature going no higher than 1.5 degrees Celsius (2.4 degrees Fahrenheit), the worst consequences of Climate Change will have been avoided. However, in terms of Climate Change disasters the situation will be worse than today, so that an aggressive policy of disaster management will be needed. The book's advanced disaster risk reduction and management plan will not only prepare all areas (land and coasts) so as to reduce the damage and impact of Climate Change disasters (floods, hurricanes, cyclones, storms, tornadoes, and catastrophic rains), but will help these areas to recover better, and then be better prepared the next time a disaster hits. We can meanwhile develop a follow up plan for 2051-2100, that will reduce greenhouse gases in the atmosphere down to levels that were closer to those in pre-industrial times, and fully solve the wider ecological crisis, such as eliminating poisonous substances and high level radioactive waste that is piling up at nuclear reactors, cleaning up the oceans, restoring all ecosystems (including coral reefs), and finally stemming the extinction of species by with further increases in biodiversity.

The book's adaptation Plan will better prepare the land areas for heat so that the temperature rises are decreased locally by using forests and ecosystems to minimize the local temperature rises, and have better facilities and planning that help billions of people survive the massive heat waves that are expected. By better water and watershed management, the plan will help water resources improve through a combination of improved coastal and land based wetlands, water harvesting, ground water replenishment and sustainable use (so that the falling water tables in many regions are arrested), through better water conservation and wise use. This will especially help regions that are prone to drought to minimize the impact of water shortages, and ensure that there is enough freshwater for urgent needs.

The book's Just Transition and Energy Democracy plans will enable the economic and financial strength and well-being of large numbers of common people to get a significant part of the action and benefits, both in terms of lower energy costs, more business ownership and employment through changes in economic development strategy. Local people will be able to enjoy and have a greater level of democratic control of the whole transition process, and many land areas (such as reforested and revived coastal areas) benefit through greater local business and livelihood development, as well as the direct local use of the food, fuel, energy and fiber from these activities, even as they grow and manage these natural resources, as well as local renewable energy development. The book's just transition plan will help all of the workers, companies, communities and nations that are currently directly or indirectly involved in fossil fuel activities to transition to renewable energy activities, or ones that involve non-carbon fuels that store renewable energy, or other employment.

Imagine a world that will enjoy plenty of clean renewable energy, will be much less polluted, will be much more beautiful with a recovery of life of every type, and will provide for a much more bountiful life for all the world's people.

That is what the implementation of something like the Plan will give us by 2050. We can then use the second half of the century to get us back to a smaller temperature rise, by doing what we will have done better, with more clean renewable energy, more beautification of planet Earth, and then go about solving the rest of the global ecological crisis. That way, we will have mostly undone the damage done over the last few centuries, and actually made planet Earth much better. We can then be truly proud of ourselves as an evolved human species.

Making It Happen

OVERALL PLAN SEQUENCE AND SCHEDULE

From 2021-2030 – Begin Replacement of all Fossil Fuel Activities with Renewable Energy

- ❏ Start with coal for electricity, and for all other uses – electrify or replace.
- ❏ All coal fired power plant construction to stop, and the replacement of all such plants with renewable energy power plants to begin.
- ❏ Then proceed to oil substitutions through renewable energy and the first establishment of solar-electric highways.
- ❏ Then begin replacing all natural gas power plants with renewable energy power plants.
- ❏ Carbon emissions to be reduced by 50% from 2020 levels.
- ❏ Major programs for RDD&D of non-carbon fuels that store renewable energy – complete all demonstration activities that fully prove these new technologies on a larger scale by 2030.
- ❏ RDD&D means – Research, Development, Demonstration & Deployment.
- ❏ Begin electrification activities and do RDD&D as needed for those for buildings, homes, industry, agriculture, and transportation.
- ❏ Begin afforestation and coastal ecosystems Identification and building in all regions of the world, and along all of the world's coastlines.

From 2031-2040

- ❏ Begin deployment of non-carbon fuels on a large scale – green production and use – establish a global agreement and then have programs to establish the safe production, storage, transport and end-use of all of these fuels (hydrogen, ammonia, etc.).

❏ Continue the global construction of solar-electric highways and roads.

❏ Reduce carbon emissions another 25% compared with 2020 levels.

❏ Begin activities for reducing emissions of other greenhouse gases (methane, nitrous oxide and fluorinated gases).

❏ Begin replacing fossil fuel cars with battery electric and non-carbon storage fuel cars.

From 2041-2050 – Complete Reducing Carbon Emissions by a Total of 100% (zero emissions by 2050)

❏ Complete replacement of ALL fossil fuel power plants with renewable energy power plants.

❏ Complete large scale deployment of non-carbon storage fuels – displace all of gasoline and diesel, and CNG (compressed natural gas).

❏ Complete electrification of all activities – extra energy totally powered by renewable.

❏ Complete the replacement of all fossil fuel activities with renewable energy, all sectors of the global economy.

❏ Complete expansion of transmission grid, smart grid and micro-grid activities, which is mostly powered by renewable energy.

❏ Complete reducing emissions of other greenhouse gases to 25% level of 2020 levels.

❏ Complete the global reforestation and afforestation Plan (1 billion hectares (Ha) added globally).

❏ Complete the Global Plan for Coastal Ecosystems – along entire global coastline.

It is totally understood that this Plan will not be implemented as written and presented. However, what is needed is the acceptance of the urgent need for a Global Plan, the modification of this Plan based on better commitments, knowledge, research, science and technology, and the implementation of a Plan – globally. That is what the book seeks to accomplish.

Glossary of Terms

INCLUDES ABBREVIATIONS AND ENERGY UNIT EXPLANATIONS

The Main Ones

Greenhouse Gases: Gases that trap the heat resulting from sunlight in the atmosphere, like the glass of a greenhouse traps heat. When sunlight falls on the earth's surface it is re-emitted mainly as heat radiation (infra-red light), which normally escapes back into space. But greenhouse gases are of a type that they trap more of this heat, leading to the warming of the atmosphere. This is like what happens in a greenhouse, where the heat is trapped by the glass, and hence the word green-house gas (GHG).

Solar PV: Solar Photo-Voltaic just means solar panels that are made in such a way that they are able to turn the sunlight (Photo) falling on them directly into electricity (Voltaic). If a Solar Panel directly faces the sun, it generates electricity that is steady (called Direct Current), but it is then run through an electronic box called an inverter, before being fed into the electric grid as an Alternating Current (which is in the form of a wave, and in most places of the world this is either 220 volts or 110 volts).

Wind Energy: Today, most of the wind energy being generated is by large wind turbines that run like propellers and turn to face the wind, and as the blades rotate, generate electricity. This type of wind turbine is called a horizontal axis turbine – when it rotates its axis is horizontal. They are usually tall as the wind speed increases with height, and are located where there is enough wind. There are also vertical axis wind turbines that are usually smaller but rotate like the rotating vents on top of buildings.

Carbon Dioxide: Is the main greenhouse gas that is a chemical molecule that consists of one atom of carbon and two atoms of oxygen (CO2) joined together. This is mostly emitted (released to the air) by the burning of fossil fuels.

Fossil Fuels: Fuels that were formed over hundreds of millions of years of the Earth's history when the plants, animals and trees took carbon dioxide out of the air and when they died, buried it in their fossils as fossil fuels. The three main ones are coal, oil and natural gas. This steady reduction of carbon dioxide in the atmosphere by the formation of fossil fuels cooled the Earth and brought it down into a range favorable for us humans.

Renewable Energy: This is energy that is made from natural sources like the sun, wind, geothermal or tidal, although if there is a fuel coming from biological sources, it is also considered renewable. Solar PV and wind energy described above are both renewable and are the best form of renewable energy. Renewable energy does not emit any carbon dioxide (or in the case of biological based fuels, recycles the carbon – so carbon is absorbed biologically and emitted back when it is burnt).

Climate Change: Where the Earth's climate in the lower atmosphere and the oceans (where we live) is changing. The problem is with human induced Climate Change occurring mainly by the burning of fossil fuels, which is changing the climate in an unfavorable way for us humans and other life on our Earth due to the increased trapping of heat.

Global Warming: This is basically a common name for Climate Change, and directly conveys the heating of the earth's atmosphere by the trapping of heat by greenhouse gases.

Carbon Source: A source that releases carbon dioxide to the atmosphere, the main source being the burning of fossil fuels. Another smaller source is deforestation, which releases carbon when trees are cut down and burned. When we breathe in we breathe oxygen from the air, and when we breathe out, we breathe out some carbon dioxide – although this amount is minor.

Carbon Sink: Something that absorbs carbon dioxide, like trees, land and ocean vegetation, and organic matter (anything left over from living things) in soils (on land or under the ocean floor). The fossils of animals, plants and trees were carbon sinks for millions of years, as they absorbed carbon and kept taking carbon dioxide out of the atmosphere, which cooled the atmosphere and gave us the fossil fuels.

Atmosphere: The atmosphere consists of a layer of gases that we normally call air that is held close to the surface by Earth's gravity. It consists of about 78% nitrogen, 21% oxygen and small but increasing amounts of carbon dioxide. In the early stages of Earth's history, there was no oxygen, until it was created by the photosynthesis of bacteria and plants. As known from people who go mountain climbing, any distance above about 6,100 meters (20,000 feet or 3.8 miles), we humans need oxygen cylinders to breathe. The lowest layer that is 12 kilometers high (7.5 miles or 39,000 feet) is called the Troposphere, and it is the layer that is getting heated by global warming.

Hydrogen Gas (H2): Chemically this gas is a molecule that is made up of two atoms of hydrogen. When it is burnt in air or in the presence of oxygen, it turns into water (which is hydrogen dioxide or H2O). So, burning it does not create any carbon dioxide, so it is called a non-carbon fuel. The important aspect is that we need "Green" hydrogen, or hydrogen that is made by, say, electricity from solar PV (or other renewable energy) by splitting up water back into hydrogen and oxygen. The world is currently using a lot of hydrogen for other purposes (like refining oil), but our purpose is to use it as a non-carbon fuel made from say solar energy, so that it can store solar energy. That is why, in this book, we have called it a non-carbon storage fuel.

Ammonia Gas (NH3): Chemically this gas is a molecule that consists of one atom of nitrogen and three atoms of hydrogen. When burnt, it also does not release carbon dioxide. Our interest is in producing "Green" ammonia, that is made by using, say, solar PV electricity. The world is using a lot of ammonia, mostly as fertilizer, but our purpose is to use it as a non-carbon fuel made from, say, solar PV electricity, so that it can store solar energy. That is why, in this book, we have called it a non-carbon storage fuel.

Abbreviations and Units

BECCS   Bio-Energy with Carbon Capture and Storage

CCS   Carbon Capture and Storage

DRR   Disaster Risk Reduction

CAFÉ   Corporate Average Fuel Economy, US Standard for Vehicles

CORSIA   Carbon Offsetting and Reduction Scheme for International Aviation

FAO   Food and Agriculture Organization

GCM   Global Circulation Model

GWP   Global Warming Potential

IPCC   Intergovernmental Panel for Climate Change

ICAO   International Civil Aviation Organization

IMO   International Maritime Organization

OPEC   Organization of Petroleum Exporting Countries

PV   Photo-Voltaic

UNCED   United Nations Conference on Environment and Development

UNEP   United Nations Environment Program, renamed to UN Environment

UNESCO   United Nations Educational Scientific and Cultural Organization

UNFCCC   United Nations Framework Convention on Climate Change

Green House Gas (GHG) Emissions Units

1 US Ton   = 2,000 pounds (lb.) = 909 Kilograms (Kg)

1 Metric Ton   = 2,200 pounds (lb.) = 1,000 Kilograms (Kg)

MtCO2   = Metric Tons of Carbon Dioxide (CO2)

MMTCO2   = Million Metric Tons of Carbon Dioxide (CO2)

How Total Greenhouse Gas Emissions are calculated

Emissions of a greenhouse gas calculated by how much it contributes to global warming. Different gases have different quantitative effects on how much warming (or heat trapping) they contribute as compared with the warming (or heat trapping) contribution of the same weight of carbon dioxide. The time frames these effects are compared are 20 years, 100 years and 500 years. These are called the Global Warming Potential (GWP) of the gas.

So over a 100 Year period the Global Warming Potential of the gases are as follows:

GWP of carbon dioxide (CO2) = 1
GWP of methane (CH4) = 28
GWP of nitrous oxide (N2O) = 265

This means that a metric ton of methane traps 28 times more heat than a metric ton of carbon dioxide over a 100 year period, and a metric ton of nitrous oxide traps 265 times more heat than a metric ton of carbon dioxide over a 100 year period.

If we calculate total greenhouse emissions (in metric tons) on a 100 year basis, the calculation will be as follows:

Total Greenhouse Gas Emissions for the three gases
= Total CO2 emissions x 1 + Total methane emissions x 28 +
Total nitrous oxide emissions x 265

These will therefore be expressed as being equivalent to carbon dioxide, or CO2e.
Hence, the total emissions will be expressed as
MMtCO2e = Millions of Metric tons of carbon dioxide equivalent.

Atmosphere Gas Concentration Units

Recent Gas Concentrations of the three main gases are:

Carbon Dioxide = 410 ppm or parts per million (up from 280 ppm in pre-industrial times)

So 410 ppm of CO2 in atmosphere means that if one looked at 1 million molecules, 410 of those are carbon dioxide molecules.

Methane = 1,800 ppb or parts per billion

So 1,800 ppb of methane, means that if one looked at a billion molecules, 1,800 molecules are methane.

Nitrous Oxide = 325 ppb or parts per billion

So 325 ppb of nitrous oxide, means that if one looked at 1 billion molecules, 325 of those will be nitrous oxide molecules.

GOAL: Peak in concentrations by 2050

The Plan in this book means that the concentrations of gases will stop somewhere a little above where they are today, and increase no more. Ultimately, if we want to get back to a comfortable position, we need to get back to gas concentrations at least close to where they were in the late 1980s. That means:

CO2 Concentration = 350 ppm
CH4 Concentration = 1,250 ppb
NO2 Concentrations = 295 ppb

Energy Units

Here are some of the energy units used in this book, that were all converted to electrical energy units so they could be compared with each other.

Millions Metric Tons of Oil Equivalents – Mtoe

Energy from all sources converted into what is equivalent to the same weight of oil or petroleum.

Quads – Quadrillion BTUs

Another Energy Unit that has been used. **BTU** – British Thermal Unit.

For convenience, these units were all converted into electrical energy units. The symbols go as follows:

Kilo = 10E3 (Or 1,000); **Mega** = 10E6 (or 1 million);
Giga = 10E9 (1 billion); **Terra** = 10E12 (1 trillion);
Peta = 10E15 (1,000 trillion); **Exa** = 10E18 (or 1,000,000 trillion)

kilowatt hours (KWH) or "units" are what you see on your Electrical bill in most nations

1 Kilowatt Hour = 1,000 Watt Hours (KWH)
1 Megawatt Hour = 1 million Watt Hours (MWH)
1 Gigawatt Hour = 1 billion Watt Hours (Me)
1 Terrawatt Hour = 1 Trillion Watt Hours (TWH) = 1 billion Kilowatt Hours = 1 billion KWH
1 Petawatt Hour = 1,000 Trillion Watt Hours (PWH) = 1 Trillion KWH

Much of the world also uses Exa Joules

The conversions of these units are as follows:
1 Mtoe = 11.63 TWH
1 Quad = 293.07 TWH
1 Exa Joule = 277.8 TWH

So Energy, in whatever units it was published, was converted into TWH (Terrawatt Hours) and then divided by 1,000 to convert it into PWH (Petawatt Hours), before being shown on the pie charts.

Energy Efficiency of Fossil fuels

The average thermal efficiency of coal and oil fired utility scale Electric Power plants is about 40%. That means that only 40% of the heat energy of coal and oil are converted into useful electrical energy, and 60% is wasted up the stack!

For Combined Cycle Natural Gas Power Plants, the energy efficiency is about 60%. That means that 60% of the energy of the gas is converted into useful electrical energy and 40% is wasted up the stack!

Bottomline: Anywhere from 40-60% of the heat energy of fossil fuels is wasted when they are used! Also, when a certain level of energy use is reported for fossil fuels, the amount of renewable energy (say solar PV) energy needed to replace it in KWH is correspondingly less.

NOTES / REFERENCES

[1] "Storms of My Grandchildren – the Truth about the Coming Climate Catastrophe and Our Last Chance to Save Humanity," James Hansen, Bloomsbury Press, 2009.

[2] IPCC 2018: Summary for Policy Makers In, "Global Warming of 1.5 Degrees C: An IPCC Special Report on the Impacts of Global Warming of 1.5 Degrees C above pre-industrial levels and related global greenhouse gas emissions pathways, in the context of strengthening the global response to the threat of Climate Change, and efforts to eradicate poverty," V. Masson-Delmotte, et al, World Meteorological Organization, Geneva, Switzerland, 32 pp, October, 2018, Intergovernmental Panel on Climate Change. https://www.ipcc.ch/sr15/chapter/spm/.

[3] "World Energy Outlook – 2018," or WEO2018, published by the International Energy Agency, 2019. www.iea.org/weo.

[4] "Global Energy Transformation – Roadmap to 2050," IRENA (2019), International Renewable Energy Association, Abu Dhabi, 2019, www.irena.org

[5] The Solutions Project, https://thesolutionsproject.org

[6] "Drawdown – The Most Comprehensive Plan Ever Proposed to Reverse Global Warming," Edited by Paul Hawken, Penguin Books, 2017.

[7] "Getting to Neutral – Options for Negative Carbon Emissions in California," January, 2020, Lawrence Livermore National Laboratory, LLNL-TR-796100, www.gs.llnl.gov/content/assets/docs/energy/Getting_to_Neutral.pdf

[8] "An Inconvenient Truth – The Planetary Emergency of Global Warming and What We Can do About It," Al Gore, Rodale Books, 2006.

[9] "Fight Global Warming Now – The Handbook for Taking Action in Your Community," Bill McKibben, Holt Paperback, 2007.

[10] Fu, Ran, Timothy Remo, and Robert Margolis, 2018. 2018 Utility-Scale-Photovoltaics-Plus-Energy Storage System Costs Benchmark. Golden, CO: National Renewable Energy Laboratory. NREL/TP-6A20-71714. https://www.nrel.gov/docs/fy19osti/71714.pdf

[11] IPCC, 2011: IPCC Special Report on Renewable Energy Sources and Climate Change Mitigation. Prepared for Working Group III of the Intergovernmental Panel on Climate Change [O. Edenhofer, et al], Cambridge University Press, Cambridge, United Kingdom and New York, NY, USA, 1075 pp. (Chapter 7 &9).

[12] "Green hydrogen and the Intermountain Power Project", Presented by the Los Angeles Department of Water and Power (LADWP), Los Angeles, California, USA, 2019. https://www.cpuc.ca.gov/uploadedFiles/CPUC_Website/Content/Utilities_and_Industries/Energy/Energy_Programs/Gas/Natural_Gas_Market/Nov13LADWP.pdf

[13] "Cost and Engineering Study of Puente Power Project Cost Effective PV Solar and Storage Capacity," Dr. Doug Karpa, August 2017, Study for the Clean Coalition. www.cleancoalition.org

[14] "Global Energy Transformation – Roadmap to 2050," International Renewable Energy Agency, IRENA, GET 2018 Report, Abu Dhabi, 2018. www.irena.org/publications.

[15] "How Geothermal Energy Works," December 2014, Union of Concerned Scientists (UCS).https://www.ucsusa.org/resources/how-geothermal-energy-works.

[16] "The Carbon Footprint of Global Tourism", Article in Nature, Climate Change, June 2018, Volume 8, pp. 522-528. www.nature.com/natureclimtechange.

[17] "Carbon Dharma – The Occupation of Butterflies", Sailesh Rao, A Climate Healers Publication, 2011-2016, www.climatehealers.org.

[18] "World Military Expenditure Grows to $1.8 Trillion in 2018," Stockholm International Peace Research Institute, SIPRI, Press Release, April, 29, 2019. https://www.sipri.org/media/press-release/2019/world-military-expenditure-grows-18-trillion-2018

[19] "Pentagon Fuel Use, Climate Change, and the Costs of War," Neta C. Crawford, Watson Institute, Brown University, June 12, 2019.

[20] "The Global Carbon Budget 1959-2011", Le Quere, C., et al, Earth System Science Data Discussions 5, No. 2, (2012): 1107-1157.

[21] The Bonn Challenge on Forests, Managed by the International Union for the Conservation of Nature, https://www.iucn.org/theme/forests/our-work/forest-landscape-restoration/bonn-challenge.

[22] A Story of Large Commitments yet Limited Progress. New York Declaration on Forests Five-Year Assessment Report." Climate Focus (coordinator and editor). www.forestdeclaration.org

[23] "The Global Tree Restoration Potential," Article, Jean-Francois Bastin, et al, Science Magazine, Volume 365, Issue 6448, pp. 76-79, July 5, 2019. Authors from Crowther lab. https://science.sciencemag.org/content/365/6448/76/tab-pdf.

[24] Example of Damage Caused by Clear Cutting Forests for Timber Harvesting, The Battle Creek Alliance, www.Battlecreekalliance.org/aerial-views.html

[25] Association of Temperate Agroforestry – Four Key Characteristics of Agroforestry. https://www.aftaweb.org/about/what-is-agroforestry.html

[26] "Multi-Hazard Risk Assessment for Schools Sector in Mozambique," Global Facility for Disaster Reduction and Recovery, GFDRR, World Bank Group, Report, May 2018.

[27] "Disaster Risk Reduction – India Country Report", Establishment of National Disaster Response Force, UNDRR. https://www.wmo.int/pages/prog/www/tcp/documents/PTC-45_4.2.5.3_CountryReport_India_DRR.pdf

[28] "Landslide Hazard and Risk Assessment- 3", UNISDR, United Nations Office of Disaster Risk Reduction, Words into Action Guidelines, 2017.

[29] IPCC 2019: Summary for Policy Makers in, "Climate Change and Land – An IPCC Special Report on Climate Change, desertification, land degradation, sustainable land management, food security, and greenhouse gas fluxes in terrestrial ecosystems," World Meteorological Organization, Geneva, Switzerland, 32 pp, October, 2018, Intergovernmental Panel on Climate Change. https://www.ipcc.ch/srccl/chapter/summary-for-policy-makers/.

[30] "One Straw Revolution – An Introduction to Natural Farming," Masanobu Fukuoka, Edited by Larry Korn, Emhaus, Pennsylvania, Rodale Press, 1978.

[31] "Fourth US National Climate Assessment – Vol. II: Impacts, Risks and Adaptation in the United States," November 2018. https://nca2018.globalchange.gov.

[32] "Solving the Climate Crisis – A Congressional Action Plan for a Clean Energy Economy and a Healthy, Resilient and Just America," US House Select Committee on the Climate Crisis, June 2020. https://climatecrisis.house.gov/report

[33] "Annual Energy Outlook 2018 – with Projections to 2050," or AEO 2018 Report, United States Energy Information Agency, US Department of Energy, February 2018. . www.eia.gov/aeo

[34] "Annual Energy Outlook 2019 – with Projections to 2050," or AEO 2019 Report, United States Energy Information Agency, US Department of Energy, January 2019. www.eia.gov/aeo

[35] "Annual Energy Outlook 2020 – with Projections to 2050," or AEO 2020 Report, United States Energy Information Agency, US Department of Energy, January 2020. www.eia.gov/aeo

[36] "The Full Cost of Electricity – Estimation of Transmission Costs for New Generation," Juan Andrade and Ross Baldick, White Paper, University of Texas at Austin, Energy Institute, UTEI/2016-09-2, January 2017.

[37] "Community Microgrids, A Way of providing Electrical Grid Resilience with local Renewable Energy." https://clean-coalition.org/community-microgrid-initiative/

[38] "Community Choice Aggregation 3.0 National Report – Reducing Greenhouse Gas Emissions 2020", Prepared by Local Power LLC, https://localpower.com/CCA_30.html, Supported by the Urban Sustainability Director's Network.

[39] "An Ocean Blueprint for the 21st Century – Conserving and Restoring Coastal Habitat," US National Oceanic and Atmospheric Administration (NOAA).

[40] "The Economic Case for Restoring Coastal Ecosystems," Michael Conathan, Jeffrey Buchanan, and Shiva Polefka, Center for American Progress and Oxfam America, April 2014. www.americanprogress.org

[41] "On Fire – The Burning Case for a Green New Deal," Naomi Klein, Simon and Schuster, 2019.

[42] "Climate Change Impacts on China Environment: Biophysical Impacts", Elisa Chih-Yin Lai, February 2009, Wilson Center. https://www.wilsoncenter.org/sites/default/files/media/documents/publication/climate_biophysical1.pdf

[43] "World and China Energy Outlook 2050 – 2018 Version," CNPC, ETRI, China National Petroleum Corporation, 2018.

[44] "India's National Action Plan on Climate Change needs desperate repair," Down to Earth Article, October 2018. https://www.downtoearth.org.in/news/climate-change/india-s-national-action-plan-on-climate-change-needs-desperate-repair-61884

[45] "India's Energy & Emissions Outlook," NITI-Aayog, 2019. https://niti.gov.in/sites/default/files/2019-07/India's-Energy-and-Emissions-Outlook.pdf

[46] "India's Ammonia Capacity to Witness Double Digit Growth over next Six Years", GlobalData Report, February 2019.

[47] "BP Energy Outlook 2019 – Insights from the Evolving Emissions Scenario – European Union," British Petroleum, www.bp.com/energyoutlook

[48] "Negative Emissions Technologies: What Role in Meeting Paris Agreement Targets," EASAC Policy Report 35, European Academies Science Advisory Council, February 2018, www.easac.eu

[49] "Decarbonizing the EU Energy System: The Important Role for BECCS," B.S. Rodriguez, P. Drummond and P. Ekins, 2016. https://discovery.ucl.ac.uk/id/eprint/1532750/1/Solano,%20Drummond%20&%20Ekins.pdf

[50] "US Energy Innovation and Carbon Dividend Act," US Congress House Resolution 763 (HR 763) – legislation for introducing a Carbon Tax, 2019. https://www.congress.gov/bill/116th-congress/house-bill/763/text

[51] "Beyond Beef – The Rise and Fall of Cattle Culture," Jeremy Rifkin, A Plume Book, 1993.

[52] "Transforming Our World: The 2030 Agenda for Sustainable Development," United Nations Publication A/Res/70/1, www.sustainabledevelopment.un.org

[53] "Rethinking Progress – Towards a Creative Transformation of Global Society," Harinder S. Lamba, Daanish Books, New Delhi, 2005.

[54] "Tobacco Institute," Wikipedia, https://en.wikipedia.org/wiki/Tobacco_Institute

[55] "Stratospheric Sink for Chlorofluoromethanes: Chlorine atom-catalyzed Destruction of Ozone," Mario J. Rowland and F.S. Molina, Nature Magazine, Vol. 249, No. 5460, pp. 810-812, June 28, 1974. Reprinted in – https://unep.ch/ozone/pdf/stratopheric.pdf

[56] "The Heat is On – the Climate Crisis, the Cover-up, the Prescription", Ross Gelbspan, Basic Books, 1997.

[57] "Climate Change Costs are Starting to Bite Business," Sierra Club Magazine, Paul Rauber, April 29, 2019. https://www.sierraclub.org/sierra/2019-3-may-june/protect/climate-change-costs-are-starting-bite-business

[58] "Climate Analysis Indicators Tool (CAIT) Version 2.0 (2014), Washington DC, World Resources Institute, June 2017, Global Greenhouse Gas Emissions as tabulated in Wikipedia.

[59] "Energy Democracy – Advancing Equity in Clean Energy Solutions," Edited by Denise Fairchild and Al Weinrub, Island Press, 2017.

[60] "No One is Too Small to Make a Difference," Greta Thunberg, Penguin Books, 2019.

What You Can Do

The Overall Situation We Face

1. WE HAVE RUN OUT OF TIME – WE ONLY HAVE 30 YEARS TO SOLVE Climate Change!
2. We have to agree globally to a plan and make it happen!
3. Global Warming is a GLOBAL problem and will take ALL of human civilization and ALL nations to make it happen
4. This Book presents a Plan to show that we can do it!
5. If we delay, the consequences will be much worse.
6. If we fully implement a plan, such as described in this book, that is quantitively and timewise enough then it will be much better.
7. As the Plan in this book seeks to show, we will have more than enough energy, we will solve the problem of Climate Change, and we will have a much more beautiful Earth! Then all of us – rich, middle class and poor, will be much better off, and our brother and sister species will see the beginnings of better conditions in expanded ecosystems.
8. Still, because things have been worsening for some time, even as we move decisively to solve the big problem, we need to prepare for Climate Change of 1.5C – we need to prepare year round for disaster preparedness and adaptation.
9. **Part of the way towards the year 2050, as we realize we can do better, then we can up our ambition even further and do things faster.**
10. Because the rich and powerful do not move easily, as they have much to lose initially if things change, it will take every one of us to make it happen.

The Personal Situations We Face

1. The global, national and local **situations** we face **determine** what we can or cannot do in our daily lives.

2. Today the world is dependent 81% on fossil fuels – this basically today determines how things are grown, made, transported, heated/cooled, and everything else we do in our lives.

3. What we can do is determined by the choices made available to us in terms of:
   a. Energy **choices**
   b. Transportation **choices**
   c. Housing **choices**
   d. Business and Employment **choices**
   e. Social Conditions **choices**
   f. Political and Security **choices**

4. The extent to which you are able to live a low carbon life style is **influenced** by these **choices**. Unfortunately, powerful political interests have made sure that our **choices are very limited**. Basically, we have almost total dependence on fossil fuels and fossil fuel driven cars and highways that enable them.

5. What this book is advocating is to use resources to make zero and low carbon **choices** available for people, discourage high carbon activities and encourage zero or low carbon choices available for people, so that the transition to the new economy is easier.

It will take all the people of the world to turn this around. Although there are many things that you will think of and do in your lives, here is what I recommend.

It is important that you become active as you are very important. Yes YOU!

Here is What I Recommend

Inform Yourself

1. Read this book and inform yourself.
2. If you have less time, go to the following website and read and download the summaries and other free information.

   www.brighterclimatefutures.com

3. The website will have more updated information, details on other items and issues, a blog and news.
4. Watch the videos and social media information for *Brighter Climate Futures.*

Become Active

1. *Insist* that your national government work on a Plan to get to near zero greenhouse gas emissions by 2050, and insist that the government push for a global agreement, plan and implementation that is effective, adequate and timely.
2. Insist that governments at all levels make available choices in each of the areas listed above, but specially in providing zero or low carbon choices at affordable prices.
3. Insist that the way in which solutions are implemented and funds are spent enable and empower people and democratic institutions at the local levels, so as to support the processes of a Just Transition and Energy Democracy.
4. In the US support of political, fiscal and financial measures that lead to an implementation of the Green New Deal – mainly so that energy, climate and ecosystem solutions are accompanied with ways of helping and empowering those at lower levels. Support all other meaningful efforts at Climate Change solutions.
5. At the same time work with local, and state or province level organizations and people to begin to phase out fossil fuels and begin to plan and implement the local aspects of the Plan as laid out in this book.
6. Form or participate in local, national and global coalitions that work on and push for plans and activities at all levels.
7. If you wish to take it up as a career, select some aspect of

the Plan and begin to devote your career life to make that happen. Look for organizations that will support jobs and employment in such activities.

8. If you can, select and support organizations financially that are working on Climate Change solutions that align with the Plan or approach described in this book.

9. The author will work to join with or form non-profit organizations that make the above activities happen, provide information, help and consultancy on the Plan, as well as join forces with and help those who wish to take up meaningful work in these areas.

10. Socially and personally push people to accept and push for the changes needed of the type that will help the acceptance of and implementation of ways of doing things as needed by the Plan – push for the Plan.

11. *Insist* that local, state and national governments implement changes in codes and standards, as well as incentives and rebates, that encourage renewable energy, electrification, and reductions in fossil fuel use, while also encouraging afforestation, protecting land ecosystems, and the expansion of any local coastal ecosystems.

12. *Insist* that your food begins to be grown by methods that lead to a regenerative agriculture that increases soil fertility, is more organic, with lower herbicide and pesticide residues, and uses less chemical fertilizer, diesel fuel, pesticides and water.

Reduce Your Carbon Footprint and Help Educate Citizens and Communities

1. Personally, if you can afford it, invest in a solar PV system for your house or your housing complex, and insist your government have in place measures and laws that enable you to financially benefit from doing so. This can also include any kind of other renewable energy system – solar thermal (hot water heating panels), small vertical axis wind systems and ground source or air source heat pumps (for heating and cooling) that save energy. In the US there are Net Metering Laws in place that enable a homeowner to get credit for the electric energy produced by their solar PV

system – insist that your government enable you and your area electric consumers to do something like this.

2. Work towards electrifying your house or building, so that all fossil fuel use is stopped and all cooking and appliances mainly use electricity, again that is powered by renewable energy (at your house) or what comes over the grid (ask your government to enable something like Community Choice Aggregation or CCA as described in this book).

3. **Insist on the highest level of Energy Efficiency** for everything you use or install in your house or apartment or building, whether it be heating or cooling units, furnaces, appliances or cooking units. Change out all incandescent and even fluorescent light bulbs with LED (light emitting diode) lights that consume much less electricity.

4. Reduce the carbon footprint of your personal transportation by selecting electric vehicles (insisting that your government come up with vehicles that are affordable), or at least use smaller electric bikes, trikes and quad bikes – with or without battery electric power. Insist that local traffic patterns and choices encourage human powered transportation.

5. Insist on your local, state and national governments to implement low carbon mass transit, electric, rail and high speed rail transportation.

6. Minimize your aviation travel as it can give big increases in your carbon footprint, using air flights only for long haul travel. Insist that governments make available high speed rail globally for travel over land areas.

7. For your tourist travels, minimize your carbon footprint and again, only use air travel for long haul flights and after you land locally, organize your local travel to all by low carbon modes – electric vehicles, buses, bikes and hikes.

8. Calculate and minimize your carbon footprint (how much you and your family emit in terms of tons of carbon dioxide in a year). The one that is available from Nature Conservancy is a good one. Run it and try to minimize your carbon footprint.

    a. http://www.nature.org/greenliving/carboncalculator/index.htm

    b. Calculates one's total carbon dioxide emissions

     c. Does not account for Solar panels (electric or thermal)

     d. Lamba Family (2 people) = 36 tons of CO2/yr.

     e. US Average (2 people) = 53 tons of CO2/yr.

     f. World Average (2 people) = 11 tons of CO2 equivalent/yr.

9. By 2050, all of these need to be close to zero.

     a. Lamba Plan – Have installed solar PV system, replaced most light bulbs with LED lights and drive a hybrid car. Lamba plan is to electrify everything, have a battery back-up system installed and switch to an electric or fuel cell vehicle. Also ride electric bike when practical.

10. Recycle everything, and insist that your nation set up a plan for at least **90% recycling of all paper.** Recycling is an area that can help produce significant employment, and reduction in energy use.

11. *Compost* all your kitchen and yard green wastes, or insist that your area government set up collection from all regions of city or small town, and set up industrial scale composting facilities for these, with the compost going all to farms.

12. Lastly, if you eat meat, reduce your consumption, especially of beef, lamb and pork. If you do not eat meat, encourage all surrounding local areas to produce for most of your fruits and vegetables consumption. If you drink milk and use dairy products, reduce your consumption, and find good substitutes for your nutrition – there are plenty.

Actions You can Take Out There!

Community, State, National and International

Many cities, counties, districts, states and nations have already begun to plan and implement energy efficiency actions, or reduce their carbon footprint. If yours has not, then begin to apply pressure that they do so. If funding is a problem, then try and find a way so that international or national mechanisms can help your local governments. In many cases, local and national level organizations may already be active in many of these activities, so the best strategy may be to support and participate in their activities. In some cases, it may be suitable to submit petitions, and demand that currently available funds be used for solar PV be installed on all public buildings.

The Need for Political Activism Within Your Nation

The biggest challenge facing most nations is how to get their governments to become solid supporters of actions to solve the Climate Change problem. This will require a lot of activism at all levels to make this happen. At each location, wherever people live, YOU should demand responsiveness on this issue, discourage those candidates for office who are clearly opposed to action and support those that are clearly for Climate Change solutions and actions. No more dirty fossil fuels – you need your government to enable you and your community to proceed towards clean renewable energy and clean energy jobs.

Global Actions

While the main focus of Climate Change may need to be on those nations that are making the biggest contributions to carbon emissions, it is important to realize that all nations and all the people of the world live and breathe the same atmosphere. Carbon emissions in one nation spread out and occupy the whole atmosphere. So, one nation, or a small of group of nations, that continue to increase their carbon emissions can wipe out the benefits of the emissions reductions by all the other nations. Hence, pushing for an effective global agreement is very important, so that something like the Plan in this book has a chance to succeed.

Push for something like the transformation plan to be accepted, globally agreed on and that implementation begin immediately.

INDEX

Adaptation, Heat and Drought, 135-138
Adaptation, Rains and Floods, 138-142
Agriculture, Regenerative, 143-151
Agroforestry, 110, 137, 143, 147, 300, 301
Afforestation, 103, 106, 183-184
American Chemistry Council, 266
Ammonia, 44, 67-72, 86, 194, 210, 221
Annual Energy Outlook, US, 160-162, 166, 167
Association of Temperate Agroforestry, 110
Aviation, 87-88

Battle Creek Alliance, 104-106
BECCS, Bio-Energy Carbon Capture and Storage, 225
Beef, 101, 103, 143, 144, 245
Bioenergy, 30, 31, 34, 84-85
Biomass, 30-33, 37, 196
Bonn Challenge, Forests, 102
Blue Carbon, Coastal Ecosystems, 111-118
Blue Carbon Initiative, International, 114
Breakthrough Energy Coalition, Paris Agreement, 23
Bureau of Reclamation, US, 159

California Energy Council, CEC, 72, 191, 193
California Energy, Climate and Ecosystem Plan, 190-197
California Public Utilities Commission, CPUC, 193
California Air Resources Board, CARB, 193
California Independent System Operator, CAISO, 53, 193
California Fuel Cell Partnership, 74
California State Board of Forestry, 104
Cal Fire, California Department of Forestry, 104
Cap and Trade Program, California, 191-195
Carbon Capture and Storage, CCS, 192
Carbon Neutral, California, 37, 192
Cato Institute, 273
China Energy, Climate and Ecosystem Plan, 205-213
Clean Development Mechanism, CDM, from Kyoto Protocol, 22, 134
Clean Power Plan, CPP, US, 157
Clinton, Bill, 278
Coal Power, Utah, 58, 59
Coastal Ecosystems, Global, 111-118, 296-297

Coastal Ecosystems, US, 184-186
Community Choice Aggregation, CCA, 47, 76, 77, 179-182
Community Microgrids, 178-179
Competitive Enterprise Institute, 18
Concentrated Solar Power (CSP), 45, 63, 64
Conference of Parties, COP of the UNFCCC, 20, 21, 236-238
Corporate Average Fuel Economy Standards, CAFÉ, US, 192, 271, 272
Crowther Plan, Reforestation, 103, 104

Decarbonization, 158, 193
Department of Defense, DOD, US, 97, 98
Desertification, 4, 97, 106, 143
Disaster Risk Reduction, DRR, 121-132, 199
Drawdown, 36
Duck Curve, electrical renewable energy, 53

Earth Summit, 20, 25, 153
Earth Summit Network, 20
Eel Grass, 118
Eco-Cities, 5, 96, 189, 299-301
Ecological Crisis, 4, 5, 309
Electrification, Global, 42, 52, 74-83, 299
Electrification, US, 170-175
Ellwood, California, 60
Energy Democracy, 248, 303-304
Energy Efficiency, 43, 44, 55, 92-93
Energy Information Agency, US, 160-162
European Union Energy, Climate and Ecosystem Plan, 223-239

Flettner Rotors and Kites, Ships, 86
Fluorinated Gases, 287, 288, 292, 295
Food and Agricultural Organization, FAO, 151, 298
Fukuoka, Masanobu, 147

Geothermal Energy, 62, 63, 259
Gelbspan, Ross, 273
Global Circulation Models (GCMs), 17, 18, 273
Global Warming Potential, GWP, 15, 16, 17, 28, 286-289
Gore, Al, 20, 38, 153, 275-279
Greenwashing, 277, 278, 302
Green New Deal, US, 198-204
Global Green Deal, 259, 260
Global Warming Treaty, See UNFCCC, 13, 24-27, 104, 134, 153, 236-238
Global Military, 96-99

Haber-Bosch Process, Ammonia, 70
Hansen, James, 18-19
Himalayan Region, South Asia, 90, 120, 130, 137
High Speed Rail, 85, 87, 88, 92, 166
Hump Curve, electrical renewable energy, 54
Hurricanes, Typhoons and Cyclones, 123-125
Hydroelectric energy, 43, 44, 213-225
Hydrogen, 44, 52, 58, 67-70

India Energy, Climate and Ecosystem Plan, 213-223
India, Pavagada Solar Plant, 46
Inslee, Jay, 157-158
Integrated Transportation System, 88-90
Intended Nationally Determined Contributions, INDCs of Nations, 13, 22, 156
International Civil Aviation Organization, ICAO, 87, 245, 253
International Energy Agency, 29-34, 40, 41, 66, 93, 243
International Maritime Organization, IMO, 85, 86
International Renewable Energy Agency, IRENA, 34, 61, 93, 240, 294
International Union for the Conservation of Nature, IUCN, 102, 114

Jacobson, Mark, 35, 45
Jobs and Economy, 294-304
Just Transition, 301, 302

Klein, Naomi, 199
Kyoto Protocol to Climate Change Treaty, 9, 13, 21, 22, 26, 37, 38, 97

Landslides, Disaster Risk Reduction, 130, 131
Los Angeles Department of Water and Power, LADWP, 58, 59

Marin Clean Energy, MCE, California, 47, 76
Mars, the Planet, 263
Mangroves, 111, 112
McKibben, Bill, 38, 39
McMichaels, Patrick, 273
Methane, 15-17, 27, 94, 284-290
Midgley, Thomas, 266
Milky Way Galaxy, 262
Military, Global, 96-99
Molina, Mario, 266

National Cyclone Risk Mitigation Project (NCRMP), India, 215, 216
National Action Plan on Climate Change (NAPCC), India, 216
National Climate Assessment, US, 155, 156
National Renewable Energy Laboratory, NREL, US, 52

Natural Farming, 147-149
New York Declaration of Forests, 102
Nitrous Oxide, 15-17, 27, 50, 157, 287-292
Non-state Actor Climate Action, NAZCA Portal, (Paris Agreement), 23, 24
North Atlantic Treaty Organization, NATO, 152
Nuclear Energy, 4, 30-33, 44, 45, 161, 197, 208, 212, 218, 219, 220, 225

Obama, Barack, 157
Organization of Petroleum Exporting Countries, OPEC, 231, 277, 278
Organic Farming, 146
Ozone Layer, 4, 266, 267, 276

Paradise, California, 127, 129, 190
Paris Agreement, 13, 21-24
Planet of the Humans, 274-276
Power Marketing Administration, PMA, US, 158, 159, 177
Puente Natural Gas Powerplant, (proposed) California, 60

Rail Transportation, electric, 79
Rao, Sailesh, 94
Reduce Emissions from Deforestation and Degradation, REDD+, 104
Regenerative Agriculture, 133, 146-151
Reforestation, US, 183, 184
Renewable Portfolio Standard, RPS, 191
Rowland, Sherwood, 266
Runaway Greenhouse Effect, 106, 128, 190

Salt Marshes, Tidal, 110-113
Salt River Project, Arizona, 178
Sanders, Bernie, 158-160
Sea Grasses, 113-118
Sendai Framework for Disaster Risk Reduction (DRR), 120-121
Shipping, 85-86
Sierra Club, 276
Smart Grids, 55, 82, 83, 159
Solar Alliance, Paris Agreement, 24
Solar-Electric Highways, Global, 74-78, 249-252
Solar-Electric Highways, US, 170-172
Solar Rooftop, 65-67
Solar Thermal, 64, 65
Steam Methane Reforming, hydrogen Production, 67-70
Stockholm International Peace Research Institute, SIPRI, 97
"Storage Fuels", Hydrogen and Ammonia, 67-75
Strong, Maurice, 20
Sustainable Agriculture Jobs, 297-298

Sustainable City, 299-301
Sustainable Development Goals, SDGs, 257-259
Sustainable Habitats Jobs, 299-301
Sustainable Transportation Jobs, 297
Sustainable Fishery Management (Jobs), 298, 299
Sustainable Forestry Jobs, 298
Sustainable Industry Jobs, 299

Tax, Aviation Transport, 244-246
Tax, Carbon, 242-244, 246
Tax, Financial Transactions, 244, 246
Tax, Meat, 245, 246
Tax, Fossil Fuel Vehicles, 245, 246
Tennessee Valley Authority, TVA, US, 159, 177
Thunberg, Greta, 39, 305
Tobacco Institute Approach, 264-270, 276, 280
Tornadoes, 125-127
Tourism, 90-92, 252-254
Transmission Expansion, Electric, 53, 82-84
Transportation, Low Carbon, 88-90

Urban Forestry, 110, 111
UN Conference on Environment and Development, UNCED, 20, 153
UN Educational Scientific and Cultural Organization, UNESCO, 114
UN Framework Convention on Climate Change, UNFCCC, 12, 13, 20, 24-26,
104, 134, 153, 234-238
US Global Change Research Program, USGCRP, 155
Venus, Runaway Greenhouse Effect, 263

Watson Institute Report, 97
Wildfires, 101, 105, 106-109, 127-130, 156, 189, 195
Wind Energy, 43-45, 61-62

ABOUT THE AUTHOR

 The author Dr. Harinder (Hari) Singh Lamba, has experience in engineering, business and ecology. He has a Ph.D. in engineering from the University of Illinois at Urbana-Champaign, with about 40 years of experience in industry, both in engineering product development and in advanced technology. He migrated from India to the USA in 1970 with a bachelor's degree in Aeronautical Engineering. He was one of the founders of the Earth Summit Network, an informal organization formed in Chicago in 1991-92 to educate the local public about the Earth Summit, or the United Nations Conference on Environment and Development (UNCED) that was held at Rio de Janeiro, Brazil in 1992, where the original global warming treaty was signed. Since then he has been active in non-profit groups, talking about and making presentations on Climate Change.

Through his volunteer work and through self-education, he has also developed a good understanding of environmental (ecological), developmental (technical, economic, industrial and financial) and political (democracy) issues. **Because of his background, he has the unique ability to understand all aspects of the Plan and its solutions needed in energy, climate, economic development and ecosystems.** He has published a number of technical engineering papers and has technical patents. He is the author of a number of books including, "Rethinking Progress – Towards a Creative Transformation of Global Society," and a "Personal Climate Change Handbook," 2016, a 40 page book that is available on Amazon. See below for a list of the author's books. The author's aim in this activity is to see the Plan accepted, and something like the Plan implemented globally in a timely and effective manner.

Books by the Author

Rethinking Progress – Towards a Creative Transformation of Global Society, **Harinder Lamba, Daanish Books, New Delhi, 2005**

This book describes the environmental and developmental crises the world faces, how nations progress and are enriched or do not progress or are impoverished, what historically happened with the planet over 4.6 billion years, and what happened with global nations after the start of the industrial revolution. The book also describes and offers alternatives types of progress that will help to solve the ecological and developmental crises, and the alternative approaches to ecology, industrialization, economics, democracy, agriculture and education that will help global society steer itself in new directions. The book also presents what the world needs to do to overcome the broader ecological crisis and improve the living conditions and opportunities for the vast masses of people.

SELF-PUBLISHED BOOKS ON AMAZON

Personal Climate Change Handbook, **Hari Lamba, 2016**

This short 40 page book provides a good snapshot of the situation as of 2016 just after the signing of the Paris Agreement, and guides the reader on how to evaluate and reduce their own carbon footprint and as to what kind of activism will be required to apply pressure at the local, national and global levels to get political movement on solutions to Climate Change.

Our Only Home – Poems for Our Planet Earth, **Hari Lamba, 2016**

This collection of 28 poems by the author is an enjoyable book if you enjoy poems about the beauty of nature and our planet. It belongs to a tradition of poetry called "verse journalism" or poetry with a purpose. After you enjoy a poem about beauty, it often steers the reader towards taking care of nature and our Earth, and developing a spiritual connection with them. It reminds us that there is not any other planet out there for us, and that Earth is our only home.

The History of Our Earth – And Our Role in its Future, Hari Lamba, 2016

This book is a fun way to get to know about the history of our planet Earth since it was formed 4.6 billion years ago. This book is unique in that it combines poetry and planetary history in an entertaining and educational way. For adults this book will provide information and understanding about the planet's environment and how it has evolved so as to be favorable for life. For children the book will provide a sensitivity towards the planet's environment – the poem can be recited, while the images are displayed. An important aspect of the book is how the planet took out carbon dioxide out of the air and buried it in the fossil fuels, thereby cooling the atmosphere that us humans and life as we know it, could flourish.

Rejuvenating America – Rejuvenate – Visions of a Better America, Hari Lamba, 2018

This book offers descriptions of visions of what the United States of America, the nation, can be like in the future, in a way that is not only good for itself but for the whole world. Besides visions that are already out there, it offers visions in the areas of trade, climate and economy. It describes in detail a four point jobs and economy vision or plan on how to develop a pro-employment and pro-environment economy – tax reform, systematic industrial policy, local production for local use (to uplift depressed communities) and transforming and starting new activities for Climate Change solutions.

www.rejuvenate-america.com

"A compelling vision of what could be."
— *James J. Greenberger, Founder and Executive Director*
NAAT Batt International

CPSIA information can be obtained
at www.ICGtesting.com
Printed in the USA
FSHW021222140321
79422FS